Collected Plays

BY CHARLES WILLIAMS

Thomas Cranmer of Canterbury
Judgement at Chelmsford · Seed of Adam
The Death of Good Fortune
The House by the Stable
Grab and Grace *or* It's the Second Step
The House of the Octopus
Terror of Light
The Three Temptations

With an Introduction by
JOHN HEATH-STUBBS

REGENT COLLEGE PUBLISHING
VANCOUVER, BRITISH COLUMBIA

Copyright © 1963 The Estate of Charles Williams
All right reserved.

This edition published 2005 by special arrangement with
The Estate of Charles Williams, David Higham Associates, London,
and the Watkins/Loomis Agency, New York.

Regent College Publishing
5800 University Boulevard, Vancouver, BC V6T 2E4 Canada
www.regentpublishing.com

Regent College Publishing is an imprint of the Regent Bookstore
<www.regentbookstore.com>. Views expressed in works published by
Regent College Publishing are those of the author and do not necessarily
represent the official position of Regent College.

Library and Archives Canada Cataloguing in Publication Data

Williams, Charles, 1886-1945.
Collected Plays / Charles Williams.

Reprint of the ed. published: London : Oxford University Press, 1963.

ISBN 1-57383-366-5

I. Title.

PR6045.I5A19 2005   822'.912   C2005-903730-X

CONTENTS

Introduction	v
THOMAS CRANMER OF CANTERBURY	1
JUDGEMENT AT CHELMSFORD	61
SEED OF ADAM	149
Appendix	173
THE DEATH OF GOOD FORTUNE	177
THE HOUSE BY THE STABLE	195
GRAB AND GRACE, or IT'S THE SECOND STEP	217
THE HOUSE OF THE OCTOPUS	245
TERROR OF LIGHT	325
THE THREE TEMPTATIONS	375

INTRODUCTION

THE nine plays in the present volume represent Charles Williams's mature contribution to dramatic writing. To most readers he is still probably best known for his novels; to a smaller number for his theological writings—such as *The Descent of the Dove* and *He came down from Heaven*; to a smaller number still for his two cycles of poems on the Arthurian myth—*Taliessin through Logres* and *The Region of the Summer Stars*. It is these last, I believe, which will ultimately be appreciated as his most important achievement. But among his other writings, those with which we are immediately concerned must take a high place and form a very distinctive and original contribution both to the tradition of religious drama, and to the development of the verse-play as a living form in our time.

Charles Williams's style, like that of several other poets of the present century, underwent a marked change in his middle years. Among the plays in this volume, *Thomas Cranmer of Canterbury* partially signalizes the beginning of this change, and it is seen in its full extent in the others, as it is also in his Arthurian poems. It is a change in style rather than in ideas; for although the latter developed and deepened, they remained remarkably consistent throughout his career. But he was long in finding a form wholly adequate to his ideas. His early poetry follows a variety of styles, all of them really a little outdated at the time when he wrote. There are verses Pre-Raphaelite, Chestertonian, Kiplingesque, Macaulayish. He had also a great facility—an all but fatal facility—for pastiche of earlier styles, that of the seventeenth century, for instance. His later style is wholly his own, but it is not a 'modern' style, in the sense

INTRODUCTION

of owing very much to the experiments, or rather renovations, initiated by Mr. Eliot and others in the twenties and thirties. The diction, though often capable of striking excursions into colloquialism, and of placing the seemingly commonplace word or phrase in a fresh light which gives it a new power and significance, remains fundamentally formal. But the formality is no longer conventional: it is related, rather, to Williams's profound sense of hierarchy and ceremony as enduring expressions of the divinely ordered nature of things. If the language does not appear contemporary, as this word is commonly understood, it is because it is a language aware of the greater contemporaneity of eternity.

The earlier verse already referred to includes some plays (not reprinted here)—*A Myth of Shakespeare* (1928) and *Three Plays* (1931). Of the first two in the latter volume, 'The Witch' and 'The Chaste Wanton', Mrs. Ridler, in her introduction to *Seed of Adam and other Plays* (1948), says correctly that 'they are better suited for reading than for acting—a kind of drama to which so many distinguished poets have contributed'. She adds the further observation that 'as long as he was writing in blank verse, after the model of Lascelles Abercrombie (whose work he much admired at the time) he was liable to write in pseudo-Shakespearian metaphors'. To the influence of Abercrombie (whom, by the way, the current fashion possibly underrates) must be added, I think, that of the early verse-plays of Yeats. I well remember Charles Williams, in conversation, speaking of the impact which first opening Yeats's *The Countess Cathleen* had on him as a boy. It is perhaps worth noting that the treatment of the dicing for Man's soul in *The House by the Stable* perhaps owes something to the central motif of *The Countess Cathleen*, though of course the image is a traditional one. The later development of dramatic form

INTRODUCTION

by Charles Williams may be better understood if we think of it as parallel to, though independent of, that achieved by Yeats in his later plays, rather than as following the line of Mr. Eliot's verse drama. All three writers realized, or came to realize, that the problem of modern verse-drama lay in breaking with the tradition of Elizabethan blank-verse rhetoric. But Yeats and Williams aimed at producing a drama on the lines of their own mature lyrical work—formal, concise, and symbolic in its basic structure, whereas Mr. Eliot has moved increasingly towards a transmutation of the naturalistic conventions of the contemporary stage into poetic terms.

The third of the *Three Plays*, 'The Rite of the Passion', is in a rather different case from the others. It was commissioned for actual performance in a church, but is rather a dramatic quasi-liturgical action than a play as we commonly understand the word. Several interpreters of Charles Williams (including Mrs. Ridler, Mrs. Hadfield, and Brother George Every) have pointed out that the figure of Satan in this work anticipates a series of figures in the later plays—the Skeleton in *Cranmer*, The Third King in *Seed of Adam*, the Accuser in *Judgement at Chelmsford*. In all these, a figure apparently representing Evil or Death ultimately appears, in the light of eternity, as the instrument of Good. This series really culminates in the Flame in *The House of the Octopus*; but the Flame is explicitly an image of the Holy Spirit guarding over and working in the Church.

While considering Charles Williams's earlier dramatic efforts we must also mention the two privately printed Amen House Masques.[1] They are occasional *jeux d'esprits*, but embody some of his leading ideas with a light touch. They have proved effective in revived performance apart from the occasions they were written for.

---

[1] Another play, *A Myth of Bacon*, is known to have existed in at least two copies. These, however, appear to have been lost or destroyed.

INTRODUCTION

All Charles Williams's work is really religious in character, and by far the greater part of it explicitly so. All the plays in the present volume (except the radio play *The Three Temptations*) were commissioned for performance either by Church groups, or at Church festival occasions. When one considers the rather low standards of theatrical competence which has all too often been regarded as acceptable for such circumstances, one must immediately be struck by the freshness and vitality of his approach. Charles Williams's religious plays are considerably more than pageants, or sermons in quasi-dramatic form, though the two festival plays, *Cranmer* and *Judgement at Chelmsford*, partake of what is best in the pageant as a form, and in all of them the doctrinal content is both central and absolutely coherent. I do not think this is the place to discuss Williams's religious ideas, important as they are in themselves, and for the understanding of his work. They have been discussed by others, and by myself, elsewhere, and will, I think, continue to be increasingly discussed. I feel, however, that there is a danger that discussion of these ideas may tend to distract attention from the purely literary merits of his work, to which so far sufficient credit has scarcely been given by accepted criticism. I wish therefore mainly to concentrate on Charles Williams's handling of dramatic form, within the limitations imposed by the particular kind of play he was engaged upon.

Thomas Cranmer of Canterbury was commissioned for the Canterbury Festival, for performance in the cloisters of the Cathedral. It is inevitable that one should compare it to Mr. Eliot's *Murder in the Cathedral*, written for performance on the like occasion, and with a theme in some ways similar. It must be emphasized, however, that neither play seems to owe anything directly to the other. *Cranmer* covers the historical sweep of the Reformation from 1529 to the Archbishop's martyrdom without becoming a chronicle play. The most original and perhaps the most significant character is (as has already been indicated) the Skeleton, who is both a commentator on the action and a mainspring of it. This (in a sense) ambiguous image, both of suffering and negation and of the Divine, is at the centre of the play's conflicts: the conflicts of King, Lords, and Commons, of Protestant and Catholic, between which Cranmer's tragedy is enacted, culminating in the triumph of martyrdom but with an ambiguity even there:

THE SKELETON. Friend, let us say one thing more before the world—
 I for you, you for me: let us say all,
 if the Pope had bid you live, you would have served him.
CRANMER. If the Pope had bid me live, I should have served him.

In *Cranmer* Williams breaks with blank-verse rhetoric, and develops his peculiar technique of the irregularly stressed line with occasional internal and end rhymes, used also in his later Arthurian poems, and apparently owing something to Hopkins.

Seed of Adam is a further advance in dramatic technique in its free, symbolic treatment of historical time. One might rather say that historical time is here swallowed up in eternity, where Adam and Augustus Caesar coincide, where Joseph is a young captain in the service of the Sultan of Bagdad (who is both the second King among the Magi and the world of the imagination), and where the Third King is also the core of the Apple. The complexities of *Seed of Adam* may seem very difficult on the printed page, though they are in fact perfectly coherent in Williams's thought; but in actual performance the play has an immediate and powerful dramatic impact. This is surely what is essential to any play of ideas, whether secular or religious. The ideas are not so much to be expounded dialectically in the dialogue as immediately incarnated in the action.

INTRODUCTION

The next three plays are simpler, and presumably an attempt on Williams's part to accommodate his peculiar manner to what are assumed to be the capacities of a popular audience, and more modest resources of production. They belong, I suppose, to the category of Morality Plays. The characters, however, though personifications, are by no means abstractions. I agree with Mrs. Ridler in finding *The Death of Good Fortune* the least interesting of the three; but this is not to say that it is without interest. Its moral—that all fortune is good fortune (present also in *Cranmer*)—will be better understood if we have read Williams's comment in *The Figure of Beatrice* on Virgil's speech on Fortune in the circle of the avaricious in Dante's *Inferno*. *The House by the Stable*, like *Seed of Adam*, is a Nativity Play, and when we realize how much they differ from each other, and from the conventional kind of Nativity Play, we see how original, and also how varied Williams's conceptions are.

The treatment of evil in *The House by the Stable* and in its sequel, *Grab and Grace*, is straightforward, but, as Mrs. Ridler says, Pride and Hell in this play are not dummies. The temptations which Pride offers, especially when in *Grab and Grace* she changes her name to Self-respect, are real and subtle enough. She and Hell are also real enough considered as prostitute and bully, as well as eternal states. Nor are the figures of Faith and Grace, the one brisk and sophisticated, the other a mischievous small boy, taken out of any pre-Raphaelite stained-glass window.

Judgement at Chelmsford like *Cranmer* is a festival play. It was originally written under the pseudonym of Peter Stanhope—this character is the poet in Williams's novel *Descent into Hell*—for the twenty-fifth anniversary of the formation of the Diocese of Chelmsford in 1939, but the war prevented its actually being performed till after Charles

INTRODUCTION

Williams's death. It was clearly designed in such a way as to give scope for small groups from the parishes of the Diocese to perform separate scenes within an over-all frame. But out of this scheme Williams has produced a grand and original design, possibly suggested by Dante. The play sweeps backwards in historical time, and upwards from initial despair through scenes of ever-increasing hope to the vision of the marriage of Church and Empire and to the finding of the Cross.

Charles Williams's last wholly finished stage-play, *The House of the Octopus*, has a dramatic structure and plot of a kind perhaps more often demanded of a play today. This may make it more accessible to some readers and audiences, though I must confess to liking it rather less than the others. The most original and poetic conception in it is that of the Flame, but otherwise there seems to me to be a touch of melodrama in the treatment of Evil in the person of the Marshal of P'o L'u. The setting suggests the Japanese invasion of the Pacific during the Second World War, but it must be remembered that P'o L'u is Williams's name, in his Arthurian poems, for the Antipodean Empire antithetical to Byzantium—not formal Hell, but as much of Hell as limited human consciousness can realize. The Octopus is also used as a symbol for P'o L'u in these poems; it has never seemed to me a wholly satisfactory symbol—partly because a real octopus is not at all formless, nor is it really necessarily sinister.

Terror of Light, here printed for the first time, is in prose, but Williams intended its final drafting in verse. Reading it as it stands, one realizes that the rather formal and mannered nature of his verse-diction and metric had an important function. It distanced the dialogue of his plays, removing them, as it were, to a timeless dimension. The prose dialogue of his novels has often been rather sharply criticized for conveying a sentimental and even cosy quality—which is, one must add, in the sharpest possible contrast with the intense spiritual realism, as we may call it, of their themes. The same paradox confronts us in *Terror of Light* as it here stands. But for the reader already acquainted with Williams's other plays and with the rest of his work it will be of the profoundest interest. It draws together, indeed, many of the themes which most deeply preoccupied him, notably in his non-dramatic works. Thus the treatment of Simon Magus recalls the figure of Simon the Clerk in *All Hallows Eve*, the last of his novels, on which he was working at about the same time. On the other hand, the relationship between John and Mary Magdalen in this play (which may seem a little embarrassing—as it does, indeed, to the unconverted Saul of Tarsus) will be better understood if we relate it to that between Percivale and Dindrane which is explored in the poems of *The Region of the Summer Stars*.

The radio play, *The Three Temptations*, shows Williams exploring a new medium with considerable grasp of the technique it requires. It is characteristic of him immediately to have seized on the greater freedom the form offered for his own ends, so that time is transcended. The events of the beginning and end of Christ's earthly ministry are brought together in a simultaneous relation, in a manner which would scarcely be possible in a stage play. Another new and striking—indeed appalling—conception is that of Judas Iscariot as Everyman. This gains at least part of its power from the fact that a radio play is addressed not to an audience in a theatre but to the individual listener by his own fireside.

I have attempted to present these plays as plays, to be performed—actually, or if the reader has not the opportunity to see them thus, in the theatre of his mind; but not to be merely read. The ideas they embody are daring and

INTRODUCTION

profound, and are expounded in Charles Williams's other writings. But to grasp them initially in terms of dramatic action may be one of the best, as well as one of the readiest ways of becoming acquainted with them.

JOHN HEATH-STUBBS

THOMAS CRANMER OF CANTERBURY

CHARACTERS

THOMAS CRANMER
HENRY VIII
MARY
ANNE BOLEYN
FIRST LORD
SECOND LORD
A PRIEST
A PREACHER
A BISHOP
FIGURA RERUM, A SKELETON
The Commons; Singers; Executioners

PART ONE

The SINGERS *enter and take their places*

THE SINGERS. God, the protector of all that trust in thee, without whom nothing is strong, nothing is holy; Increase and multiply upon us thy mercy; that, thou being our ruler and guide, we may so pass through things temporal, that we finally lose not the things eternal: Grant this, O heavenly Father, for Jesus Christ's sake our Lord. Amen.

The PRIEST *and the* PREACHER *run on* Cambridge 1528
THE PRIEST. The Lord remember you!
THE PREACHER. The Lord remember you!
THE PRIEST. Because you have forsaken him alone,
 The Lord shall smite you with scabs and emerods.
THE PREACHER. Because you have followed lying gods,
 The Lord shall set over you gods of stone.
THE PRIEST. Atheist!
THE PREACHER. Idolater!
THE PRIEST. Beast!
THE PREACHER Devil!
 Will you silence God's Word?
THE PRIEST. Will you touch God's altar?
 You shall come to the fire with your hands in a halter:
THE PREACHER. And the Lord shall fling you to your own evil.

They fall apart. CRANMER *enters*

CRANMER. From riding to reading sweetly the days go.
 I praise God for his space of Cambridge air,
 where steeds and studies abound, that my thighs,
 body and mind, have exercise,
 each o'erstriding his kind, in beast or word.
 Steed and speech go reined and spurred. I learned

easier the riding than the reading; I took
tenderness rather than tyranny and made my gain:
but now in strengthened brain I master the twain.
Coming in from the gallop, I vault on language, halt
often but speed sometimes, and always heed
the blessèd beauty of the shaped syllables. I would let go
a heresy or so for love of a lordly style
with charging challenge, or one that softens a mile
to a furlong with dulcet harmony, enlarging
the heart with delicate diction. Come,
today's journey waits: open gates! Blessed Lord,
thou hast given me horses, books, Cambridge, and peace:
foolish the man, having these, who seeks increase.

THE PRIEST. Roar, Antichrist: reach a ravin of hands.
THE PREACHER. Rage, Antichrist: wrap the Lord in bands.
THE PRIEST. Here is Christ, in a secret sacrificed.
THE PREACHER. Here, the Word witnessing, here is Christ.
CRANMER. Yet ah for the wars! here too must we wring
souls duty out of that beauty: *verba verbera*—
even sluggards as I; I have sought,
read, thought, these three years, thought, read.
Appears now what was said:
In the beginning was the Word.
The Word was with God and the Word was God—
his disciples heard; his feet ran to the rood;
he gave himself to the souls of all holy living—
This is my body; take, eat:
Drink this; this is my blood:
feed on this in your heart by faith with thanksgiving.

The BISHOP *enters, vested with acolytes and incense,*
and goes round the stage

But now is man's new fall: now the fresh creature,
his second nature, nurtured by grace from the old,

THOMAS CRANMER OF CANTERBURY

lusts to withdraw itself and withhold
from the lawful food of God's favour; it lies
on the sea-broad floor of the Church, and its eyes
shut themselves on the steep sacramental way,
for it beats its heart in a half-sleep,
blindly covered by that panoply's art it was bid
rid itself of; multiple show and song
throng in its dreams the bare step of the Lord
and are adored in comfortable fearful respect.
It rises to genuflect where ceremony and rite
compose a moon-bright image. O in Paradise—
cries the tale—when Adam saw
himself in Euphrates, false awe and false delight
threw him to a plight of self-circling adoration,
where salvation's way was lost, which Christ restored
in means of communion; now are means of communion adored
yet dyked from approach; untrod, unexplored,
is the road; instead of God are God's marvels displayed,
rivals to Christ are Christ's bounties made,
and dumb are our people: negligent they lie and numb.
> [*The* PRIEST *and the* PREACHER *take their places at the back of the stage*

Our Father, in whom is heaven, thy kingdom come.

The SKELETON *enters, carrying the crozier. He crosses the stage to the steps*

THE SINGERS. Blessed is he that cometh in the name of the Lord; Hosanna in the highest.
THE SKELETON. Fast runs the mind,
and the soul a pace behind:
without haste or sloth
come I between both.

THOMAS CRANMER OF CANTERBURY

There blows a darkening wind
over soul and mind:
faith can hear, truth can see
the jangling bones that make up me:

till on the hangman's day,
and along the hangman's way,
we all three run level,
mind, soul, and God or the Devil.

CRANMER. O that the King, O that God's glory's gust
from heaven would drive the dust of the land, smite
his people with might of doctrine, embodied raise
their subservient matter, set with his fire ablaze
their heavy somnolence of heavenly desire, his word
bid what God said be heard, what God bade be done!
that the King's law might run savingly through the land:
so might I, if God please, outcast from my brethren stand.

THE SKELETON. We of heaven are compassionate-kind;
we give men all their mind;
asking, at once, before they seek, they find.

We are efficacious and full of care;
why do the poor wretches shriek in despair?
They run; after each, entreating him, runs his prayer.

Populous with prayers is the plain of Paradise,
skirring after the men who prayed, whose cries
beseech heaven to refrain; heaven hears not twice.

THE SINGERS. O how amiable are thy dwellings, thou Lord of hosts!

THE SKELETON. We see our servant Thomas; we see
how pure his desire—Amen; let his desire be.

THOMAS CRANMER OF CANTERBURY

Trumpet. The KING, ANNE BOLEYN, *the* LORDS, *and the* 1529
COMMONS *enter. The* KING *takes his throne; the* LORDS
retire to the back of the stage; the COMMONS *go to their
own place*

THE SINGERS. Give the King thy judgements, O God; and
thy righteousness unto the King's son.

Then shall he judge thy people according unto right;
and defend the poor.

The mountains shall also bring peace; and the little
hills righteousness unto the people.

He shall keep the simple folk by their right; defend
the children of the poor, and punish the wrong doer.

They shall fear thee, as long as the sun and moon endureth: from one generation to another.

He shall come down like the rain into a fleece of
wool: even as the drops that water the earth.

In his time shall the righteous flourish; yea, and
abundance of peace, so long as the moon endureth.

His dominion shall be also from the one sea to the
other: and from the flood unto the world's end.

THE KING. Hither, Thomas.

> [*The* SKELETON *goes to* CRANMER, *touches him, and
> brings him to the* KING. *He kneels. The* SKELETON
> *stands between and behind them*

                       Thomas, I am married to a Death.
The lives I sow are slain in the woman's blood.
Corpse-conceived is the heir of my kingdom and power.
My soul is the power of God over this land:
my soul pines; the land dies; counsel the King.
CRANMER. Omnipotent sir—
THE KING.   The Pope's throat is thick.
His cold was caught in the Alps; Christ's image
is worked by German cords to mechanical glory.

My mind misgave me; God confirms me; my children
die, for my seed is drowned in my brother's blood.
CRANMER. Sir, the doctors deny the dispensation:
Oxford, Cambridge, Paris, Orleans, Toulouse,
Padua, Bologna; the Pope at first refused it.
ANNE. Henry, Henry, Henry, make me a wife.
THE KING. I saw a face that set me free from fate,
and made me pure to free the fate of the land,
by love, by a daughter of England, by Anne Boleyn.
I must have Anne, Anne with an heir by Anne,
legally mine, canonically mine.
There are no ghosts of children in her chamber
frightening me with white bones when I go in;
the mitred skeleton of Rome at the door
points in with the hand and trips me with the foot
spectrally mouthing secret words; on the bed
beyond him is Anne, live children playing by her.
I labour, I labour, with the need of the deed.
Can any man anywhere unmake the King?
CRANMER. The imperial crown and jurisdiction temporal
of this whole realm are drawn direct from God:
within Christ's law there is none above the King.
THE KING. There must be found a means to make the marriage.
The Pope nods from a corner. Archbishop Warham
is dead, as dead as Catherine's sons; he swore
that I was head of this Church, saving Christ's law.
Am I not head?
CRANMER.   Absolute head.
THE KING.   The oaths to Rome?
CRANMER. Great sir, no oath has any force,
nor can be taken, nor should be understood,
to spoil a tittle of a subject's duty
unto the absolute Crown and Seat of England.

THOMAS CRANMER OF CANTERBURY

ANNE. Henry, Henry, Henry, make me a queen.

THE KING. There must be an archbishop to beget me an heir

legitimately and canonically.

I am the head. Be Canterbury, Thomas.

The Pope nods to me; he will send the pall.

The Archbishopric 1533

CRANMER. Sir!

THE KING. Be Canterbury: help me beget an heir.

I am turmoiled each way with desire and hope.

Be swift; determine the cause; pronounce this month

the dispensation invalid, the marriage null.

Terrible to the land is the trouble of the King.

CRANMER [*standing up*]. I am no man for this; I am purblind,

weak, for my courage was shouted out of me

by schoolmasters and other certain men.

My thought is slow, uncertain of itself,

willing to serve God and its friends and peace—

THE KING. The will of the King is as the will of God.

THE SKELETON [*giving the crozier to the* KING, *who hands it to* CRANMER]. Besides, even your thoughts must consider your world,

and a little hurry to be of use to your world.

Even a shy man must make up his mind.

Has not much adoration quenched communion?

Must not Christ intend to restore communion?

Now is your chance, Thomas, to serve Christ!

CRANMER. I am God's servant and the King's.

THE KING.   Go then,

and make me, as I am, irretrievably Anne's.

[CRANMER *is vested*

THE SINGERS [*during the vesting*]. O how amiable are thy dwellings: thou Lord of hosts!

My soul hath a desire and longing to enter into the

courts of the Lord: my heart and my flesh rejoice in the living God.

Yea, the sparrow hath found her an house, and the swallow a nest where she may lay her young: even thy altars, O Lord of hosts, my King and my God.

Blessed are they that dwell in thy house: they will be always praising thee.

Blessed is that man whose strength is in thee: in whose heart are thy ways.

Which going through the vale of misery use it for a well: and the pools are filled with water.

They will go from strength to strength: and unto the God of gods appeareth every one of them in Sion.

[CRANMER *goes to* ANNE

ANNE. Make me irretrievably, irretrievably the King's.
CRANMER. The King is masked with his majesty; all we are tasked
to be shaped at his will, infiltrated with his colour,
whether for dolour or peace. You must have no sense,
madam, but of this spiritual obedience
to make you in mind and feature the King's creature,
as the King is God's; be you the image of God's image.
ANNE. I have seen an image of myself:
a golden-shoed, crowned, and red-mouthed image,
which the King holds in his hands over his lands.
Some kiss its feet, some its mouth.
CRANMER. Feet to run, mouth to bless the King;
he is the stress of our hearts to heaven. Come,
madam, I will bring you to him; you are his bride.
ANNE. Henry, I am the queen; I will be your wife.
Henry, Henry, Henry, kill my enemies.
THE KING. Why, sweetheart, this is a holiday in heaven:
God is placable to the land, as I to you.
Look now, the land has peace

THOMAS CRANMER OF CANTERBURY

for I am quiet, and you are placable to me:
this will be sealed and revealed in the coming of an heir.
You have done well, Archbishop; get to your tasks.
Make a single kingdom for the prince of the kingdom.
              [CRANMER *goes out.* ANNE *sits at the* KING's *feet*
THE SKELETON. Anne had a vision of an image in the
   King's hand.
The land also has visions. Speak; I permit you.
VOICES FROM THE COMMONS. Adoration!
                          Communion!
                          Adoration!
                          Communion!
Up with the clergy!
                 Down with the clergy!
Texts and the Councils!
                 Texts and the Fathers!
Jesus, have mercy!
             Antichrist!
                          Antichrist!
They lie in hell; death gnaws upon them!
Shibboleth!
         Shibboleth!
                  Abracadabra!
THE SKELETON. Hark, the images go abroad!
Once in a way, once in an age,
when men's spirits rage, I set the images free,
all idols of hall, chapel, and marketplace,
spectral images, lacking love's grace, of me.
Their foreheads' phosphorescence shines;
they make signs; then one man walks, one talks,
under those moons, and in action and speech
each grows a wicked automaton to each,
a diseased bone, to be flung to Gehenna;
yet I only am the pit where Gehenna is sprung.

Brother reason and sister experience spew at each other,
sister dogma and brother denial run askew.
Then all but the hearts of the blessed ones dance
askance from love of Christ to love of corruption,
crying maniacally *Abracadabra,
abracadabra, abracadabra.*
But through their delirium I walk like a blind
beggar, pleading for a man to be kind;
the Son of Man walks backwards on their way,
crying *Do you hear me? where is the way?
O my people, where is the way?*
       [*He goes round the stage, as if blind and begging,
       saying*

O my people, where is the way?
Do you hear me, zealots? where is the way?

THE PRIEST. Accipe; this is the way.
THE PREACHER.   Audi; this is the way.
THE COMMONS. This, we heard, was the way.
THE LORDS.   This, we feel, is the way.
THE KING. This that I bid is the way.
THE COMMONS.   This—is not this—
   the way?
THE SKELETON [*to the audience*]. Yet, O my people—can
   you believe it?
blessed and chosen are they who receive it—
there is a way; I am the way,
I the division, the derision, where
the bones dance in the darkening air,
I at the cross-ways the voice of the one way,
crying from the tomb of the earth where I died
the word of the only right Suicide,
the only word no words can quell,
the way to heaven and the way to hell.
                          [*He goes round the stage, singing*

THOMAS CRANMER OF CANTERBURY

I am the way, the way to heaven;
who will show a poor blind beggar the way to heaven?
I am the way, the way to hell,
who will teach a poor blind beggar the way to hell?
            [*The figures break into movement*
I am the way, the way to salvation,
who will desire the way of salvation?
      [*He runs round the stage; they all follow him. Presently he stops, and sits on the steps*
I am the jawbone of the ass
on which, it is said, it came to pass,
Christ rode into Zion; Zion gleams askance.
Let us hear what my people make of this dance;
especially what my Thomas makes of the dance.
            [*The figures are still—the* KING *stands up*
But what, in the interval, is this? the King had his desire;   1534–6
does he run so soon after heaven to be rid of his desire?
      CRANMER *re-enters.* ANNE *falls at the* KING'*s feet*
THE KING. Thomas, Thomas, Anne is not what I thought.
THE SKELETON [*speaking over the audience*]. A remark few
    of you die without making,
                  [*Over his shoulder to* CRANMER
nor shall you die without making,
but, for your comfort, of a lordlier substantive.
                        [*To the audience*
That is all I can ever promise any of you,
but much peace depends on the kind of substantive.
THE KING. Go; question; report; find out all.
THE SKELETON [*rising*]. Come, Thomas; we will go to Anne
    who also had her desire and now cries to heaven.
Good or bad, you all come to it in the end.
            [*He and* CRANMER *go to* ANNE *and raise her*
THE SKELETON. Is your image broken, Anne?
ANNE.   I wanted so little:

13

only the Crown because it lay in my way,
and a few small pleasures—variations from Henry.
THE SKELETON. If you had asked for the greatest conceivable things,
as Thomas does unintentionally, they would cost no more.
The price of heaven or hell or the world is similar—
always a broken heart, sometimes a broken neck.
ANNE. My neck is small: will the King have it cut?
He loved me—once.
CRANMER. Madam, repent, confess,
entreat; the King is gracious.
THE SKELETON. Heaven is gracious,
but few can draw safe deductions on its method.
Turn your eyes; look at me.
ANNE. Archbishop, I have a secret—
hark!—that may save me.

        [*She whispers.* CRANMER *goes to the* KING

THE KING. She shall die.
CRANMER. Sir—
THE KING. She shall die.
CRANMER. If indeed—I can hardly believe—
THE KING. I say, she shall die.
She has taken my image of her love and broken it: she dies.
CRANMER. Sir, all men have sinned: your highness has sinned.
THE KING. You are full of a silly innocence, Archbishop.
I say, she dies.
THE SKELETON. Turn your eyes; look at me. I
am the broken image, the bones of the image, the image taken away from me and I from the image.
ANNE. What does King Henry say?
CRANMER. Alas, madam,
ira regis mors—the wrath of the King is death.

        [*The* SKELETON *covers* ANNE *with his cloak; they*

go out, CRANMER *following. The* KING *seats himself. The* LORDS *kneel at the sides of the Throne*

THE FIRST LORD. Most mighty sir, regard the spirituality.

THE SECOND LORD. Regard, most mighty sir, the sins of the monks.

THE FIRST LORD. Reckon meadow and pasture—one-fourth the realm.

THE SECOND LORD. Compute paten and pyx, chalice and cope.

THE FIRST LORD. Sir, the need of the government!

THE SECOND LORD. The simplicity of Christ!

THE FIRST LORD. Sir, for the Crown's need's sake—

THE SECOND LORD. for Christ's gospel's sake—

BOTH THE LORDS. it were right the Lord of England received the richness.

THE FIRST LORD. Inflaming their bestial appetite with spiritual lust,

THE SECOND LORD. fornications with pomp, adulteries with power,

THE FIRST LORD. betraying the poor vows they swore to keep,

THE SECOND LORD. abusing their virginal conformity with Christ's mind,

THE FIRST LORD. basely and turbulently collecting earth's treasure,

THE SECOND LORD. besides fornications and adulteries of the common sort,

THE FIRST LORD. such as we dare not name for mere modesty,

THE SECOND LORD. whereby their hearts' brothels enrich damnation,

BOTH THE LORDS. it were well the Lords of England had their wealth.

THE FIRST LORD. Sir, behold a formula—a device fitted,

THE SECOND LORD. a confession due to the King of criminal follies;

THE FIRST LORD. those that will sign—simple men misled,

THE SECOND LORD. Sir, dissolve them graciously; take the land.

THE FIRST LORD. Those that stand obstinately in sin, contending

THE SECOND LORD. that they never did what we have written they do—

THE FIRST LORD. or that some do; if they deny that all do,

THE SECOND LORD. Sir, dissolve them mightily; seize the gold.

BOTH THE LORDS. It were good the gentry of England had their goods.

CRANMER returns; and the SKELETON

THE KING. This many ancient Catholic kings have done, even my predecessor, Henry the Fifth.
If the monks and the guilds are as sinful as they say
it were well the King of England had the land.

THE FIRST LORD. It were better, sir, that it were given to us.

THE SECOND LORD. Then we shall know you right defender of the faith,

THE FIRST LORD. And that Anne was either legitimate or not—

THE SECOND LORD. as your Highness pleases; she having died somehow,

THE FIRST LORD. and your Highness having a quite undoubted heir,

THE SECOND LORD. as long as the lands are quite undoubtedly ours.

THE KING. Thomas, Thomas!

[CRANMER *comes to the* KING
Thomas, am I afraid?

Boars and bulls root at me and butt me.
Anne confessed; you went to Anne; she confessed.
CRANMER. Sir, she confessed.
THE KING. When you went friendly to her?
CRANMER. God help me, sir, I cannot bully; I went
friendly. I have searched my heart often to know
if I went too friendly; she and the Nun of Kent,
poor creatures, shut in prison, and I went,
speaking them softly; did I speak too soft?
I cannot shout, but what they said I told.
If I deceived—did I deceive? I desired
justice to the prisoners, justice to the King.
THE SKELETON. You shall have it, Thomas, justice for
yourself;
trap for trap, honour for honour, prison for prison;
love, in the end, for love. We will play fair.
THE KING. Stand by me, Thomas. I am the King.
I need no help; only stand somewhere near me.
There is blood running over gold in all men's eyes,
yours are clear, but worn with looking on books.
THE SKELETON. With the grand hydroptic desire of humane
learning,
as says a priest of Paul's, bended and boned
to my frame, a master of this same wisdom,
but of deaths also and other lores disowned;
and a greater than he, another John than Donne,
felt Christ's feet spurning such learning:
But you, poor man, think it good and better than Anne!
THE KING. You have been a picker of quarrels with me,
my lord,
over my book: I told the Bishop of Winchester
you were too old a truant for him and me.
CRANMER. Archbishop and the King's servant though I
be,

THOMAS CRANMER OF CANTERBURY

I am everywhere out of place but among books
where past voices make canticles of peace.

THE SKELETON. Anne had an image of the Crown—she is dead;
it is sped, the image that the King had of Anne.
Are words wiser than women or worship? safer,
securer, purer? will you hierarchize the glancings
of everywhere the translucent golden-tinctured wafer
on men's eyes, the webbed light of the glory
wherein is the angle of creation? along those lines,
up and down my sides, communion and adoration
flow and ebb and flow. Beckon your image,
call and repel it, serve and slay it.
Till the day when I sound its knell and yours as well,
have, have, have your will,
for what it is worth, precisely what it is worth;
have, have, have your prayer.

<small>The English Bible 1537</small>

CRANMER. Pray we, all humble readers, for the grace of God:
Blessed Lord, which hast caused all holy Scriptures to be written for our learning

THE SINGERS. grant that we may in such wise hear them, read, mark, learn, and inwardly digest them, that, by patience, and comfort of thy holy Word, we may embrace,
and ever hold fast the blessed hope of everlasting life,
which thou hast given us in our Saviour Jesus Christ.

CRANMER. Sir, I have a book to offer the King:
a sacrament of the Word; deign, sir, to behold.

ONE OF THE COMMONS. In the wall of the creed
the stones of doctrine hold,
built there, at need,
by prophets and doctors of old:
maxims of James and Paul
and John, master of all;

THOMAS CRANMER OF CANTERBURY

    out of the Sacred Books
    the True Faith looks.
ANOTHER OF THE COMMONS. Great are the logical schools
    but greater are myths and songs:
    Solomon's lions and bulls,
    Jael and Israel's wrongs;
    the books are filled with shapes and sounds,
    and heaven opening thunderous bounds
    where feet-and-face-hidden seraphs burn
    and eyed wheels turn.
ANOTHER OF THE COMMONS. Maxim and myth are shaped to bones;
    mine grow older and truer to these.
    Where Absalom dies and King David moans
    my head with Job is bowed to my knees.
    Dry is the green, brittle the tree
    where the Lord sits to throw taunts at me;
    this book is man's breath
    'twixt the first and second death.
                      [CRANMER *brings the Bible to the* KING
CRANMER. Many identities hath the Sacred Word,
    so widely is he bestirred for our beatitude:
    always, in each good, somewhere he hath his height
    that the flight of man's heart must find. O but speech
    never found reach of wing or vision more
    than soars here! since the Catholic faith began
    man here has had his shelter, light, and food.
    It were good, might it only be so, for men
    with this alone to live, Nazianzen said,
    and do no song other. Apollyon's thong
    hath bound this now for these hundred years
    from native ears and native sound. O now
    our common English, whereto we were born, left
    forlorn to this health, yet having and meant to have

wealth so great of words, language of power,
this hour receives its consummate miracle; the Word
takes the sound heard natively around,
the excelling grace of speech; in our proper land
deigns He—O marvel!—to stand; this is His type,
ripe for communion, this His image. Sir,
let the King's grace bountifully prefer
this; enfranchise Christ into English speech.

THE KING. Is not your coat of arms badged with three cranes?

CRANMER. Sir?

THE KING. Three cranes, I say?

CRANMER.   Sir, yes.

THE KING.   They shall be pelicans,
pelicans in their love, feeding their thankless young
on their own blood. I have changed them; see it done.
You are like to be tested, if you stand to your tackling:
but have your will, publish it under my seal.

THE SKELETON. Under my seal, too, whereby I promised it to you.

1545 My hour is not yet come, but I will show
a little prelude of the hour of you and me.
                    [*He goes and stands behind the* LORDS

THE FIRST LORD. Who stands by the King?

THE SECOND LORD.   The King's friend.

THE FIRST LORD. A silly innocence lives in his face.

THE SECOND LORD. It hath caught the King—unlike to unlike.

THE FIRST LORD. Is he apt to be used?

THE SECOND LORD.   Apt to be used,
being shy of his own heart and mind,
but not so apt—none of his kind are—
if you trouble his incalculable sense of honesty,
which holds the King; who now has none,
only a kind of clinging to honesty in others.

THOMAS CRANMER OF CANTERBURY

THE FIRST LORD. He prayed the Court to renounce the holy days
   forbidden to the Commons; he has a daemon
   of peace and the poor.
THE SECOND LORD.   They are quite dangerous,
   these hankerers after peace and goodwill;
   they are provoked by I know not what
   to be a stone everyone stumbles on—
   except the King.
THE FIRST LORD [*after a pause*]. Except the King.
THE PRIEST [*coming up to them*]. Lords, Master Cranmer
      hath the King's ear,
   urging heresies, hurrying destructions,
   preaching impossible simplicities of doctrine.
THE FIRST LORD. He thinks Christ as simple as he is.
THE PRIEST. Save, Lords, the ancient miracle.
THE FIRST LORD. We are altogether against miracles, new or
      old.
THE SECOND LORD. But the old are better,
   since men forget how miraculous they are,
   and the King gives more land to their protectors.
   Come, let us put an end to this fellow.
THE FIRST LORD. He has had none of the abbey lands.
                              [*They go up to the* KING
   Sir, please your Highness permit
THE SECOND LORD. an examination of Dr. Cranmer.
THE FIRST LORD. He has infected the realm with heresy
THE SECOND LORD. desperately provoking perilous commotions,
THE FIRST LORD. dangerous to your Majesty,
THE SECOND LORD. dangerous to your Majesty.
BOTH LORDS [*speaking in the* KING's *ears*]. Commotions, uproars, rebellions, conspiracies!
   hear the Commons!

THOMAS CRANMER OF CANTERBURY

THE COMMONS [*murmuring*]. Grievances, grievances!
Where are the abbeys?
                        the rites?
                                      the mystery?
Give us back the things our fathers had!
Strange men are sitting on top of the abbeys,
stamping on our rites, stealing our rents.
Come to the King: grievances, grievances!
THE LORDS. Sir, you were best commit him to the Tower;
it is clear your Commons do not care for communion;
that, we think, is the meaning of their noises.
          [*They come between the* KING *and* CRANMER, *back
          to back, with outspread arms. The* FIRST LORD
          advances, driving CRANMER *back before him; the*
          SECOND *stands over the Throne*
THE SKELETON. If these men had their way now,
they would save him difficult life, difficult death;
and me the working, but I must divide
his life to the last crack and pull his soul
—if it lives—through the cracks; therefore—
                        [*He whispers in the* KING's *ear*
THE KING [*roaring*]. Thomas!
            Where is Canterbury? where is the Archbishop?
Keep him waiting, do you, among your boys,
in the scurvy noise of your lackeys, your runabouts,
   hey?
I say, by my faith I have a fine council; this man
that is better than the proudest of you, the King's more
than any in his true heart, what, you would start
as a cony, would you, and dog-chase on to his doom
with fellows that will find room to spare and to swear
this or that slander for a crown or two? I will put you
   down,
masters: come hither, Archbishop; this is the man

THOMAS CRANMER OF CANTERBURY
I owe much, by my faith in Almighty God.
I will nod you to your death before him; I vow
there shall none of you touch the man the King loves.
                                        [*The* LORDS *retire*
They are gone; I have saved you awhile; but yet
this life, lord Archbishop, is a catcher of men,
aye . . . aye . . . it shall catch you.
        [*The* SKELETON *comes up and sits at the* KING's *feet*
CRANMER. Sir, I desire no more.
THE KING. Y'are an honest man. Listen: I had a dream.   *The*
I saw a creature run about the world,   *death*
everywhere at all times, that would be caught   *of King*
   Henry
but would not stay for catching, or mayhap   *1547*
the thing was still, it was everything else ran by,
and I ran also, too slowly or too fast;
sometimes I could see, sometimes I could not see,
but when I saw I wept for the joy of it—
a crimson flashing creature, full of power.
All my life I sought for it, and then I died,
and it was gone and everything was gone,
except a voice calling, *Where is the prey,*
King of England? but I was not the King: it called
Henry, where is the prey? but I was not Henry.
In the nothingness, for the creature was not, I stood
and answered: *I*—and before I added more
the nothingness broke over me in a peal
of laughter, all the angels crying *You!*—
Here is a fellow calls himself I,—and their mirth
filled me, but I was weeping; there were streams
of mockery running to misery; and I woke,
the tears upon my cheeks, and the chamberlains trembled
beside me, hearing me roaring in my sleep.
What did I say that was wrong—am I not I?
am I not I myself? what did this mean?

CRANMER. Sir, I do not know.
THE SKELETON. You will know.
[*To the audience*] So will you.
THE KING. I have always lost the thing I sought to find
you are the nearest thing I ever found
to the thing that I looked for; you are an honest man,
God shall be honest with you and play you fair;
God help you in the hour when he plays you fair.
Yet I am the King, and Henry, and myself.
I always lose the thing I seek to find.
Catherine was forbidden, and Anne was false, and the Howard.
Why have so many been false to me—to *me*?
Yet one man pleaded—who? for Anne, for the monks,
for Mary, for the traitor Fisher, the traitor More,
and the worse traitor Cromwell. Who, I say?
CRANMER. Sir, I believed they loved you.
THE KING. Nor they nor me.
You are the nearest thing to a friend I have.
I have saved you, Archbishop; come up to me; what is this?
THE SKELETON [*touching the* KING]. Give the King thy judgement, O Lord!
THE KING. Thomas, I am dying: hold me, speak to me.
CRANMER. Highness!
THE KING. I have saved you; I have loved you.
CRANMER. Sir, my lord,
think upon Christ!
THE KING. I have loved you, if not them.
You are the only thing that was true to me.
I have loved you.
CRANMER. King Henry, think on Christ alone.
THE KING. I shall be I, shall I not?
CRANMER. Sir, if God please.

THOMAS CRANMER OF CANTERBURY

THE KING. Love me, Thomas; hold my hand; look to the
heir.   [*The* KING *sits rigid*
THE SINGERS. In all time of our tribulation, in all time of
our wealth, in the hour of death, and in the day of
judgement:
ALL THE PERSONS [*kneeling except the* SKELETON *and the*
KING]. Good Lord, deliver us.
> [*The* SKELETON *removes the crown and leads the*
> KING *out,* CRANMER *following. The* LORDS *whisper*
> *in a corner. The* SKELETON *returns and crouches at*
> *the top of the steps*

THE SKELETON. Ohé, the King is dead.
Protection is taken away; the world grows unkind.
The man must carry himself; his mind
follows its vision after its mode
through the uneasy palace to its god's abode;
Ohé, the King is dead.
The twin hungers are loosed; an amphibian shape
monstrously crawls from dungeons of need;
from bedchambers of greed a chattering ape
stands hatted by the man's side.
Yet bounty and beauty and others' thoughts abide
still at his back for belief.
He finds not awhile the place of derelict grief,
the mean little oubliette,
where he and I, cheek by jowl, shall be comradely met.
Ohé, the King is dead.
Now there is no sure face in the man's mind;
fingers are fumbling at his wrists, trying to bind;
feet tripping his feet, to throw him down;
the lords and the commons come crying about the town.
THE COMMONS [*moving towards the Throne*]. King Henry is   Edward
dead.   VI
                                                              1547–53
> King Edward is on the throne.

25

Long live the King!
      God save King Edward the Sixth!
He is a pretty boy!
    and pious.
        Where is he?
God bless him!
    bring him out!
        show him!
          where is he?
Show us the King!
THE LORDS [*putting on their hats and standing by the Throne*].
  Be silent.
THE COMMONS. The King! show us the King!
THE LORDS.   Be silent.
    [*They perch on the arms of the Throne*
We have the King in our guard; the King is a child,
though a paragon of precocity, much too precious
to march through a hubbub of hurras; his state of health
renders it rash to let him shine in public.
        [*They lift up the Crown*
Be still, and know that we are the Lords.
THE COMMONS.   The King!
THE LORDS. The King is behind us and in us; we are the King:
we shall rule England for thrice a hundred years.
   [*The* COMMONS *maintain a continued subdued murmur.* CRANMER *returns, habited in a gown*
CRANMER [*going up to the* LORDS]. My lords, King Henry
  had in mind to make
a ritual for communion, that men should find,
by nourishment on the supernatural, the natural
moving all ways into the supernatural,
and the things that are below as those above.
Do not forget this work; our honour, Lords,

is to order the land according to God and the King,
if King Edward permits.

THE FIRST LORD. We are the King's protectors.
Go to it, Archbishop.

THE SECOND LORD. Go to it, Archbishop.
We are making a ritual for our own communion
on lands, houses, chantries, abbeys, guilds,
which are broken for us, and blood is given for us.
Feeding on that body, we grow; we grow into houses
lustily foundationed over leagues of land.
Our bodies are made space and our blood time.
Enlarged so, a man's spirit has nothing,
nothing at all between himself and God.
Sacraments of nature are better than those of grace,
and a simple noble heart than copes and mitres.
But do not you trouble for that; go you
and use your patterns of words, versicles, responses,
formulae, vain repetitions, muttering and mummeries.
We will deal with you at need as you deal with words;
the King permits you to write your soul in words.

CRANMER. My lords, the purified Church is the truer Church,
Catholic and Apostolic; a simple heart
may err without the means.

THE SECOND LORD. We will not err.
One King is dead; the gentry do not die.
One King is a child; the gentry are never children.
Whatever bruises their heel, they bruise its head,
and now the older miracle seems the more troublesome.

THE COMMONS [*crying out*]. Down with new-fangled communions! down with the rich! *The rebellions 1549*

[*Some of them run down the steps and face the stage*

ALL. Grievances! grievances! hear the Commons' grievances!

VOICES. Give us back something we can pray to!
  Give us back the thing that hangs in the Church.
  Give us back our shows and songs!
  We will not have the Mass said in English!
  We desire Latin and processions and a great to-do!
  We will not have the Bible printed in English!
  We will not have two sorts of communion.
  We will not have communion more than once a year.
  We will have a mystery, a wonderful thing.
  Everybody shall bow and touch their foreheads,
  and any one who does not shall immediately be slain.
  Grievances! Grievances!
ALL. Hear the Commons!
                    [CRANMER *speaks from the top of the steps*
CRANMER. You ignorant rough creatures, you rocks and heaths,
  who will have the mystery of Christ to be no more
  than an unintelligible monster, risen
  from your and your fathers' past, the lapse and beat
  of time through something hung in a shell of gold,
  you ask you know not what: because of my office
  and my duty to God and the King, now will I say
  what you should know and cannot: therefore hear.
THE SKELETON [*while* CRANMER *continues to address the rebels*]. How absolute we are! now in your night
  is there no ravage? does nothing, Thomas, roar
  like seas or winds or the crowds of the poor marching?
  is all hushed down to those sweet-sounding collects
  where reason and charity softly kiss each other?
  You were less certain in old days at Cambridge.
  This is the ruinous nonsense of the mind,
  that men come mightily to believe their causes,
  because of their mere rage of controversy,
  and without morality to believe in morality.

CRANMER. Alas, it was never anywhere heard till now
that this sweet and comfortable food
Christian folk should curmudgeonly deny!
and yet be willingly stupefied with substitution—
ceremonies, genuflexions, adorations.
Has not our Lord the King made you a path?
To rest in images is clear superstition;
refuse them; come from them; come into gentle peace.
THE SKELETON. You speak well, Thomas, but you do not know all.
No man ever refused adoration yet,
but in it was something which was death to refuse;
death of one kind or another, I say not which kind.
CRANMER [*stumbling in his speech*]. And this . . . and you think . . . and you, children,
want a thick mystery to gaze at. Mystery
is there to be resolved by the soul's mathematic.
There are two classes of men—godly and ungodly;
those who desire experience of the only good,
those who refuse it. Children, will you refuse?

[*The* LORDS, *with drawn swords, fetch him back*
THE FIRST LORD. Leave them to my Hungarians, Archbishop.
THE SECOND LORD. I have collected a great unity of Christendom—
Germans and Italians, Lutherans and Catholics,
mercenaries from abroad of every faith,
gospellers and idolaters; all's one.
They shall teach the English to defy the Families.
THE FIRST LORD. Seymours, Dudleys, Pagets and Howards.
Down, dogs!
THE SECOND LORD. To your mire, swine!
CRANMER. My lords, the poor—
THE FIRST LORD. Leave the poor to us, Archbishop;
we will see to the security of Crown and Gospel.

THOMAS CRANMER OF CANTERBURY

THE SECOND LORD. We are the things below as the things above;
  the source, not to say father, of word and spirit,
  the word of our culture and the spirit of our gospel.
            [*They run down, threatening the* COMMONS
THE SKELETON. Beautiful on the hills are the feet of the heralds
  of the kingdom, bloody as Christ's but with others' blood.
  Since the Adam in Eden invoked and dividing yoked
  themselves separately to the bitter angel of possession,
  since the secession and embroilment of the sons of Noah,
  to certain chosen spermatozoa is revealed,
  semper, ubique, the propriety of proprietorship,
  the rite and religion of themselves;
  see how they fight for their Vincentian canon,
  which, among those who believe it for a season,
  is called natural Decency and obvious Reason.
THE SINGERS. Thy word is a lantern unto my feet: and a light unto my paths.

  I have sworn, and am steadfastly purposed: to keep thy righteous judgements.

  I am troubled above measure: quicken me, O Lord, according unto thy word.

  Let the freewill offerings of my mouth please thee, O Lord: and teach me thy judgements.
            [*The* LORDS *drive the rebels out and follow them*

<small>The Book of Common Prayer 1549–52</small>

A WOMAN [*running out from the other* COMMONS *and kneeling to* CRANMER]. Hear of the thing, Sir, you have made dear!
  Sir, how it clings and sings, this Bible, this book,
  lifting one look to scry heaven, speeding the sound
  underground of power; joys
  and griefs, mingling in its noise, spring from our Lord

30

who works deep down; there is Christ adored,
and his Spirit lurks, more than ourselves, in our mind
behind moons and suns: no day
but expands, as it may, from this. My mother died
with whispers of it; I make a guide
for my son's mind of portions I hear read.
Let it spread, Archbishop, let it rise,
this is a good way for a man to be wise.
CRANMER. It shall blow as the wind of youth; it shall take youth
with wonder, nor age lose it nor death deny.
The Word to wayfaring men shall testify
how his graces transubstantiate times and places,
nor shall any release from the claws of John's eagle
this land, till the poor find peace, and the rich goodwill,
and the course be one with its end.
Faith herein shall befriend for ever our folk,
hope, and the thing that is more than hope or faith.
Thus it saith for ever: O gift, O grafted power
in the power of men's souls: Christ singer, Christ voice, Christ song,
in hamlets, towns, ages: rejoice, rejoice,
heart! feed on this! what remains?
O but this—that words be as muscles and veins
to Christ's Spirit bringing communion, the shape
of his advent, nor none there to escape
into the unformed shadow of mystery mere,
but find a strong order, a diagram clear,
a ladder runged and tongued; now my hand,
my unworthy hand, shall set itself to that end.
Be for the need of the land the ritual penned.
[He goes to his desk
THE SKELETON. Rungs and tongues! the anatomy! the ladder
and the scale!

Your hand shall be a banner, friend, in another manner,
when another fire burns than this sweet desire.

[*To the audience*

And you, whose hands are still, lying now so quiet,
one day, against your will, I may bid them move
in their own life; then they shall crawl
slowly up sides, shoulders, and heads,
till each spreads
palms and fingers there, and waggles assent
to all sins I call against them. Thomas, you may think,
was fortunate in his hand beyond you. But that can wait.

CRANMER [*writing*]. Almighty God, unto whom all hearts
be open, all desires known, and from whom no secrets are
hid; Cleanse the thoughts of our hearts by the inspiration
of thy Holy Spirit, that we may perfectly love thee, and
worthily magnify thy Holy Name;

THE SINGERS. Through Christ our Lord. Amen.

THE SKELETON. Take heed, my people, take heed to your
praying.
You shall give account of your least saying:
who knows how far your words may go?
It were good you said but *yes* or *no*.

CRANMER [*writing*]. Lift up your hearts:

THE SINGERS. We lift them up unto the Lord.

CRANMER [*writing*]. Let us give thanks unto our Lord God:

THE SINGERS. It is meet and right so to do.

CRANMER [*writing*]. It is very meet, right, and our bounden
duty, that we should at all times and in all places, give
thanks . . .

THE SKELETON. Ah how the sweet words ring their beauty.
it is meet, right, and our bounden duty.
but will you sing it with unchanged faces
when God shall change the times and the places?

CRANMER [*writing*]. . . . here we offer and present unto thee,

O Lord, ourselves, our souls and bodies, to be a reasonable, holy, and lively sacrifice unto thee; humbly beseeching thee, that all we who are partakers of this holy Communion, may be fulfilled with thy grace and heavenly benediction. And although we be unworthy, through our manifold sins, to offer unto thee any sacrifice, yet we beseech thee to accept this our bounden duty and service; not weighing our merits, but pardoning our offences, through Jesus Christ our Lord; by whom and with whom, in the unity of the Holy Ghost,

THE SINGERS. all honour and glory be unto Thee, O Father Almighty, world without end. Amen.

THE SKELETON. Many a master hath made device,
in words, of incomparable sacrifice,
but woe, woe,
to any who see not where the words go:
it were better they had said but *yes* or *no*.

CRANMER [*writing*]. We praise thee, we bless thee, we worship thee, we glorify thee . . .

THE SKELETON [*leaping up*]. We praise thee,

THE SINGERS [*joining with the* SKELETON]. we bless thee, we worship thee, we glorify thee, we give thanks to thee for thy great glory, O Lord God, heavenly King, God the Father Almighty.

CRANMER [*writing*]. The peace of God which passeth all understanding . . .

THE SINGERS. keep your hearts and minds in the knowledge and love of God.

CRANMER. These to the will of God in the will of the King. Who waits?

THE SKELETON. I. After such a prologue,
whatever faces you see, or hear feet go by,
they are only I, points and joints in me;
I only waiting for what I only am working.

THOMAS CRANMER OF CANTERBURY

CRANMER. Who waits?
THE SKELETON [*going to him*]. My lord!
CRANMER.   Friend, do I know you?
  Are you of my household?
THE SKELETON.   An indweller, my lord;
  a copier-out, a carrier-about
  of works and words, an errand-runner.
CRANMER. My eyes are weak; forgive me, if I should know you.
  Much study, it is written, tires the flesh.
THE SKELETON. Much study of such communion tires the flesh,
  though perhaps less than the communion itself tires;
  your eyes, my lord, need certain sovereign balsams
  of spittle worked in clay and cleansed by fire
  I may one day bring; it will help not a little.
CRANMER. What are you called?
THE SKELETON.   Anything, everything;
  fellow, friend, cheat, traitor.
  I was born under Virgo, of an outlandish house,
  to keep account of such vows as there are written.
  My name, after today's fashion, is latinized
  into Figura Rerum. Anne prized me at first;
  later she found my bones and called me a cheat.
  King Henry found me a servant, and then a traitor.
  I am the delator of all things to their truth.
CRANMER. My mind and eyes are blind; what are you?
THE SKELETON.   To truth;
  to what you say you would find: I believe you; find it.
CRANMER. I am blind; I am afraid; what are you?
THE SKELETON. A moment's geometrical formation of fate;
  a functioning spectrum of analysed eternity;
  eternity always insists on being analysed.
  I will call you, for you bade me show you the end,

no more servant now, but friend.
Do you run to me or do I run to you?
CRANMER. God, without whom nothing is strong—
THE SKELETON. I respected you, Thomas; I heard; I am
   here.
Do not fear; I am the nothing you meant.
I am sent to gather you into that nothing.
Do you run to me or do I run to you?
CRANMER. Christ or devil, leave me to lie in peace.
THE SKELETON. If I leave you to peace I shall leave you to lie,
   to change without changing, to live without living.
I will not. Do you run to me or do I—
CRANMER. God, God, stop the world moving!
THE SKELETON. Stop me loving, would you? stop me proving
   the perfect end in the diagram of bones?
You believe in God; believe also in me;
I am the Judas who betrays men to God.
Friend, friend!
CRANMER.   Ah, ah, ah!
         [*As he falls forward, his hands clutch his papers; he
         seizes them and straightens himself*
My work! I have a work.
I am nothing except—
THE SKELETON.   I must run then after you.
You will choose the rack instead of the cross?
I am sorry, friend; it takes longer.
I will remember your prayers and meet you
in the core of the brain, in the coasts of the heart,
drawing apart, doubling and troubling you.
Of all my Father gave me I will lose none.
CRANMER. The Council: I must go to the Council.
The King is dead; the book goes to the Council.
Almighty God, unto whom all hearts be open—
                              [*He hurries out*

THOMAS CRANMER OF CANTERBURY

THE SKELETON [*calling after him*]. Yours is; a little while, and
we meet at Oxford,
and she who is to come, the Queen who sends you there,
I will have her too; I will catch her as well as you.

> [*He turns suddenly on the* COMMONS *who are moving. They rush out in confusion*

And all you—I will lose none.
In your lives and tongues I will bring you to climb
at my time, without haste, without sloth,
the rungs of my ladder, where the redeemed
walk; his lordship dreamed
it was set from his English hand in the English land,
but the anatomy itself talks, talks of itself.

> [*The* COMMONS *have gone out; he continues to the audience*

How I speed, how heedfully I speed!
Can you wait? can you see me coming? can you wait?
for a little while and where am I? lo,
a little while and here am I; spin,
spin each of you his brave platter,
his work his life! how it topples and falls!
No matter; spin, platter! spin, world; spin,
air and prayer, without and within, but one
twirling twy-flash dazzle of soul and sun
down the hangman's way on the hangman's day;
can you pray now or be shut-eye dumb?
can you pray: *Even so, Amen, Lord, come?*
as my singers—O hark! as my singers say.

> [*He backs out, beckoning to the* SINGERS, *who rise and follow him*

THE SINGERS. Here we offer and present unto thee, O Lord,
ourselves, our souls and bodies, to be a reasonable,
holy and lively sacrifice . . .

PART TWO

The SINGERS *enter and take their places*

THE SINGERS. My God, my God, look upon me, why hast thou forsaken me: and art so far from my health, and from the words of my complaint?

O my God, I cry in the daytime, but thou hearest not: and in the night season also I take no rest.

And thou continuest holy: O thou worship of Israel.

CRANMER *enters*

CRANMER. Lambeth and Westminster are full of strange song.
A voice but now cracked from the street like a thong
high to the sky, stinging all ears with *Wait,
wait,* singing *the day of the hangman's way.*
I sit in my study; a fit of fear takes my heart
while in my mouth the grand art
fails, speech fails; the thong cracks to the sky;
at the song the souls out of each part of heaven fly;
heaven is thick with spirits flying and crying,
fleeting towards me, and fleeing off ere we meet:
Tyndale was burned; Forrest was cruelly burned—
behind them the souls of the righteous ride in the air;
God be witness I never turned in my mind
or denied, but always sought and desired to spare;
the souls come rushing, flushing, with crimson light,
and the words in my book slither out of my sight
as if they were that creature the King's look
caught, new creatures my thought cannot find
while my mind shrinks from an unknown singer in the street.
Hark now, hark!

THOMAS CRANMER OF CANTERBURY

ONE OF THE COMMONS [*coming in secretly*]. Archbishop, Archbishop,
now when the shaft is shaped from the quill
to aim at the brain, to whistle shrill
against us who are slain for need and not for will,
who saved others and ourselves we cannot save—
Christ pardon us talking on the edge of the grave—
Archbishop, Archbishop,
against us who all our lives on our tongues have rolled
for sweetness of taste God's terms, now we take hold
on a saint unhallowed, a martyr unaureoled;
saying, *so Christ made us, Christ be merciful so,*
Christ pardon us, speaking more than we know.

[*He goes to his place*

CRANMER. The world is full of a threat that forms not yet.
O peace, peace! all we are strangers
each to his brother, each for another
ingeniously inventing temptations and cruel dangers.
Once and twice I have written Melanchthon to come;
he who ingeminated peace to Germany,
he who is nearest in kind of all men to me;
he writes not, he comes not. And we,
we ever reform our books and not ourselves,
but the storm in the street is whipping our books from their shelves,
stripping torn pages, driving white-breasted prayers,
to swoop and stoop and trouble the day,
blinding and stunning us running on a sloping way.
Melanchthon my brother, come from Germany, come,
let us make a council of peace for Christendom.
Is it he? is it he? not he, but now for our sin
time's anguish and anger and bitter clangour begin.

THOMAS CRANMER OF CANTERBURY

The COMMONS *enter noisily; the* PREACHER *runs in, dragging the* PRIEST

THE PREACHER. My lord, my lord, here is a knave
whose parish is weary of him; his bells ring
in the time of sermon; sometimes he sings
in the choir ere sermon is done—nay,
even challenges godly preachers in the pulpit.
The whole parish is a witness to it all.
CRANMER. This were ill done indeed; is it truly so?
THE PREACHER. My lord, he was once an abbot on Tower Hill;
shows his breeding.
THE PRIEST.   I do not say, my lord,
but sometimes, ere sermon is ended, a bell will ring,
or I cry *hem* and turn in my seat, or even
think the preacher were done and begin to sing
before the good man had unburdened all his stuff.
Old habits die hard, my lord, and accidents happen
in churches as well as out.
CRANMER.   What is your church?
THE PRIEST. I am Vicar of Stepney, if it please your Grace.
THE PREACHER. But the people of Stepney are weary of him, my lord.
CRANMER. It is very ill; we must be tender to consciences
when we suffer by them; we must in charity
believe that a good man labours at his duty,
though it should please God plague us by his duty.
Get hence to Stepney, vicar, and hear the sermons.
THE PRIEST. At your Grace's bidding.   [*He retires*
THE PREACHER.   My lord, ye are over-gentle
to so stout a papist!
CRANMER.   Why, we have no law to punish them.
THE PREACHER. Were I Archbishop, I would fast unvicar him;

and put sharp sentence on such rogues as he.
If it come to their turn, they will show us none
of this foolish favour.

CRANMER. Well, if God provide it so,
we shall abide it.

THE PREACHER. God shall snatch the sword
from those who will not use it on his foes.
Y'are warned.

CRANMER. Be off, good fellow; do we serve Christ
by running round with torches, bludgeons, and oaths?
Who was it the torchbearers once found in the garden?
the bludgeon-brandishers brought into court?
the oath-takers smote and smothered?
I am troubled often because, in my jurisdiction,
I have signed and sent obstinate men to the fire.
Amend your life; love all; make your communion
on love and peace—this is the body of the Lord.

THE PREACHER [*retiring*]. Now I see why the great people
  laughing say:
*Do my lord of Canterbury a shrewd turn,
and he is your friend for ever.* But God—
God has only us to defend his glory,
and what will happen to that if we leave off killing?
  [*He goes over to the* LORDS *who have entered, the*
  SKELETON *following*

THE SKELETON [*coming down*]. My hour is nearer; I will
  show myself again.
The way he treads is turning into a rope
under my hands; he pauses; I pick it by a trick
from under his feet, and fling it to these hands that fling
  it to those,
each time circling his body: he feels the pain
constrict his rich arteries—love, and faith, and hope:
tight round his drawn muscles the pressure grows.

THOMAS CRANMER OF CANTERBURY

Did he gird himself to tread my way? he is girt
now by the way, and borne therein to his hurt
by my multitudinous hands. I am his match
to delay and dismay. Catch, my children, catch!
    [*He makes a motion of throwing a rope to the* LORDS
    who, with the PREACHER, *come near* CRANMER

THE SECOND LORD. In this order for the supper of the Lord, 1552
what is this, Archbishop, about kneeling
to a memory, to a past day, to creatures and men?

THE PREACHER. In the Word of God there is no word of kneeling.

CRANMER. Nor standing nor sitting; lie then on the ground—
bivouac as Turks or Tartars, around salvation.

THE SKELETON. Or—might it be said—after the mode of the Apostles?
Controversialists are apt to forget the facts
till a certain jangle of my bones comes to remind them.

THE SECOND LORD. No kneeling; the grace lies in the memory.

CRANMER. I grant it is not given by measurement,
weight, or solidity; it is immaterial;
how can the flesh absorb spirituality?

THE SKELETON. Ah, you do not quite know, incredulous Thomas,
what the flesh can do when it is put to it.
You shall do a thing one day with the flesh of that hand
to astonish men as God may astonish you.
Is not the world full of his witness?
what of the light that lighteth every man?
    [*Running to the edge of the stage and calling to the*
    COMMONS

Have you forgotten, have you forgotten,
how you saw and handled aboriginal glory,

sown from spirit, seeding in flesh?
what is the plot of each man's story
but the wonder and the seeking and the after-sinning,
O bright fish caught in the bright light's mesh?
      [*The* COMMONS *stir. He swings round*
O master and doctor, have you forgotten
when the woman Joan came out of the tavern,
and her face was moulded of heavenly fire?
or how you looked from your Cambridge cavern
and saw King Henry God's spoken splendour?
Shall I, the splendour and the glory, tire?
  [CRANMER *staggers. The* SKELETON *runs and leaps*
  on the Throne
Have you forgotten, have you forgotten,
O my people, have you forgotten,
The moment of central and certain vision,
when time is faithful and terrors befriend,
when the glory is doubled by the sweet derision,
in the grace and peace of the perfect end?

Have you forgotten, have you forgotten,
O my people, have you forgotten,
the moment when flesh and spirit are one,
—are they ever separate, but by a mode?
Though the skull look out, will you fear, will you run?
will you forget how the glory showed?
        [*He pauses and leaps down*
But I intermit the metaphysical dispute
between my lord of Canterbury and his peers.
There is this to be said for my lord of Canterbury,
he dimly believes in something outside himself—
      [*He adds generally to the audience*
Which is more, I can tell you, than most of you do.

THOMAS CRANMER OF CANTERBURY

[*As soon as the* SKELETON *descends, the* SECOND LORD *sits down on the Throne*

THE SECOND LORD. Y'are slack, y'are slack, Archbishop: why do you loiter?

CRANMER. It is rumoured, my Lord, you have shut up in the Tower
 one of the Bishops; that the revenue of the See
 must be accommodated to your Grace.

THE SECOND LORD. We will say to the King: it is put so in the papers.

CRANMER. I must tell you this is against all honesty.
 It were good you stayed till the King came of age.
 I must tell you we serve the King; where is the King?

THE SECOND LORD. I am King enough; you shall not see the King,
 unless by me. I have a plan for the Throne.

[*He plays with the Crown* 1553

 The judges agree; the Council agrees; all men
 agree to the plan I have made. The King agrees.
 The King commands you to agree.

CRANMER.   I will see the King.
 It is my right: I will see the King alone.

THE SECOND LORD. You shall not see the King more than I let you,
 nor alone, nor with any of your loyal, simple sort.
 The King commands you, on your allegiance, agree.

CRANMER. If the King commands—

THE SKELETON.   The rope begins to constrict
 Something happens Doctor Cranmer had not foreseen
 when the King commands something against the kingship.
 There may be worse coming. Hark!

ONE OF THE COMMONS [*running out*]. The King is dead.

43

THOMAS CRANMER OF CANTERBURY

Queen Mary 1553–8

  A trumpet sounds at the entry. The COMMONS *rush on to the stage. The* PRIEST *runs forward. The* SECOND LORD *rises*

THE COMMONS. God save Queen Mary!
THE SECOND LORD [*to the first*]. Shall we stand together?
THE FIRST LORD. I doubt we cannot stand.
CRANMER. Is King Edward dead? I must wait then for the Queen.
      [*A second trumpet. The* COMMONS *shout*
THE SECOND LORD. Can she alter the world?
THE FIRST LORD.   That we shall see presently.
CRANMER. I would I were not so afraid.
THE SKELETON.   The rope constricts.
 Hope is beginning to feel a little choked:
 Faith soon. Love—we shall see presently.
   [*A third trumpet. The* QUEEN *advances. A* BISHOP *accompanies her*
THE SKELETON [*leaping up and down the steps*]. Fly, Thomas.
CRANMER. Bid our friends fly, not me.
       [*The* PREACHER *runs out*
THE SKELETON. Your Bishops fly.
CRANMER.   Well; but I cannot fly.
 I will not turn from the things that I have done.
THE COMMONS. God save the Queen.
THE SKELETON. She is coming on you; you will lose your See.
CRANMER. It was given by God and the Prince, and it is theirs.
THE COMMONS. God save the Queen.
      [*The* LORDS *take off their hats*
THE COMMONS AND THE LORDS. God save the Queen.
THE SKELETON. She is coming; you will lose your honours.
CRANMER.   Have I any?
 Neither honours nor dignities—nor money hardly:

THOMAS CRANMER OF CANTERBURY

I was richer when I came to Lambeth first.
But money and life belong to God and the Prince.

THE SKELETON. She is coming; you will lose your honour.

CRANMER. If God please;
they roared my courage out of me when I was young.
Yet, if God please, I will stand to what I have done.

THE SKELETON. Your mind and your world make nonsense of your life.

She is here; my hour is at hand; now I am yours.

[*He goes to the back*

ALL. God save Queen Mary.

> [*All the* PERSONS *kneel, while the* QUEEN *takes her throne, the* BISHOP *beside her.* CRANMER *rises. The* QUEEN *kneels. The* SKELETON *exhibits himself in the attitude of one crucified*

THE SINGERS.

> Tantum ergo sacramentum
> Veneremur cernui:
> Et antiquum documentum
> Novo cedat ritui;
> Praestet fides supplementum
> Sensuum defectui.

> [*The* SKELETON *comes down the stage; all the* PERSONS *crouch lower as he passes. He faces* CRANMER *at the opposite corner*

THE SKELETON. The writings yield to the Rite; the Rite to me.
This is the end, friend, of all translation,
when your bones are translated to what you loved and hated. [*The* QUEEN *rises and sits*

CRANMER. When King Henry told me his dream I dared not speak
of the beak of the King's falcon, but well I knew
how it flew through my sleep, as now; a slither of wings

45

beats on my face and brings
a hot iron to my heart; in the dream I cannot shriek
nor speak; my heart stops; I am nailed,
impaled by that motionless heart to the air or what there
where I hang the air is. I float; each limb
at its own whim begins to jerk and gyrate
or at some power's ruling the hour; they dance,
I live askance in a jest, the puppet of the prince
of the air, long since damned, I damned long since.
Christ help me! my heart dead,
my body spread, my mind lusting to walk,
handle, learnedly talk: but each jerk
of the limbs lurks in the brain, becoming babble
of words, words unmeaning, insignificant gabble,
words infinitely dividing; infinitely sliding
smoothly, faster and faster, before and behind each other:
mind and body, nothing stops or drops or ends till I wake.
God have mercy upon me for Christ his sake!
First when I came to Cambridge, wretched man;
in the night ere Anne died, again when the lords
accused, or of late were fain destroy: but this last
darkness was wholly passed so, dream into dream
cast, sweat into sweat, fear into fear;
when the Queen from the depth came rising, riding so near:
when the Queen came riding yesterday into the town;
she had no head, over her shoulders the Crown
threw a golden light; her hands emerged on the rein;
at her horse's pacing my limbs jerked in pain,
as the Queen rising, riding, came steadily in.
Purge, O God, a sinful man of his sin.

                                            [*He bows himself*

THE SKELETON [*standing over him*]. When the heart has no motion, the brain no thought,
  we shall see what we shall see;
  he shall find into what plight he was brought
  when we bade his desire be.
  He had his way; if he trod his way,
  where there's a way there's a will;
  many there be that find the way,
  few that find the will.
THE SINGERS. Lighten our darkness, we beseech thee, O Lord, and by thy great mercy defend us from all perils and dangers of this night.

[*All the persons rise*

ONE OF THE COMMONS. Master Cranmer has made submission.
ANOTHER. He has made adoration.
ANOTHER. He has set up the mass again at Canterbury.
ANOTHER. It is false; he gave the Bishop of Rochester a paper.
THE PRIEST. God has put down the mighty from their seats.
THE FIRST LORD. It is fortunate then that he chose to put down the Archbishop
  whom the Queen's grace can heartily condemn for heresy;
  the question of sedition may be quietly dropped.
THE SECOND LORD. After all, the Dudleys were never really gentlemen,
  Lady Jane was making difficulties already.
CRANMER [*standing up*]. I raise again the mass at Canterbury?
  It was a false and flattering monk who did so.
  Have I erred? let them show me then where I have erred.
THE SKELETON. In thinking, though it was important for you to be right,
  it mattered at all in the end whether you were right.

CRANMER. I stand by all the doctrine of the Church.
　　The Scripture and the Fathers are agreed—
　　it was given for communion and not adoration,
　　and it was made idolatry everywhere.

The Degradation 1555–6

THE QUEEN. Thomas Cranmer, falsely called Archbishop...

CRANMER [*going to her*]. Madam,
　　your father made me...

THE QUEEN. 　　　　　　　　who unmade my mother,
　　discrowned her and disthroned the Holy Thing...

THE SKELETON. O tares! O wheat; that grow together to harvest:
　　I run with you, O my people, through the dark air.
　　Thomas, your heart that was double with God and the Devil
　　must be choked by a heart double with the Devil and God.

THE QUEEN. ... will you recant now?

CRANMER. 　　　　　　　　What should I recant?
　　Madam, your Grace, by God's grace, is the head
　　of all the people of England, therefore the head
　　of the Church they are: one folk, one Church, one head.

THE BISHOP. The Queen has denounced you to the Holy Father.

1555 CRANMER. Ah, that the Queen should denounce her subject to a stranger!

THE FIRST LORD. Madam, this treachery shocks me.

THE SECOND LORD. 　　　　　We have come, Madam,
　　to entreat your Grace to restore adoration and the Pope
　　who has been of late a stranger only by accident,
　　by a slight misunderstanding about motherhood.

THE FIRST LORD. We have drawn up an act for the restoration,

THE SECOND LORD. adding
　　a second part to prevent interference with property.

THOMAS CRANMER OF CANTERBURY

If the abbey lands were ours when we were Protestant
they will clearly be closely ours when we are Catholic—
not that we are ever anything in fact but ourselves.

We are the proprietors; we are time and space.

THE FIRST LORD. With that corollary, behold us wholly yours.

THE SECOND LORD. And dispose of the Archbishop in any way you choose.

Every contract involves a little sacrifice.

THE SKELETON. When time and space withdraw, there is nothing left

but yourself and I: lose yourself, there is only I.

THE BISHOP. The Holy Father, by his sentence, here
deputes us to degrade you. Thus—and thus.

CRANMER. Which of you hath a pall to take my pall?   1556

THE SKELETON. I.

> [*He wrenches the crozier from* CRANMER'*s hand, and
> gives it to the* BISHOP. CRANMER *is unfrocked and
> a coarse gown is put on him*

THE SINGERS. O Lord God of my salvation, I have cried
day and night before thee: O let my prayer enter into
thy presence, incline thine ear unto my calling.

For my soul is full of trouble: and my life draweth
nigh unto hell.

Thou hast laid me in the lowest pit: in a place of
darkness, and in the deep.

My sight faileth for very trouble: Lord, I have called
daily upon thee, I have stretched out my hands unto
thee.

I am in misery, and like unto him that is at the point
to die: even from my youth up thy terrors have I suffered
with a troubled mind.

Thy wrathful displeasure goeth over me: and the fear
of thee hath undone me.

THOMAS CRANMER OF CANTERBURY

> They came round about me daily like water: and compassed me together on every side.
>
> My lovers and friends hast thou put away from me: and hid mine acquaintance out of my sight.

THE BISHOP. Now you are no lord any longer, nor priest; you are excommunicate.

CRANMER. I appeal from all
to the Council of the Universal Church.

THE BISHOP. But the Universal Church has cast you out.

THE SKELETON. Thomas, what is happening now is more like the counsel of the Universal Church,
the operation of the body of Christ,
than any language.
Things spoken seem unfamiliar when they happen.
[*He stands opposite* CRANMER *at the top of the steps, in the attitude of a priest in procession*

The Recantations 1556

THE QUEEN. Will you recant?

CRANMER. I will always submit myself
to the Church, and the Pope if the Pope be head of the Church,
if they can prove me that out of the Scriptures.

THE SKELETON [*taking a step*]. That just unfrocked you; will you be unfleshed?

THE QUEEN. It shall not serve; will you submit yourself to adoration and our Father at Rome?

THE BISHOP. Hilary, Augustine, Ambrose, Chrysostom, Tertullian—
will you set yourself up against these?

THE QUEEN. We are the Prince, as our father was the Prince: will you set yourself up against us?

THE BISHOP. If the Pope is head of the Church, obey; if the Prince
and the Prince admit the Pope, why, still obey.
Will you set yourself up against your principles?

THE SKELETON [*taking a step*]. There is an hour—this,
   Thomas, is the hour—
  when the pure intellectual jurisdiction
  commits direct suicide: the minds and the world
  die, and the life shivers between their bones.
CRANMER. If the Queen serve the Pope, I will serve the
   Queen.
THE QUEEN. This shall not serve; we have signed the writ
   for the burning.
THE BISHOP. But see, what quiet might come instead of
   burning!
THE SKELETON [*taking a step*]. And no man can think clearly
   while he is burning!
  Though, we agree, that is neither here nor there.
  What is incineration compared to truth?
THE QUEEN. Consider the command of the Prince who is as
   a god.
THE BISHOP. Consider the witness of doctors to the will of
   God.
THE SKELETON [*taking a step*]. Consider anything with a
   remote resemblance to God
  that is likely in the least degree to save you from burning.
                                                        [*A pause*
CRANMER. General Councils have erred and Popes have
   erred:
  is it not like that my word went wrong?
THE SKELETON.   It is like.
CRANMER. That when I strove at winning the land for
   Christ
  I erred from the beginning?
THE SKELETON.   From the beginning.
CRANMER. Christ my God, I am utterly lost and damned.
  I sin whatever I do.
THE SKELETON.   Whatever you do.

CRANMER. As well sin this way and live as that way and die.
It is folly and misery all.
THE SKELETON. Folly and misery.
CRANMER. Did I sin in my mother's womb that I was forsaken
all my life? where is my God?
THE SKELETON. Where is your God?
  [*After a pause*
When you have lost him at last you shall come into God.
  [*The papers of recantation are brought to* CRANMER
CRANMER [*signing them*]. I will sign anything, everything. I have burned,
and the flame is returned on my soul: if it saves from hell
I may well recant; they may be right; they are,
for they say they are, they are sure, they are strong. O Christ
—Christ leaves me to myself, I lose myself,
as I lose him; I will believe adoration,
I will receive the Catholic Church of the Pope,
I will put my hope in images and substitution;
I sinned in the false dissolution of King Henry's matter.
Bring me all; I will acknowledge all.
I was the master of a whole college of heresies—
faster! faster!—I am the worst
that ever the earth bore, most outcast, most accurst
... Korah ... Saul ... the penitent thief ... O Christ, what have I done?
THE SKELETON. What have you done?
THE BISHOP. These
unforced, with a pure consent, you freely deliver?
CRANMER. I have signed, I will sign, all; freely I will sign.
THE SKELETON. There are two freedoms, brother; this is one.
Between now and tomorrow's sun you shall come to the other.

THOMAS CRANMER OF CANTERBURY

THE BISHOP [*returning to the* QUEEN]. Madam, the apostasy
  is ended; Cranmer recants.
THE QUEEN. Tomorrow then, let him be given to the fire,
  and let the recantation be publicly proclaimed.
ONE OF THE COMMONS. Master Cranmer hath recanted.
THE PREACHER [*creeping in*]. No; he dare not!
ANOTHER OF THE COMMONS. He has sworn the Pope back
  again into England.
ANOTHER. No; that was done but now in the Parliament.
ANOTHER. They will not burn him then?
ANOTHER.   Yes, he will burn.
THE PREACHER. He has betrayed—
THE PRIEST.   He is restored to—
BOTH.   truth!
THE SINGERS. Dies irae, dies illa, *The Martyr-*
  Solvet saeclum in favilla, *dom*
  Teste David cum Sibylla. *20 March 1556*
CRANMER. They will burn me; I know it; I denied God for
  naught.
THE SKELETON. Some men deny, some men declare; un-
  less I,
  who shall try the denial and the declaration?
  I will try it in my way, not yours nor any man's else.
CRANMER. They will burn me.
THE SKELETON.   What is that, O soul, to
  thee and me?
  Thomas, all your life you have sought Christ
  in images, through deflections; how else can men see?
  Plastic, you sought integrity, and timid, courage.
  Most men, being dishonest, seek dishonesty;
  you, among few, honesty, such as you knew,
  in corners of sin, round curves of deception;
  honesty, the point where only the blessed live,
  where only saints settle, the point of conformity.

Mine is the diagram; I twirl it to a point,
the point of conformity, of Christ. You shall see Christ,
see his back first—I am his back.

CRANMER. Can life itself be redemption? all grace but grace?
all this terror the agonizing glory of grace?
but what will they do? will they pardon or burn?

THE SKELETON. I am Christ's back; I without face or breath,
life in death, death in life,
each a strife with, each a socket for, each,
in the twisted rear of good will, backward-running speech,
the derision that issues from doctrines of grace
through the division man makes between him and his place.
Christ laughs his foes to scorn, his angels he charges
with folly; ah, happy who feel how the scorn enlarges!
I am the thing that lives in the midst of the bones,
that (seems it) thrives upon moans, the thing with no face
that spins through the brain on the edge of a spectral voice.
Rejoice, son of man, rejoice:
this is the body of Christ which is given for you;
feed on it in your heart by faith with thanksgiving.

CRANMER. Will they burn me?

21 March 1556

THE SKELETON. Friend, do you hear the horses, the horses?
Do you hear the gentlemen riding to town?
Lord Williams of Thame and Sir Robert Bridges,
and Sir John Brown and his Oxford neighbours,
the gentlemen riding into town?

[*He begins to sing*
for the burning of a poor man, a very poor man:
a poor man in duty, God save him from duty!
a poor man in honour, God save him from honour!

THOMAS CRANMER OF CANTERBURY

a poor man in misery, God save him from misery!
All Christian people, pray for a poor man!
   [*He runs to the edge of the stage and sings outward*
All Christian people, God save you from riches!
if you have duty, God save you from duty!
if you have honour, God save you from honour!
if you have misery, God save you from misery!
God make you poor men for the burning of a poor man.
THE SINGERS. He hath filled the hungry with good things,
   and the rich he hath sent empty away.

Two EXECUTIONERS *enter, carrying torches. They stand in the middle of the stage. The* SKELETON *turns, still at the edge of the stage, and looks at* CRANMER

THE BISHOP [*coming to* CRANMER]. Master Cranmer, have
   you any money?
CRANMER.   No.
THE BISHOP. Here are fifteen crowns to give to the poor.
THE SKELETON [*singing*]. At the bringing out of a poor man,
   a very poor man.
CRANMER. Why does he talk of crowns?
THE SKELETON [*running to him*].   Friend,
   traitors and heretics, common criminals, lazars,
   are given alms for the poor. Lazar, set forth.
   Mayhap someone will give you such alms on your way
   as shall make you rich for ever with another's riches.
CRANMER. They will burn me then?
THE SKELETON.   Friend, it is necessary,
   they will tell you; love necessity; I am he,
   I am coming, run—run hastily to meet me.
   You shall find that in me is no more necessity. Run.
CRANMER. I will run, I will run . . . [*He stops, choking*].
THE SKELETON.   I will run faster than you.
   I will run faster than this man's words or yours.

THOMAS CRANMER OF CANTERBURY

I am the only thing that outruns necessity,
I am necessary Love where necessity is not.

> [*They fetch* CRANMER *to the centre of the stage. The* BISHOP *goes as to a pulpit, the* SKELETON *following him and standing behind him. A noise from the crowd*

THE BISHOP. Behold him, good people!

THE SKELETON [*copying the* BISHOP'S *gesture*]. Behold him, covenant of Christ!

THE BISHOP. Though he repent, it is needful that he burn
to make equilibrium with the Lord Cardinal John
who died for defending as this man for destroying.

THE SKELETON. I have made equilibrium; I have drawn him level.

THE BISHOP. And for other just causes known to the Queen and Council
which now must not be opened to the common folk.

THE SKELETON. For the cause of the justice that I will thoroughly open
on the day when I do so well that ye cannot think.

THE BISHOP. He that stole from England the food of the soul
weeps, repents, is saved as the thief that rose
from a cross by Christ to the promise of Christ's own cross.

THE SKELETON. The Son of Man comes as a thief in the night.
After my mode I have gathered many souls;
who shall prevent me, coming swiftly for all?

> [*The* QUEEN *rises*

THE BISHOP. This child of Apollyon is saved; infinite grace!

THE SKELETON. Infinite, without measurement or dimension,
the contradiction of measurement and dimension;
I only measure what I only am.

THOMAS CRANMER OF CANTERBURY

THE BISHOP. Lest any man doubt his repentance, his conversion
he shall tell you ere he die; Master Cranmer, speak.
THE SKELETON. I am equated now to his very soul:
I am his equilibrium; Thomas, speak.
CRANMER [*kneeling*]. Blessed Omnipotence, in whom is heaven,
heaven and earth are alike offended at me!
I can reach from heaven no succour, nor earth to me.
What shall I then? despair? thou art not despair.
Into thee now do I run, into thy love,
that which is all the cause thou wert man for us,
and we are nothing but that for which thou wert man,
these horrible sins the cause of thy being man,
these sins to thy love the cause of motion in love,
where is stayed no sin nor is merit of ours marked,
nor aught can live but the hallowings of thy Name,
through which thy kingdom comes, in earth and heaven
thy will being done, the bread of which be our food.
THE SKELETON. And I lead you all from temptation and deliver from evil!
THE SINGERS. Amen.
CRANMER [*rising*]. Good people, give not your minds to this glozing world,
nor murmur against the glory of the Queen;
love each other, altogether love each other;
each to each be full of straight goodwill,
wherethrough let the rich give naturally to the poor
always, and especially in this present time
when the poor are so many and food so dear.
What else? yet for myself I will something say:
I am quite come to believe in Omnipotent God
and in every article of the Catholic Faith.
But since the Queen will have me cut from obedience,

outcast from her, I must have an outcast's mind,
a mind that is my own and not the Queen's,
poorly my own, not richly her society's.
Therefore I draw to the thing that troubles me
more than all else I ever did—the writings
I let abroad against my heart's belief
to keep my life . . . if that might be . . . that I signed
with this hand, after I was degraded: this hand,
which wrote the contrary of God's will in me,
since it offended most, shall suffer first;
it shall burn ere I burn, now I go to the fire,
and the writings, all writings wherein I denied God's will,
or made God's will but the method of my life,
I altogether reject them.
> [*A pause. The* SKELETON *goes to the top of the steps. Then an uproar*

FIRST LORD. Are you in your wits?
SECOND LORD.   Do not dissemble.
CRANMER.   My lords,
I am a man loved plainness all my life,
nor ever till lately dissembled against the truth,
which now I am most sorry for.
THE BISHOP.   Stop his mouth.
VOICES. Away with him to the fire!
> [*The* EXECUTIONERS *run out*

                         He is mad with rage!
He despairs, he despairs!
                         The devil hath his soul!
Blessed be God for the good man's word!
                                    Blessed!
He does not know what he says!
THE SKELETON.   But I know all.
Friend, let us say one thing more before the world—

THOMAS CRANMER OF CANTERBURY

I for you, you for me: let us say all:

if the Pope had bid you live, you would have served him.

CRANMER. If the Pope had bid me live, I should have served him.

THE SKELETON. Speed!

CRANMER. Speed!

ALL THE PERSONS. Speed!

[*They all hurry out*

THE SINGERS. Glory be to the Father, and to the Son; and to the Holy Ghost; As it was in the beginning, is now, and ever shall be: world without end. Amen.

JUDGEMENT AT CHELMSFORD

*A Pageant Play in Celebration of the Twenty-fifth
Anniversary of the Diocese of Chelmsford*

SYNOPSIS

Judgement at Chelmsford, unlike most pageants, combines all its Episodes into a complete whole. Each, therefore, must be understood not as a separate incident, but as an incident related to all the others and to the final climax. Each episode also has, for those who care to take it so, two sides: the historical and the spiritual. Thus the complete pageant offers a representation not only of the history of the diocese, but of the movement of the soul of man in its journey from the things of this world to the heavenly city of Almighty God.

PROLOGUE

Chelmsford, on her birthday, comes to the gate of heaven to talk with her elder brothers, the Great Sees of Christendom. There are five of these—Canterbury, Rome, Constantinople, Antioch and Jerusalem, representing the chief bishoprics of the Universal Church. Her approach is prevented by a figure called the Accuser, who warns her that before she can enter heaven she must see herself as she really is. He asks, if she were called to death and judgement that night, by the destructiveness of war, what she could say on her own behalf, and he calls on the Five Sees, ministers of justice, to listen to her defence. They enter, to the sound of aeroplanes and bombs, and also call in St. Cedd, the Apostle of Essex, to defend and befriend his spiritual child. The stage is thus set for an exhibition of her 'ways of living', that is, how far and with what energy she has followed God.

JUDGEMENT AT CHELMSFORD

FIRST EPISODE—MODERN TIMES

The modern diocese in its dual aspects of town and country life is represented by machine-workers and agricultural labourers. The commonest accusation thrown at the Church is that of futility, and in this episode the accusation is presented at its face value. A young girl, eager for life, is met by a priest who, sincerely but inadequately, proposes to her the Christian religion; she refuses it because she does not feel it to be 'as strong as the blood in her'. A Committee discuss ways and means of attracting the young people into the churches. A tendency arises to consider the whole world of grace in terms of the attractiveness of this world. But underneath this there remains, as the Sees point out, the undoubted power of God and the courage and faith (however badly expressed) of Christians. This episode as much as any other is therefore an assertion of Christianity.

EPISODE 2—THE CHELMSFORD WITCHES

The Accuser, taking advantage of this first presentation, points out the false way in which such words as Love, Power, Grace are used on earth. To exhibit this he calls up Matthew Hopkins, a lawyer of Manningtree, who under cover of the love of God, bought himself comfort by getting money for witch-hunting, and shows himself as much a son of the devil as any witch. It is here that the character of the Accuser is explained. If the witches desire to see the devil, they see the Accuser in his place, for

> God made me to be the image of each man's desire—
> A king or a poet or a devil—rarely Christ.
> Most men when at last they see their desire,
> fall to repentance—all have that chance.

JUDGEMENT AT CHELMSFORD

The Chorus recall our Lord's saying that Satan cannot cast out Satan and mock at Satan's kingdom. Rome and Canterbury ask pardon of each other for the follies and evils done in the history of Christ's Church on earth.

EPISODE 3—THE REFORMATION

This episode depicts the two opposing parties of Papalists and Reformers, the former fighting for the Rites and the latter for the Bible. A Catholic and a Protestant martyr are seen at the same stake. A seraph descends to release their souls to peace. They turn to each other and recognize that the mission of each was given by the other's need, and that both brought honour to Christ and joy to heaven.

EPISODE 4—BARKING ABBEY

After the foregoing episode, Chelmsford asks to be allowed to show ordinary lives, gay as they can be, and St. Cedd calls up the girls of Barking Abbey at the Christmas feast of the Triduum, when for three days, including Holy Innocents, the girls elected their own Lady Abbess and ruled the convent as they wished. A play, supposed to be written by Nicholas Udall, one time vicar of Braintree and author of *Roister Doister*, is rehearsed.

EPISODE 5—
JOHN BALL AND THE PEASANTS' RISING

The Accuser enjoys as much as any the beautiful and mild moments of life, but 'wit flashes to heaven more from a full stomach than ever from an empty'. He accuses the Church through the ages of being negligent of man's earthly needs. He calls up the Peasants of 1431, who, inspired by the Priest, John Ball, went to King Richard to demand that the principles learnt from Holy Church should be put into practice. The needs of the poor are always the indirect, if

JUDGEMENT AT CHELMSFORD

not the direct, concern of the Church. The King fails them and they are driven back by the 'wall of gold, iron and steel'. As the prophets of old pronounced the doom of Babylon, so now the Chorus pronounces doom on that great city London. She shall stumble into the judgement away from God to feed evermore on the chaff she proffered the poor. Chelmsford and the Great Sees join in a psalm of penitence.

EPISODE 6—MARTYRDOM OF ST. OSYTH

St. Cedd asserts that in spite of many fallings away from the faith, and the many times when it seemed almost to be extinguished, there have always been some who maintained belief in Love; that is, in Love as being a real actual and dominating principle. As witness to this, St. Osyth is called from heaven. A fierce band of Danes put the nuns to flight and kill Osyth. The Chorus recall her to heaven, but Chelmsford, in need of the support of the saints, implores her to stay. Jerusalem assures her of Christ's permission, and Osyth goes to find her old homes of Essex, and many others. At this present promise of divine life, Chelmsford feels a pang of relief and understanding. She cries a little as the stress of her anxiety grows less, and she begins to believe that self-knowledge and repentance are a preliminary to the Communion of Saints.

EPISODE 7—OLD KING COLE

The Chorus speak of the extravagance of the love of God in creating man and filling him with that same desire for extravagance of loving joy. Chelmsford proclaims that God's grace has kept joy in her, as seen in the love and friendship of man with man, woman with woman, man with woman. Legends and tales tell the same story, and she calls up 'Old King Cole' (King Coel of Colchester, who was, of course, an historical character) and his daughter Helena, who, according to some legends, married Constantius, the Western Caesar, and became the mother of the first Christian Roman Emperor, Constantine the Great. Constantius discusses with King Cole the merits of the City as opposed to the Nation, and finds the City 'where all nations can know themselves through others' the greater name. He admits that the one thing Rome lacks is a soul—a vision worthy of her. For the Pagan, the City and a little friendship within the City is man's total sum of good. At the sight of Helena, Love, 'the only untired god that is left', reveals to him the vision that Rome lacked. To this hour of greatness he dedicates the child of the union, who, he prophesies, will draw a new doctrine into the heart of Rome. Constantinople confirms the view that the body is holy and valuable, because our Lord is incarnate and not a mirage in a desert of piety. As Moses saw the glory of God in the burning bush, so the glory of God may be revealed through 'the actual unveiled beauty of flesh to eyes of love'. Canterbury describes how God has been pleased to send rumours of Paradise—the invisible world of greatness—to man through his senses, and asks where witness of this may be found. Chelmsford replies that these may be found in her now as in the earliest days. The call from that other world is shrill, and whoever hears, sows a seed from Eden's giant tree of life. Man's experience is full of divine things. But, Canterbury asks, where does man reap and glean the results of these?

It is Jerusalem who answers this question: 'In me' and strangely, 'in the gloom of the tomb that is no tomb'. In speaking thus, Jerusalem has a deeper knowledge than the other Patriarchs, knowing that without the tomb there can be no Resurrection. He describes the violent and inflamed horror that sweeps over man, and the pain that drives along the nerves and lives of mankind, and the desolation of the soul when everything is but a vision of pain. He asks who bears witness to this. Chelmsford, too, knows the terror and the horror of life, and she knows that everyone who lives in her knows it. Remembering our Lord's promise never to fail those who call upon Him, she commands Him to come to her aid.

'Be quick, be quick; it is I; you love me; come.'

EPISODE 8—
ST. HELENA AND THE INVENTION OF THE CROSS

As the Choir sings of the 'glorious battle and the ending of the fray' Chelmsford's prayer is answered, though her struggle is not yet ended. Two seraphs descend the heavenly stairway with a covered burden. Thomas Ken, one time vicar of Little Easton, is called to explain the 'mystical legend of the finding of the Cross'. Preaching as to his parishioners on the day of the Invention of the Cross, he tells how St. Helena found in Jerusalem the place of the true Cross, but 'find you the Cross within you, you shall find Christ Himself, so holy, so fresh, so sweet and fragrant a Cross that you shall laugh to find how you have mistook Him'.

EPILOGUE

The Chorus and Jerusalem make an impassioned appeal to Chelmsford to bend and loosen the rigid sinews of her soul. The appeal is not in vain. Chelmsford, in accepting and binding herself to the Cross, finds that grief brings joy and that peace awakes through all moments at once. Jerusalem is no longer seen as a stern father, but her final home and resting place. The Accuser is her lover, who through love of her, has made her see and face facts as they are, and brought her humble repentance. All who are in her, past, present, and to come, unite themselves to her in the great exchange of mortal and divine love through the Incarnation and Atonement. He leads her to the Great Sees, who welcome and embrace her, while the whole company sing the Te Deum 'Thou art the King of Glory, O Christ' and the Diocese of Chelmsford achieves its end in God.

Prologue	71
Episode I. Modern Life	77
Episode II. The Chelmsford Witches	85
Episode III. The Reformation	94
Episode IV. The Girl Abbess of Barking	101
Episode V. John Ball and the Peasant Rising	115
Episode VI. St. Osyth and the Danes	123
Episode VII. Old King Cole	128
Episode VIII. The Invention of the Cross	139
Epilogue	145

PROLOGUE

*The place is outside the gates of Heaven, considered as in
the air above the diocese.* CHELMSFORD *enters*

CHELMSFORD. I am a young See, yet I am one
with all the rest of Christendom, blest as they—
Canterbury, Rome, Constantinople, Antioch,
Jerusalem, my predecessors, my brothers and lords.
My house is in the plains beyond the mouth of Thames,
and built by the rushing wind and the tongued flames
where the coast of heaven borders the English coast
and the byres of Essex are the shires of the Holy Ghost.
I am as old as the whole Church in Britain.
Cedd raised the first rough fold of my sheep
and I hallow his name wholesomely where the plough
shears the fields still as in his own years,
but otherwise now towns are much of my ministry:
mark them, the might, mirth, and misery of England,
spreading, treading hard on each other's heels, making me
changed from what I was once, before the charge
of my children was wholly mine, before the mitre
touched my brows with something darker than age,
to assuage their need, comfort, console, cherish,
lest if they perish I too be cast from the place
with my peers, the patriarchates, the heavenly thrones
whose zones map Christendom, in England, and beyond
where the great ships float from my river. To-day
the fledged heel of Contemplation strikes the edged wheel
of Time, to spin it, and heaven opens within.
It is my birthday; on this feast I come to the place
of grace in vision, to the gate of heaven, to walk
and talk with the grand celestial princes, they
who assess the deeds of the Church militant on earth,

and confess in clear light the fulfilment of their needs.
I am come shyly to meet them; blessed be he
who made me also in Christendom holy and free.
  A kind of gentle discord. The ACCUSER *comes in*
THE ACCUSER. Halt there, sweet!
CHELMSFORD.   Whose feet here
  interpose between me and those who await me?
THE ACCUSER. Child of the Apostles, do you hope to come
  quite so easily into heaven? think again.
  The Apostolic Sees will have something to say
  to that; and I too, whether they do or not.
CHELMSFORD. Who are you? where do you come from?
THE ACCUSER.   I come
  from going with time up and down the earth,
  testing the worth of the confessors. David and Job,
  Peter and Paul, Becket and Wesley knew me;
  there are few who do not. The Creator of all,
  Primal Wisdom, primal Justice, primal Love,
  made me and bade me to my work. I stand
  at the right hand of all men in their hour of death;
  but also they may see me at any hour. Their breath
  catches, their blood is cold, they remember their sins.
  They see what they have made of their lives.
CHELMSFORD.   But why
  to me now, to-day, at the gate of heaven?
THE ACCUSER. Sweet, your world is become perilous to you.
  This is no age with long peaceful hours
  fastidiously changing young things into old;
  families, cities, churches gradually thriving
  through the happy quiet virtues, as the corn grows.
  The air is dangerous with flames other than Pentecost
  and a host other than angelic rides—hark!
              [*The noise of aeroplanes at a distance*
  Day and dark alike carry the things

that strike bitterly and awfully at bed and board
leaving the dead in the shelters and in the streets.
Hark!
> [*The distant sound of bombs; a faint scream or two.
> Aeroplanes*

If you were called to-night to be judged, how
could you answer? do not speak; I have come to show.
> [*The aeroplanes seem to pass over*

CHELMSFORD. I take refuge with God.
THE ACCUSER. So do; but I too,
I shall be there. Call on your refuge, call.
I will call for you. Ho, heavens of creation,
ho, ministers of justice, vengeance, mercy,
ho, foundations of grace; come down and hear.
CHELMSFORD. Mercy of God, justify me.
THE ACCUSER. Truth of God,
exhibit her!
> [*The* CHORUS *without begins the* Dies irae *interrupted
> by the bombs*

THE CHORUS. Dies irae. . . .
> [*The procession of the* SEES, *accompanied by*
> MUSICIANS *and* CANDLE-BEARERS. *When they have
> taken their places they speak*

CANTERBURY. I am Canterbury; Augustine taught me;
  beside Augustine
I gathered to myself the fruits of Iona and Glastonbury;
I have fathered many children; you, daughter,
loved as much as any. I will know what you know.
ROME. I am Rome; Peter made me and blessed Paul;
no small history is mine, and yet all
is to be the servant of servants and intercede
as Peter at need was lamb-like bidden to do.
CONSTANTINOPLE. I am Constantinople; I raised
a Church to Holy Wisdom; it turned to a mosque.

JUDGEMENT AT CHELMSFORD

The East famished; the West forgot; but God
discerned through all how I praised the Unity.
ANTIOCH. Antioch am I; in me the faithful were named
Christian first, shamed a little in the naming,
a scandal to others. O Christians, are you to yourselves
a scandal now? or by yourselves unblamed?
JERUSALEM. I am the oldest and youngest of all the Sees,
Jerusalem; the body of my Bishop was never shrined
after it was twined on the criss-cross pontifical chair,
and a mitre there of a sharp kind on his head.
ALL THE SEES [*stretching their arms upwards and outwards to touch their fingers*].
Blessed and hallowed and praised be the Thing in us
communicating each to other and other to each,
Blessed and hallowed and praised in the beginning
and in the ending be God, in time and beyond time.
CANTERBURY. Daughter, when Contemplation called to us
that you were waiting at the gate of the third heaven
we arose and came; the fame of all the bishoprics
comes up to us; we have loved you much
for the souls that sprang into heaven by the touch
that took from our own the power of your hand; and the speech of your voice
that learned to teach others as we taught you.
But it seems the Accuser of all things, living and dead,
the dweller on the threshold of love, is here too,
new-set to hinder and hamper your coming.
THE ACCUSER. Neither to hamper nor hinder; I show fact
outward and inward. It is her business
if the facts of her history rise between her and you
to shut the gate of heaven in her face, and her fate
leaves her outside.
CANTERBURY. When the High God made you,
brother, he bade you interpret in your fashion—

JUDGEMENT AT CHELMSFORD

  the worst of the worst; accuracy without compassion,
  curst things always shown as guilt—
  often, not always, they are. Call some other,
  some friend of our child, to show the other side
  of truth: even truth has always two sides.
THE ACCUSER. Call anyone you like; call all you can.
  I desire neither her damnation nor her salvation.
  Sister, who will you have to defend and befriend you?
CHELMSFORD. Who more than he who first taught me?
  brought my shires through the shining water
  into Christendom? these places that were I
  before I was named? shamed though I be
  for ill following his way, yet am I still
  his mystical child. Blessed one, blessed Cedd,
  sped long since to your saving, to the Prince of Zion,
  cry to your Lord that he send you down now;
  how should he be content to let you lose
  your love's effort, the incarnate news of grace?
  Cedd, come from Christ, come once more
  to this shore betwixt earth and heaven; speak for me.
THE ACCUSER. Come, listen to the world in which you lived.
  Christendom has thrived well since you died,
  in some thirteen hundred years to rend the sky
  with flaming fleets, and the streets shrieking below.
  O it has made a good thing of your speaking.
      The aeroplanes and bombs: ST. CEDD *enters*
ST. CEDD. I was with holy Aidan, come from Iona,
  lord of Lindisfarne in the spiritual land:
  the cry reached me there, now as before,
  when the East Saxons called; then being thralled
  in a sacred servitude to Aidan my overlord,
  I was sent by him to lead a raid into Essex;
  I obeyed; forest and ford heard the sound
  of the northern sea of Christ crying *Alleluia*.

JUDGEMENT AT CHELMSFORD

So there we stamped the sacraments on them.
At Maldon and Tilbury I made a house of monks
to be hosts of adoration, nor forget I
the vows between me and my folk, the yoke we carry
each for other: what was spoke then
lasts while men do, on earth or in heaven,
liege of lastingness, sworn faith of the Saviour.
What may I do now for England and Essex?
Say, pontiffs, say, child of love.
Say you also, well-belovèd brother,
who have of all tasks the ungratefullest toil.

THE ACCUSER. Cedd, we have often met, and now again.
Neither can grudge other, but that these
may judge rightly, do what you can and may.
Explain, as best, what has happened in Essex
since your day ended: your daughter is mitred,
very princely, prinked in modest pomp,
habitually sedate in her seat along the water.
Good; I will show you her soul—

CHELMSFORD.   Ah no!

THE SEES. Show; show; show; show; show—

THE ACCUSER. Her history, her ways of living.

ST. CEDD.   Show.

THE ACCUSER. Sweet, what say you? judgement or no judgement?

CHELMSFORD [*after a silent horror*]. I have believed; I take refuge with God; show.

THE ACCUSER. See then; this is your belief in God.

EPISODE I

The sound of aeroplanes again, but this time, instead of fading, it changes into a louder noise which develops into the hum of machines and the clang of steel. There rises out of it a song. The MACHINE-WORKERS *enter on one side; on the other the* AGRICULTURAL LABOURERS. *The song is accompanied by a mechanical dance. When it stops, the* LABOURERS *begin their dance. A* YOUNG MAN *and a* GIRL *break away from them suddenly*

Song

> Belly is barking, barking aloud,
>   Lacking a good square meal.
> Fire him and fill him, fatten him well,
>   Stodge up the stiff on steel—

THE GIRL. This isn't the kind of life I want.
THE MACHINE-WORKERS [*in a subdued murmur*]. This wasn't the kind of life we wanted.
THE LABOURERS. This wasn't the kind of life we wanted.
THE GIRL. I'm not going to live in this end-of-the-world pig-sty all my days. Can't you get a job in the town? There's a noise there.
THE YOUNG MAN [*more doubtfully*]. I might; I don't know. It's not easy to get a job.
THE MACHINE-WORKERS. It's not easy to keep a job.
THE LABOURERS. It's not easy to live by your job.
THE GIRL. I can—in the factories. My sister's got one and she and her boys have something like a time. Couldn't we—*darling*?

> [*She hangs on him and cajoles him. He looks over to the machines*

THE YOUNG MAN. We might try.
> [*They move a little; the machines break out; he hesitates; the* GIRL *drags him on*

THE GIRL. Hark! Come on, come on! That's life, that is!
> *A* PRIEST *appears near them*

THE PRIEST. Our Lord said: 'I am come that you might have life and that you might have it more abundantly.' Think a little of what this means. It is no good looking for life in the loud streets of our large towns with their showy lights—that is not the kind of life you want. The kind of life you want is the quiet life that is found in the peaceful heart—and how do we find that? That is what the Church can tell you. A little self-denial, a little attention to—

THE GIRL. I've had a packet of self-denial ever since I was born, it's time someone else had a turn. And when I want more life—and don't I?—it's not in churches on Sunday evenings I'm going to look for it. No [*she chokes back the adjective*] fear!

THE YOUNG MAN [*more politely*]. Some other day perhaps, sir, if you'll excuse us. I've got to see about getting a job now.

THE PRIEST. Yes, of course. Only after all we do want something to fall back on, don't we? something to keep you straight in your job and to keep you happy outside your job. Something everlastingly good. Our Lord wanted the young people to be happy and . . . .

THE GIRL. Did he? I can tell you one thing, if he thought singing hymns was the thing a girl wanted to keep her happy, he was a good way off. When the heart's kicking in me and my throat's dry, and that fellow and the other fellow, what good are hymns going to be then? they're nothing to bite on. Jesus! what do you know about it? Don't do this and don't do that and you don't want a noise—I do want a noise, I want a noise as loud as the blood in me; I mean to make a fight of it and give as good as I get—or very nearly; and that's what I'm out for and that's what I'm going to have, so there's for your church-going and your don't, don't, don't. Come on, *darling*.

THE YOUNG MAN. Excuse us, sir.

> [*The two of them reach the machine circle; as they do so, the dance (on both sides) begins again. The* YOUNG MAN *is knocked down by a hammer, and his body is flung out. The* GIRL *gives a scream, but she is caught up in the dance, and whirled round. The* PRIEST *looks round and beckons. The* MEMBERS OF A COMMITTEE *appear and join him. The dance ceases.*

THE PRIEST. Ladies and gentlemen, fellow-Christians! It's very kind of you to come to this meeting. The subject to-night is *What can we do to get the people into our Churches?* I'm sure this is a very urgent question nowadays when Communism and Fascism are making such inroads. And Science—not that I'm against Science, for after all where should we be without it? But we ought to be attracting the young, and we don't seem to be attracting them as much as we might wish.

A WELL-MEANING LADY. I think the music's too solemn; we want brighter tunes.

A FIRM MAN. We want to make them *welcome*; we're too standoffish.

THE PRIEST. But how can one welcome them if they're not there to welcome?

THE FIRM MAN. Welcome them first and then they'll come. Brotherly love. Joy. [*He practises a cheerful smile*

A CRITICAL LADY. Too much excitement—that's what's the matter with them. Look at the books they read and look at the films they see and look at the dog-races!

JUDGEMENT AT CHELMSFORD

AN EAGER MAN [*breaking in*]. Yes, but why not give them these things *in* the churches instead of outside?

THE PRIEST [*startled*]. What, dog-races? O really, no-one's more anxious than I am to find some way of getting into their—shall we say hearts? but I don't think we could have dog-races.

THE WELL-MEANING LADY. Not up the aisles!

THE EAGER MAN. Well, I don't say *dog-races* exactly, but that's the kind of thing you've got to compete with, and that's what we've got to realize. Show them the Church wants *them*. Other days, other ways. In the Dark Ages it was different; everyone went to church because there wasn't anywhere else to go. Now there is.

ANTIOCH. There were a good many other places to go to in my time. But we managed.

THE FIRM MAN. I agree with this lady; we want to make the services brighter. Brighter tunes—and more candles. And perhaps even a little incense—quietly, of course. Nothing to show. There's something about the *smell* of incense that's attractive.

THE WELL-MEANING LADY. I don't think candles are much of a draw nowadays—not with the electric light everywhere.

THE FIRM MAN [*proceeding*]. And no sermons.

A CURATE. There I think you're wrong. We want more sermons—more sound doctrine. Modernism is ruining lives.

THE CRITICAL LADY. There's not much doctrine I hear that I can approve of. It's all High Church or Low Church or Broad Church or something. Teach them to be honest and punctual and clean—that's what we want them to be, and it's what they want to be themselves if they only knew.

THE WELL-MEANING LADY. Yes—isn't it a pity they don't seem to know?

THE CURATE. The Church is not meant chiefly to teach morals.

THE CRITICAL LADY. More's the pity.

[*The* PRIEST *hastily suppresses the indignant* CURATE

THE FIRM MAN. The trouble is that all these extra things cost money, and we can't afford it. As it is, even after the jumble sale, we're in debt. Whereas a cheerful smile doesn't cost anything.

THE WELL-MEANING LADY. O don't you think so?

THE CRITICAL LADY. It does if it's due to drink, as it often is.

THE EAGER MAN. Now, there you are. Why not have a Bottle Service? They have Bottle Parties; why not a Bottle Service? I don't say *in* the Church; why not in the Parish Hall? and everyone bring his own bottle, and have a really splendid time. Lemonade or beer or even cold tea.

THE CURATE. The Church is not a drinking club.

THE EAGER MAN. No—but why not make it one?

[*The* COMMITTEE *become agitated*

THE PRIEST. Well, we must think it over, think it over. I think the discussion has not been without its point, and I'm very grateful for this friendly co-operation. Now, before we break up, just to encourage ourselves as I may say, shall we sing *Onward, Christian Soldiers*?

[*They begin. After about three lines the noise of the machines joins in and presently dominates the tune. The dance begins again; this time the* MACHINE-WORKERS *enlarge their movements till they absorb the* COMMITTEE—*except for the* PRIEST—*and the younger of the* LABOURERS; *the older ones disappear. The dance becomes more automatic, and at last the dancers move off mechanically. As the sound dies away, the aeroplanes are again heard*

THE PRIEST. Well, perhaps it is a little disheartening, but

one must just go on. Our Lord didn't come in vain—
we know that.

> [*He begins to sing* Onward, Christian Soldiers *again by himself. The bombs are heard. He starts, but pulls himself up; the light fades a little and in a kind of dusk he moves off, his solitary voice defying the destructiveness of the world. The* ACCUSER *begins to speak but is interrupted*

CONSTANTINOPLE. And the odd thing is—that he is quite right.

THE ACCUSER [*passionately*]. This then, Christians, is your exhibition
to-day of what once—you say—happened,
the alteration of the whole world's orbit, souls
caught in the thunderstorm of grace and so struck
by the luck of the heavenly lightning that their branded flesh
loosed their expanded spirits into the air
of Christ's ascension; on earth they were dead to earth
being by a new birth remade into passion—
And this now is the latest fashion of the glory
that burns at every point in man and yearns
to escape, will he yield it way, into the strong
radiance of Christ in him and he in the world.
Sweet, was Christ crucified to create this chat?
some other, less notable, sacrifice might have served.

CANTERBURY. This is indeed your habit, brother; often
through many centuries I have heard you talk so:
I know your plausible tongue; it has trapped many.
Yes, certainly; this is the creation of Christ—
more foolish than need be, selfish often, often
misguided, slothful; but it is this or the world—

THE ACCUSER. Let her answer; this is she; can she at this gate of heaven

JUDGEMENT AT CHELMSFORD

honestly believe she is not the same as the world?
She loses her children daily and gains none;
she refuses to understand her own gospel;
she prefers always the second-best. You [*to* CHELMSFORD],
answer: since you have failed neatly to slip,
without being exposed completely, into divinity,
answer: what is the difference between you and the world?

CHELMSFORD [*faltering*]. I do not know . . . . I see I am
poorer than I thought.

CANTERBURY. Any of us could answer for her; do you,
Cedd, son of Christ, show us some other vision.

ST. CEDD. God, for his reasons, did not choose to bless
everyone with the violence of grace; the world's axis
was not turned as the temple veil was torn,
whirled into wisdom. Rather, as boys toil
to raise a pole too heavy for their hands and backs,
the common people, age by age, were bid
struggle against hell to set up heaven:
if they have not stormed the frontier of one kingdom
they have been recalled from the worst edge of the other.
The common people are the brightness and darkness of
existence,
since God chose to bid Adam multiply—
not heroes, geniuses, saints. Folly and foulness
have they in plenty, and plentifully practise love.
They are each a category of Christ's own identity
which they can turn to Antichrist. It is no small thing
that love should work so steadily in their lives.

THE ACCUSER. Love?

ST. CEDD. Love.

THE ACCUSER. Curiously are heavenly names
used on earth—love, power, grace.
Have you ever heard in your heaven of Matthew Hopkins
who between the first King Charles and the second

JUDGEMENT AT CHELMSFORD

in the towns of England traded foul bargains
in stuff of evil no less detestable than he?
He bought himself comfort by hunting the covetousness
 of others.
See in him and in the dark devices he harried
how wildly the imagination in Christian lands
loosed itself into a lurking delirium,
and the witch-hunters ran with the witches through the
 ditches of the soul.

EPISODE II

ELIZABETH CLARKE *and an* IMP *with a toad's head enter on one side and seem to sleep. On the other* MATTHEW HOPKINS *and* JOHN STEARNE *enter*

HOPKINS. Master Stearne, Master Stearne, now we must be busy. The Lord has called us to discoveries.

STEARNE. Sir, he has blessed you greatly; he has made of you an instrument of salvation against hell.

HOPKINS. Yes. I think he has. He would not have me be a lawyer; no-one came to my house at Ipswich. I waited all day and caught nothing, and then I came to Manningtree and waited, and still I caught nothing. There are too many lawyers in these parts, and the fees that the people pay them are very paltry. I could get no reasonable living here.

STEARNE. Sir, it was the Lord's working that you should be his chosen vessel.

HOPKINS. Yes—yes, certainly. Certainly it was the remarkable work of the Lord. I see a way opening that shall be popular and profitable to me—as his servant, of course, as his servant. It is written that they shall not muzzle the ox that treads out the corn.

STEARNE. I have thought often that I sniffed hell in the streets. Essex is a devil's parlour for witchcraft.

HOPKINS. It is fortunate that I should choose a house so near their parlour. I have been awakened by their voices night after night.

STEARNE. Sir, it is the Lord's doing and it is marvellous in our eyes. Sir, give him the glory.

HOPKINS. So I do, so I do. But we must honour the poor vessel he uses; we must pay it respect and keep it—

polished, as I may say. Good John, we must not forget that they who serve the altar should live by the altar. I do not mean it papistically. I hope the magistrates are godly men; they shall have profit to their souls if they spend well now. My costs will be high if I am to search out this iniquity to its conclusion. I must be highly advanced—for the Lord's sake, John, for the Lord's sake.

STEARNE. Sir, we are all altogether abominable to him except in the mystery of his predestination—

HOPKINS. Yes, that is what I say—his predestination; that is what I say—he predestinated me to be a remarkable finder of witches. I am a man of no learning, it is true; I have not read many wise books; I do not know what they did in France and High Germany. I am a simple man, good John, but I hope I can recognise evil when other people commit it: the Lord bless us all! Have you warned the magistrates and the soldiers?

STEARNE. Sir, they are waiting for us; when I call them they will come.

HOPKINS. It is time then; come this way. I have made a little opening into the room. Don't be afraid, John: the devil will not hurt us.

STEARNE. Sir, our Lord's hand is over all His saints.

[*They settle down to watch. The* IMP *nudges* CLARKE

THE IMP. Mistress, mistress; it is time, mistress.

CLARKE. Aigh, aigh, it is time. Aigh, chuck; precious chuck to wake me!

THE IMP. Give me a sup of blood, mistress.

CLARKE. Little glutton, little glutton!

[*She lets him suck*

THE IMP. Ai, ai. [*It runs about*]

CLARKE. Little sweet imp. Here! [*She speaks in his ear*] Will *he* come tonight? will he? Ann West is bringing her daughter at last; will *he* come?

JUDGEMENT AT CHELMSFORD

THE IMP. Do I know, mistress? Here again and gone again and one in the corner to be cold in the vitals; is she pretty? is she young? is she neat for him and meat for him? he will not come for nothing. Ai, ai: who is at the door, mistress, who is at the door?

> [*A knock.* CLARKE *goes, and an* IMP *with a cat's head runs in, then* ANN LEACH

LEACH. I wouldn't shut the door, Elizabeth; there are others coming. Mistress Gooding is at the corner, and I saw three shadows beyond her. They'll all be here soon. It's a cold night.

> [*The* IMPS *sit down in the shadows at the back. The music grows stronger. A knock.* CLARKE *goes.* GOODING *enters; her* IMP *slips in after her; it has a kid's head*

GOODING. Where is she?

LEACH. Who?

GOODING. Who? the girl! Where is she? where is she? isn't she here? isn't she coming?

CLARKE. No need to be so vexed; her mother's bringing her. She'll be here without doubt, for she met me in the market this morning and said she to me: 'Goody Clarke, Goody Clarke, shall I be made a witch tonight?' 'You shall that, my maid,' said I, 'to go with your mother wherever you will, and not sitting at home with toad in its hole till she comes back.' And then she looked *so* and she smiled *so*, and all sideways—*so*; she'll be a fine one.

LEACH. They've stopped maybe by Farmer Edwards' house to oversee his daughter again: he was bitter enough once to all of us, but now his child is mazed this sennight, and her eyes rolling. Horses, cows, child. [*She leans to* CLARKE] Will *he* be here?

> [*A knock: the door flies open;* ANN WEST *and her daughter* REBECCA *are seen. They come in. The*

music takes charge. The four witches bob at each other, REBECCA *standing still by her mother, who presently lays a finger on her daughter's lip and seems to bid her go and sit on the floor with the imps. She does so. The witches,* GOODING *directing, bring out a brazier and throw in herbs; afterwards, behind it, two black candles, which they light from the brazier. The witches kneel round the brazier and sing. Presently a kind of green light flashes up. The witches rise and begin to move round the brazier from right to left against the sun; they walk one after the other, but holding hands: their motion becomes quicker till they are almost running. The foremost, whose hand is stretched in front of her, cries out*

THE WITCH. The hand! the hand! he has me.
THE OTHER WITCHES. Ha, master!

[*The dance becomes very fast for a moment or two and ceases. The witches break off and stand as if worshipping. Then they revive and go between the brazier and the candles*

GOODING [*between the candles*]. The girl.
ANN WEST. Rebecca.

[REBECCA *goes round the stage and comes to the brazier. The music ceases, the light disappears and illuminates the upper stage*

ANTIOCH. England, I see, has not forgot the things
that once were done in me by different rites,
altars, rich lamps, balsams, and thuribles,
magical summons to the heart to express death;
before the apostolic trumpet shook
the image the necromancers sought to look on.
But this is under the apostolic shield;
how comes this, daughter?

JUDGEMENT AT CHELMSFORD

CHELMSFORD. This was here before
 ever the Cross grew on the English shore;
 this is the seed of Eden under the curse,
 and he, he waters it; it is his work.
THE ACCUSER. Not much mine either. I have done no worse
 than to exhibit to men their own desires,
 their love, their hunger, their hold on hell. If
 they strongly deceive their bodies with their hope
 they see me in the image of false belief,
 as these perhaps this night. You Christians,
 you are not responsible for hell, but only
 for how you help high heaven to deal with hell
 whether in a hellish way or in a heavenly.
 See how you did once.
HOPKINS. It is time now. We shall catch them in their own
 pestilential wickedness: let us bring the guard in on them.
STEARNE. Sir, will you not stay while I fetch the guard? If
 you could testify that you had seen the Prince of the
 Power of the Air—
HOPKINS. No, no. Good John, we have seen enough. They
 will tell us everything presently. Come, fetch the guard
 and godly men.   [*They slip out*
  [*The light appears again on the lower stage.* RE-
  BECCA *is now in her white shift; the brazier is moved
  and she kneels in its place.* GOODING *is still between
  the candles. She speaks, in a voice quite unlike her
  own*
GOODING. Do you renounce your baptism?
  [REBECCA *bends forward:* GOODING *pinches out the
  candles. The music begins:* GOODING *calls above it*
GOODING. Jarmara, Pechin, Panu!
  [*The imps run forward. Two of them catch* RE-
  BECCA'*s hands and hold them out: the other goes to*
  GOODING, *who kisses him and gives him a thin knife.*

He runs round behind REBECCA *and seems to prick her: she screams*

ALL THE WITCHES AND IMPS. Witch's mark, witch's mark, witch's mark!

> [REBECCA *kisses the imps; she leaps up, and dances with them. Then the witches set* REBECCA *before the candles which are again lit and stand behind her. They present a ceremony of invocation. As they crouch at one point the music pauses, and the voice of the* ACCUSER *says*

THE ACCUSER. Little time is left them now,
before the gallows is built and the pyre; in their fire
they shall have this single help: they shall see me.
God made me to be the image of each man's desire—
a king or a poet or a devil—and rarely Christ.
Most men when at last they see their desire,
fall to repentance—all have that chance.

> [*He goes down, and suddenly as the light becomes bright is seen standing between the candles.* REBECCA *falls flat; the witches cry out. There is a great knocking at the door. The lights come fully on. There is a noise of a breaking door, and the* MAGISTRATES, SOLDIERS, *and* STEARNE *enter. The imps slip away. The witches run about in disorder and are seized and bound.* HOPKINS *comes in*

HOPKINS. Hold them, hold them. Have them away. Let them be watched tonight; let them be run to and fro about the room and have no rest, that, being kept awake, they may be the more active to call their imps and familiars the sooner to help and hearten them. Let them not lie down or so much as sit in a chair; and for the better effecting it, get others to help you, and change among yourselves two or three times an hour, and let some watch the doors and walls, and if you see a spider or any such

vermin about the room, kill it, but if you can by no means
come at it to kill it, then take note that it is his shape who
comes to them, and you may know that he is confounded
by cause that his firebrand darlings are put away from
him. Watch and walk them! watch and walk them.

THE MAGISTRATE. Sir, the town is in your debt tonight. This
is a very awful thing that such devilish practices should
go on so near us. I have heard that children have been
overlooked by them and are near sick to death.

HOPKINS. It is my calling, sir. I have it in mind to go
through all these counties, through Essex and Suffolk,
and wherever good pious folk ask me, to find what evil is
done. Sir, it is a holy thing to seek after the evil that other
folk commit—but, sir, it needs money. Proof is dear and
travelling is dear.

THE MAGISTRATE. I will speak of it to the Council; we must
not miss the salvation of the Lord. But as for these—

> [*The witches are run to and fro. Presently they
> collapse, except* REBECCA *who seems all this while to
> be in a kind of trance. There is finally a procession
> across the stage, while a lurid light, as of fire, glows
> everywhere*

THE ACCUSER. Fire always over Christendom, always fire!
How shall God not require the ashes at your hands,
patriarchs? ashes of burned men, when
you swerved from the Will to keep the word, when
you abandoned God's heart for the philosophical art
of argument, and outraged men's bodies to save their
  souls,
lacking love's decencies! fire over Christendom, fire!
Protestants at Smithfield, Jesuits at Tyburn, fire!
and at Colchester the hid school from overseas
toiled for the Religion, while the last abbot
died for the Faith—fire over Christendom, fire!

Will you destroy Satan by the help of Satan?
or establish Christ by shedding the blood of Christ?
JERUSALEM. Satan falls always by his own divisions
but the blood of Christ being shed brings forth Christ.
THE CHORUS. When the Jews came forth to accuse Messias
he answered them riddling, playing with words,
saying: 'If Satan cast out Satan,
if hell be divided to ruin hell,
tell me, can Satan's kingdom stand?'

Lord, let thy children now let show
the answer the Jews seemed not to know,
losing their heads in their eager rage;
now let thy servants answer unchid:
'Lord, whoever supposed it did?'

Let the angelic armies smile,
seeing it topple all the while:
'How shall Satan's kingdom stand?
Lord, it crashes on either hand,
and where is its substance of delight?'
JERUSALEM. Yet here and now, for the follies and evils
done in the history of Christ's Church on earth,
reconcile we again ourselves to each other.
CANTERBURY [*to* ROME]. Brother, we have exchanged too much pain;
Once more I entreat your pardon—without condition.
But if it should please you now to do so too
we might begin a new revision of Christendom.
ROME [*to* CANTERBURY]. Ah brother, well may I seek pardon
from all Christendom for that which weak men
and wicked, or rash saints even, have done in my name.
The immaculate doctrine is wounded seven times by their shame.

JUDGEMENT AT CHELMSFORD

CANTERBURY [*embracing*]. Blessed be God that pardon is laughter in heaven.

ROME [*embracing*]. And the laughter pierces to degrees seventy-times-seven.

ANTIOCH. Pardon is love-in-freedom and pardon pierces
—since first men were called Christians in me—
down to new delight and new love
which else in the hard surface could not grow:
what did one of your own poets say?

THE CHORUS. 'Thus through all eternity
              I forgive you, you forgive me;
              as our dear Redeemer said—
              this the wine and this the bread.'

CHELMSFORD. Bring us, my lords, to look, forgiving and forgiven,
on the trouble of our honour that shall be joy in heaven.
When one for the Bible and another for the Church fought
and still Christ from either his own honour brought.

EPISODE III

A ROYAL PURSUIVANT *enters, with an officer*

THE PURSUIVANT. Go, seek; if you hear woman or man speak
of this English Bible, have an eye on them.
There are those who about Colchester and Essex ply
Tyndale's trade in heresy; go—watch.
His brother lives hereabouts; watch carefully.
Catch as catch can—and take all the haul to the Bishop.
  [*They go out separately. A* MAN *and* WOMAN *enter*
THE MAN. I have a copy of it here; I bought it in London.
I can read a little in it, and our vicar more,
wonderful new things, as true as Christ,
as strange as grace, and as strong as the heart's stir.
THE WOMAN. Hide it, be careful; must you dally with death?
Why not be content with what your mother
taught you, a child, and I teach our children?
no, you must have some bravery, some bold danger;
what will happen to our babies if you are hanged?
THE MAN. Wit may hide it well; have no fear.
But the Bishop shall whistle in vain; it has come to abide,
swimming up Thames with the tide against the river
from Germany and the Low Countries; a wind shall blow
in the flame of the spirit against their corrupt rites,
and the bishops may try to clutch lightning as well as this.
They will burn all they find; it has such a touch
to cleanse their poisonous doll-dusty air;
and there they will be again, back at the beginning
with God and the Bible always winning against them.
It is indeed a New Testament to us.

JUDGEMENT AT CHELMSFORD

THE WOMAN. I do not know but the old things were best.
Those changes of heart bring bitterness everywhere.
My gossip's brother has become a hot gospeller,
and none in her house have had quiet hours since.
I think our Lord did not mean us to be so pious
as to interfere with the day's brewing and churning.
THE OFFICER [*running in and calling—as the* PURSUIVANT *re-enters on the other side*].
Sir, have you heard the Abbot is caught for treason?
THE PURSUIVANT. He said that all the water of Thames would not wash
the King's Majesty of covetousness—false traitor!
He . . . ha, sir, what book is that you have?
THE MAN. Sir, what is that to you? it is no evil,
though maybe Antichrist, were he here, might think so.
THE PURSUIVANT. Sir, by your leave: we carry the King's commission
to examine all books; there are eggs that hatch
vipers out to-day in the Essex sun.
THE MAN. Nay, I will match you for that; there are a fine brood
of adders snuffing incense and—
THE PURSUIVANT.   Do you say so, friend?
Show it; nay, do you tussle? I will mend you for that.
          [*He catches the book. The* WOMAN *screams*
THE WOMAN. O blessed mother of mercy, help us all!
          [*The* MAN *and the* PURSUIVANT *wheel round, clutching the book. More run in calling and striking. The struggle becomes a whirling belligerent dance*
VOICES. The Lord strike you!
                    The Lord strike you!
  Atheist!
          Devil-worshipper!
                    Heretic!

JUDGEMENT AT CHELMSFORD

Blasphemer!
        Traitor!
                Schismatic!
                        Idolator!
Will you touch God's church?
                        Will you silence God's word?
Here is Christ!
        here is Christ!
                here!
                      here!
Therefore curse them!
                Give them great pain!
Hurt them!
        Kill them!
                Hang them!
                        Burn them!

THE ACCUSER. When Messias promised once that he would dwell
within his Church for ever, you did not think
that this was all you would let him do for you;
this the only way you would have him walk,
and his merciful talk twisted to terrible agonies.

CANTERBURY. Hark yet, brother! I heard a voice
speaking, and another: God's choice is other than ours.

From the heavens the figures of the last LORD ABBOT OF
COLCHESTER *and of the protestant martyr* ROSE ALLEN
*appear. They come a little down the steps and stand.
The dance pauses in a rigid tableau*

THE ABBOT. I was Thomas Becke, Benedictine, abbot
of St. John Baptist at Colchester. Four hundred years
had passed since the Norman founded it before I
followed my centuries of predecessors to the chair.
There I looked to serve my Lord in quiet,

JUDGEMENT AT CHELMSFORD

but bare presently stood our abbey against
King Henry's rages; there came a flood of axes
that had cried havoc on many great glories
and made cells of holy contemplation cellars
for bats winged to other flights than heaven's.
The King called me to his new oaths, but I
was thralled by the old. I denied his will; then
here they took me and hanged me by my own door.
I died—unworthy I—as many before
died for God's glory; therefore by his will now—
O unworthy, unworthy!—I glow among the martyrs.
ROSE ALLEN. I was Rose Allen, a girl of Essex;
few knew me then, and of you now none.
Fresh I ran with other younglings in the fields,
grew, and helped, I too, with the brewing and churning;
till God spoke to me out of my heart
in a blessed simpleness; grace woke,
and I—poor I—had to brace myself to the post.
The Holy Ghost would fare through me; then
bare I stood, with my mother and my fellows, against
Queen Mary's rage; there came a flood of fire
over the Essex flats; there was I;
on a day, on a day, I would not deny my Lord,
a cord was round my waist and laced tight
was I to the stake and the faggot—covered to the middle.
I burned—unworthy I—as many before
burned to God's glory; therefore by his will now—
O unworthy, unworthy!—I glow among the martyrs.
THE ABBOT. Blessed Essex, be known in love for ever!
ROSE ALLEN. Blessed Essex, be known in love for ever!
THE ABBOT. Thus it was once, sister!
ROSE ALLEN.   Brother, thus it was!
    [*They run down and are swallowed in the crowd*

JUDGEMENT AT CHELMSFORD

VOICES. Down with those who preach the new gospel!
Down with those who keep the old canons!
Down with the abbots!
                         Down with the gospellers!
                                              Burn!
hang, torture, kill! Let none escape.
                    THE CHORUS
He that does it to the least of these
for ever and ever does it to me.
It is I they hunt, it is I they seize,
it is I they slay—and I do not flee,
for it is my will always to bring
a good thing out of iniquity.

He that hates the least of these
for ever and ever has hated me:
much though he sorrow when he sees,
and be pardoned much, yet this must be—
that he hardened his heart against gentleness
he shall confess to eternity.
          [*The crowd fall back, showing the bound figures of
          the martyrs back to back*
CHELMSFORD. Did I do this?
THE ACCUSER.   Those who were of you did.
And wisely Augustine chid those who thought
they were free from the sins of those who went before
   them.
CHELMSFORD. O rid me—can any? can Messias?—of this
   woe!
ST. CEDD. Nay, since this cannot change, know
rather the range of his mercy. Man is one
in sin from beginning to end, nor otherwise within
sin's consummation, sin's opposite, the work of Man's
   Son,

JUDGEMENT AT CHELMSFORD

God's Son, Christ of the double Nature; now
he brings as ever from the worst hour a power
bounteous with all good of all kind.

THE SEES. Be with us, be with us, be with us, to the end of
the world!

     [*They stretch their hands towards the martyrs*

THE ABBOT. Pater Noster
ROSE ALLEN. Our Father
THE ABBOT. qui es in coelis
ROSE ALLEN. which art in heaven
THE ABBOT. Panem nostrum quotidianum da nobis
ROSE ALLEN. give us this day our daily bread.
CANTERBURY. Their souls in death intercede with the one
Christ,

and that heavenly breath hath sufficed; the thing is done.
Christ hath won himself again out of the pit:
go, one of you, release their souls to peace.

   [*A seraph runs down and touches the cord; it falls.*
   The martyrs turn to each other

ROSE ALLEN. Brother, what you said was true in the Church:
see now, here are the Rites saved,

beyond me, beyond you, by your doing; beyond both
saved through Christendom by true men's contrition.
I see I was not the only one with a mission,
though indeed mine was given me by your need.

THE ABBOT. Sister, what you did was great in the Church:
see now here is the Book saved,

graved in English words upon English hearts.
It shall blow as the wind of youth; it shall take youth
with wonder, nor age lose it nor death deny.
The Word to wayfaring men shall testify
how his graces transubstantiate times and places,
nor shall any release from the claws of John's eagle
this land, till the poor find peace, and the rich goodwill,

and the course be one with its end.
Faith herein shall befriend for ever our folk,
hope, and the thing that is more than hope or faith.
Thus it saith for ever: O gift, O grafted power
in the power of men's souls: Christ singer, Christ voice,
   Christ song.

ROSE ALLEN. Hark, we are called back!
THE ABBOT.   The spiral beauty
cries us again to the strain of its song: come.

       [*They re-ascend, while the song of the diocese is sung
        by the crowd*

See now the Church of thy choosing, fair Spring of Salvation;
design of the universe, hasten our hearts to thy using;
incline into glory thy cherished and changing creation
till thy kingdom be come and we lift in a living oblation.
Wonder and Splendour, exhibit the truth of thy making;
bidding us choose, thou hast sworn by thyself to be tender;
ridding our evil away, thou hast met us, forsaking
all things but thee; we are thine, O our Love, for the taking.

The death, that in thee was abiding, redeem us from dying,
we hiding in thee as in Manhood thy Godhead was hiding;
guide through the Life that was fair from thy mother our sighing,
and close in the Church of thy choosing man's uttermost crying.

Thou wert the only beginning, O soon be the ending;
we move, at thy thrust, to the joy that is ours for the winning;
O Love that art victory, thine was the gracious expending;
thou hast made us for thine, and thy heart is the full comprehending.

ST. CEDD. Disperse, lords of heaven, the sorrowful shadows
of those that wrought the woe; disperse hate,
folly, false love; bid all be gone.

THE SEES [*as they speak, the crowd disperse unhappily*]. O
Lord, who hast taught us that all our doings without
charity are nothing worth; Send thy Holy Ghost, and
pour into our hearts that most excellent gift of charity,
the very bond of peace and of all virtues, without which
whosoever liveth is counted dead before thee: Grant this
for thine only Son Jesus Christ's sake. *Amen.*

EPISODE IV

ANTIOCH. Wise were you, brother, in what you showed,
and well may all we take note of the action,
the fraction of the Sacred Body: yet Christendom
has caught the style of Christ; brother, how?
Cedd, where have you seen him this long while?
ST. CEDD. Men's fires were lit not only for destroying
but fit to warm households, to help the enjoying
of the commonness of life; nay, perhaps the rage
of prophets and patriarchs is no greater thing
than in every age the mere stirring of goodwill.
True that our Lord was God, but then Man too;
and he dined and drank wine and slept and wept and knew
his mother and his friends: this is a sweet mystery
how he could love all and yet love some
after his flesh, therefore he laboured for flesh,
and gave us lords and learners to help flesh.
And blessed be he that they left here their names—
as at Hempstead William Harvey who first found
how the blood moves in the body, or at Upton
Joseph Lister who purified hurts and stayed
Death's creeping germs, and brought to be
healing of many multitudes; at Maldon and Witham
Rayleigh who framed the constitution of the air,
and named a new thing from its mere idleness—
no wise idle he; nor William Byrd
who at Stondon, devising 'strange chromatic notes,
compassionated his voice to the choice of music'.
CHELMSFORD. These were great masters, and worked secretly;
their doing lurked in the cells of their own brain.
But rather bring now, lord, a wider thing to the viewing;

JUDGEMENT AT CHELMSFORD

 show ordinary lives, gay as gay they can be,
no remonstrant distress or remarkable delight,
but bright in their own tinctures of every day
and descended from the blood of the great knight Adam
when first he bore manfully his coat of arms
through the desert and by grace won the wilderness with
 charms.
Adam are we all; this is more than all degree.
ST. CEDD. To this therefore, see, we let grow the young
in fullness of fragrance when the Faith from its own fate
kept holiday in churches, in convents and schools,
as on the feast of fools, of boy-bishops and girl-abbesses,
nor least at your house of Barking; there the maids
by legal licence overturned law and saw
the abbess deposed and her quiet closed in riot,
when rudeness was shrived, and goodness of laughter
 thrived,
and fathers and friends and all the world's folk
came to the feast of the Triduum at Christmastide.

The GIRLS OF BARKING ABBEY *enter, chasing the* NUNS *and then bringing the* GIRL-ABBESS *in procession, two or three* NUNS, NICHOLAS UDALL *and another priest, the* CONVENT CONFESSOR, *and a few of the* GENTRY

ONE OF THE GIRLS. Make way for the Lady Abbess Catherine!
ALL. Make way.
ONE OF THE GIRLS. High day keep we under own our abbess;
prioress and novice-mistress are put down
and we govern them now as they year-long
rule us, poor creatures, with frown and bitter saying.
Now is our feast and all they plight to our playing.
           [*She breaks off*
I am thirsty with making proclamations; Dame Margaret, bring me a drink of milk.

THE GIRLS. Forfeit, forfeit! Anne, you called her Dame!
ANNE. I . . . [*she gives in*] I did!
ANOTHER GIRL. Bring her to the Lady Abbess; she shall ask pardon of all of us—
ANOTHER. And flat on her face, of the whole convent of us. Get you down, Anne.
ANNE. I appeal to the Lady Catherine!
THE GIRL-ABBESS. I do not think she need go *flat*. Sister Anne, you must kneel and ask pardon of me and the whole blessed sisterhood for high scandal and offence done against the time of the Triduum and our high feast and the rule of your unworthy sister me, your abbess, by calling the deposed mistress of the novices Dame.
ANNE. It would be me, of course.

    [*She kneels down; the girls are round in a circle*
Please you, my Lady Abbess, and you, my venerable sisters, to pardon me for this wickedness: mea culpa, mea culpa, mea culpa!
THE GIRL-ABBESS. We excuse you. [ANNE *rises*] And listen, all of you. You know that our Reverence, having been sick of a fever these three weeks, has seen nothing of your play for Holy Innocents, and we are determined to mend this piece of ill-luck. It is quite indecent that we should be compelled to wait until every nun in the convent sees it; so we will have it done before us now.
ONE OF THE YOUNGER NUNS. O come! Not another rehearsal!

    [*She stops suddenly, clapping her hand on her mouth*
THE GIRL-ABBESS [*awfully*]. What did you say, Sister Felicitas?
THE NUN. Nothing, Lady Abbess.
THE GIRL-ABBESS. If I thought you were insubordinate—
THE NUN. Not at all, Lady Abbess.

JUDGEMENT AT CHELMSFORD

THE GIRL-ABBESS. I would have you read aloud a homily of the blessed Saint Augustine instead, by yourself, where we could hear your voice and need not listen. Take care. Produce your company of wholesome actors.

THE NUN [*meekly*]. Do you want *all* the play?

THE GIRL-ABBESS [*glancing round*]. What does everyone think?

> [*There is a general murmur which suggests definite dissent*

Well, perhaps not *all*. A scene or so. Which is the most amusing? What about the Temptation of St. Mary?

THE NUN. That is very amusing.

THE GIRL-ABBESS. We will have that then. Who wrote the Play?

NICHOLAS UDALL. Your servant, Lady Abbess.

THE GIRL-ABBESS. What, you, Nicholas! We didn't see you. Is it a good play?

NICHOLAS UDALL. A very good play indeed, Lady Abbess.

ONE OF THE GIRLS. It is poetry, is it not?

UDALL. It is.

THE GIRL. Do you like writing poetry?

UDALL. It is rather difficult sometimes. One has to work extremely hard at it, even though I am one of the best poets in the kingdom.

THE GIRL-ABBESS [*with interest*]. Really? I thought it all just . . . [*she waves her hand vaguely*] came. Did King David have to work when he wrote the psalms? are they poetry?

UDALL. They are, Lady Abbess, and he did. If anyone tells you that poetry comes [*he waves his hand as she did*] Lady Abbess, tell him—tell him he is an infidel and an unbeliever. Almighty God does not give those things as easily as all that.

THE GIRL-ABBESS. Really? You astonish me, father. The Lady Abbess whose place Our Reverence has the honour of filling for a few hours always gave us to understand that that was the way in which she composed her hymns for the use of the convent. [*She looks round*] Shall we make them have a disputation about it?

THE CONFESSOR [*tactfully interrupting*]. I think, Lady Abbess, it travels rather far into matters of theology; it becomes almost a matter of the operation of the Holy and Blessed Spirit; a matter reserved to His Holiness at Rome.

THE GIRL-ABBESS [*a little disappointed*]. Well, if you say so....

UDALL [*supporting his colleague*]. And what about the play?

THE GIRLS. Yes, yes, the play.

THE GIRL-ABBESS. Yes, the play. Sister Felicitas, proceed. Stand you back, fathers, and you, gentlemen, and give them room.

THE GIRLS. Come on, come! Where are the Seven Deadly Sins? Mary—where's Mary?

ALL. Mary! Mary Magdalen!

THE PRODUCER [*taking over*]. Come, come, to your places, all of you! Obey your Lady Abbess!

> [*The* SEVEN SINS *go on one side*; MARY *and the* GIRLS *on the other. While they do so, the* CONFESSOR *takes the* PRODUCER *aside*

THE CONFESSOR. It is a little late now and I don't want to interfere, but I'm not happy about Mary Magdalen. She's a good girl, of course, but she's young and a little flighty. I wish you could have someone more devout. Now there's Tabitha—I never quite knew why you made Tabitha take the part of Sloth; one of the quietest and devoutest girls in the school. Why couldn't she have been the Magdalen?

THE PRODUCER. She's a worse actress, Father. She does much better as Sloth. Mary makes a finer show.

THE PRIEST. But she's not so pious.

THE PRODUCER. If piety can't act, Father, piety ought not to be in a play. Our sweet Lord told us that piety ought to be private, and devotion in the inner room. He said nothing about it doing anything outside. Tabitha's only got to look lumpish as Sloth, not—whatever Mary Magdalen looked. You must forgive me; every one of us to a proper job!

> [*The* CONFESSOR *retires. The* PRODUCER *turns to the* ACTORS

Now, are you ready? Away. [*She claps her hands*

MARY AND THE GIRLS.
> Dull it is in tide of spring
> to sit and hear the birds sing
> but never our eyes to be waking
> on any goodly show.

MARY.
> But see now by Bethany
> who may these bright gentles be,
> clothed in such gay livery?
> 'Fore heaven, I love them so.

THE SINS [*in procession*].
> Clothes many have we to wear,
> jewels rich and head-gear fair;
> come, you people all who care
> for a fresh day and a fine—

THE PRODUCER. Now, now, for shame! is a sin so dull? come, tempt! one would think none of you had ever sinned in your lives. Luxury, lavish yourself more; and Anger, start and brandish your sword. You have all the rest of the year to repent in; come now! Only Sloth is to look as sleepy as she chooses.

THE CONFESSOR [*as the* PRODUCER *comes near him*]. Do not be profane, sister; we must not mock at holy things.

THE PRODUCER [*indignantly*]. Who is mocking at holy things,

Father? I am as good a Christian as yourself, and what these girls don't know about the sins I shall never be likely to teach them. To them, Mary!

MARY. Gentles, if it please you, say
who ye are that walk so gay,
and why ye go this way:
we marvel how ye shine.

GLUTTONY. Happy are they to me thralled:
Gluttony am I called;
I have what I will to eat.

SLOTH. But comfort much in peace have I
who can hardly open an eye;
Sloth is my name and seat.

HATE. I am a high lord in man's life,
having in me all roots of strife,
and Hate I have to name.

ONE OF THE GENTRY. I don't understand that.

ANOTHER. No, nor do I. Ask her what it means.

THE FIRST GENTLEMAN [*to the* PRODUCER]. Sister, what does that mean?

THE PRODUCER [*absently watching the* SINS *dance*]. What does what mean, sir?

THE SECOND GENTLEMAN. What Hate says—about roots of strife.

THE PRODUCER. I can't explain now: ask Father Nicholas— he wrote it.

THE FIRST GENTLEMAN [*to* UDALL]. Hi, you, Nicholas man, what do you mean by what Hate says?

UDALL. That? O well, my lord . . . that . . . that . . . that means . . . Well [*he talks very quickly*] my lord, that means that Hate is one of those sins which have most power over men, out of which spring all the worst kinds of evil, as cruelty, buffetings, quarrellings, angers, bloodsheds, affrays, slanderings, and the rest, for all these have indeed their beginnings and fertile growths in that hatred which is engendered between one man and another, and so this hatred is a lord, as one might say, Dominus, but the short word is the better here, and so he calls himself, and takes pride in it, which is indeed the very root mark of all sin, for it is its nature to be delighted with itself and not with another, as all love's true disciples be.

THE PRODUCER. Sh'h!

UDALL. Do you see now, my lord?

THE FIRST GENTLEMAN. A very difficult way of saying a very simple thing.

UDALL [*aside*]. Go and hunt rats with Beelzebub.

MARY AND THE GIRLS.
>   Hear you, girls, how they say?
>   Methinks to go with them away
>   were a good roundelay
>   on a morn of spring.

ANGER.
>   Anger am I, a lofty lord;
>   with any who dare my sharp sword
>   I have a bold reckoning.

ENVY.
>   Envy's dress has colour quiet
>   but rich as any in this riot,
>   and her venom sharper than steel.

PRIDE.
>   I am Pride; I need no stuff
>   rich or fair; it is enough
>   for me never to kneel.

THE SECOND GENTLEMAN. And why should Envy have a sad-coloured dress, I should like to know? Why, the plays they give at Court are not as difficult as this, and there all the learned men of Europe come. But they dance prettily enough.

> [*He catches hold of* ENVY *as she passes him, interrupting the rehearsal*

Do you understand that, my girl?

ENVY [*curtseying and impertinent*]. Of course, father.

THE FIRST GENTLEMAN. Why your dress is to be so sober, hey?

ENVY. Of course. It's as simple as the Holy Gospel.

THE SECOND GENTLEMAN. Ha, indeed. Is the Gospel simple, Nicholas?

UDALL. Well—in a way, yes, sir.

THE CONFESSOR [*in an undertone*]. Brother, the Gospel is not simple, and you know it.

UDALL. Well—in a way, no, brother.

THE GIRL-ABBESS. My lords, we are waiting for the rehearsal to proceed. We are to remind you that you are here only by our courtesy and our invitation. Release Sister Envy and pray stand back.

THE SECOND GENTLEMAN. Baggages, aren't they? [*He cuffs* ENVY *lightly back to her place*] Get away with you, daughter. [*To his friend*] The money they cost us and the airs they put on.

THE PRODUCER. Now, Luxury!

LUXURY. I am sovereign of this whole cartel,
> ruler of the pits of hell,
> but the world is mine as well:
>> will you not walk with me?
> I am pleasant and satisfying
> to all men's easy lying.
>> I am called Luxury.

THE SINS [*to the* GIRLS]. Ah, flowers of sweet worth,
> will you not come and have great mirth
>> with us in our house?

LUXURY [*to* MARY]. But you are the fairest of them all;
> we will have each other, whate'er befall,
>> by everlasting vows.

[*The* GIRLS *pair off with the* SINS

THE FIRST GIRL [*to* GLUTTONY]. Ever I had a sweet tooth,

JUDGEMENT AT CHELMSFORD

THE SECOND GIRL [*to* SLOTH]. and I loved slumber well forsooth.
THE THIRD GIRL [*to* HATE]. Dove's eyes have you, my dear;
THE FOURTH GIRL [*to* PRIDE]. I in your arms be without fear.
THE FIFTH GIRL [*to* ANGER]. Sweetly, fair lord, you frighten me.
THE SIXTH GIRL [*to* ENVY]. Cover me well, sweet Envy.
MARY MAGDALEN. Cover me well, and I will abide,
> noble Luxury, by thy side
>> for ever and a day;
> unless there come a king so dread
> that he could harry the very dead
>> shall none draw me away.

THE PRODUCER. O passion, passion! My good girl, you are Mary Magdalen giving yourself up to sensuality. For heaven's sake! Our fair lady Magdalen was no coy cloisterer of sin; whatever she did I warrant she did it with an air, even if she only wore red gloves. Come, come! you are defying the whole world! Yes, and more, for now you are plighting yourself to the Lord who is to come, and you do not know it! Heartbreak, heartbreak! Come, again.

MARY [*as before*]. Cover me well, and I will abide,
> noble Luxury, by thy side
>> for ever and a day;
> unless there come a king so dread
> that he could harry the very dead
>> shall none draw me away.

THE PRODUCER. Now, all of you, clap and carol.
> [*The dance of the* GIRLS *and the* SINS, *the spectators accompanying*

THE CONFESSOR [*to the* GIRL-ABBESS]. It is almost time for Compline.
THE GIRL-ABBESS. It is very good, isn't it? We thank you, sisters. You will come with us now to the chapel where

we shall enthrone ourselves in the Lady Abbess's chair
and listen to Compline. Let us proceed in peace.
ALL THE GIRLS [*ranging themselves in a sudden change to a real beauty of devotion*]. In the name of Jesus.

[*They file out. The* PRODUCER *stops* UDALL

THE PRODUCER. O Father, may I speak to you? Look, we really need some of St. John's speeches cut, and two more written in for the tormentors; and we ought to have something funnier for the Court of the Emperor—it's rather dull as it stands. O and the Archangel Gabriel says that the names of the devils are hard to remember, and could you find her some easier ones? Where did you get these from?

UDALL. From a learned Jew in London: they are the real thing.

THE PRODUCER. They may be but I think we should have Christian devils. The Lady Abbess will like it better. It is no use having learned devils—plain simple Satan is enough for her.

UDALL [*as they go out*]. Much too much for all of us, my sister.

THE ACCUSER. Beautiful are the mild moments; fair and fit
are feasts and fasts in the season's flight; wit
flashes to heaven more from a full stomach
than ever from an empty, save only where
those who are called to it climb the steep stair
of convents or rigour of rules: else—
forget you, gentles, the tale the Gospel tells?
Messias came eating and drinking; men said,
behold a gluttonous man and a winebibber. Cedd,
what did he leave for his folk?

ST. CEDD.   Flesh and blood,
meat and drink for the heart's grace.

THE ACCUSER.   Good.

JUDGEMENT AT CHELMSFORD

Why now does the Church outface his blessing?
Where is the meat and drink meant for the poor?
ST. CEDD. What do you mean, brother? what word
of scandal against us tingles now on your tongue?
THE ACCUSER. Scandal? Judge! I accuse the Church thus—
I accuse her that always and everywhere—now and here—
she has been comatose to man's earthly need;
I accuse her that she has given no heed to the poor,
that she has allowed kings and rich men
to be masters of the poor and of herself, and a den
full only of foulness left for the dispossessed;
I accuse her of offering heaven as an excuse for horror,
of the abuse of Christ's flesh and blood; more—
I accuse her therefore of making schism in the unity
of flesh and spirit, of spoiling the seamless robe;
more—of heresy and thrice heresy,
of foiling the Single Person, God and Man,
by abusing the flesh that is his in the forms of others
and digging God's grave in the gaunt bodies of his brothers.
Answer if you can—
ROME.   No slow answer;
I may speak for all the West, for little rest
have the preachers in a thousand years had from declaring
it is ill faring for the Faith and small comfort
when the rulers of realms leave the poor to grieve;
parish priests and princes of the paparchy bear
witness against this tyranny everywhere.
THE ACCUSER. Is it so? make answer then—not to me! not to me!
Be your answer to the people! ah, do you shake?
What have you done when the people began to wake?

did you not make a refuge of the ark of salvation
when the hail peltered and the flood rose? Hark!
                              [*He calls down*
God and the people, speak! speak, you
who by the body of his passion are his true kin!

EPISODE V

A number of men and women begin to enter

THE CHORUS. All these years we have heard from heaven
   the prayer that out of his mouth was given:
   Give us this day our daily bread.
   We have heard priests and preachers teach
   young children to say in their small speech:
   Give us this day our daily bread.
   Cakes of offal and beds of straw
   are easier to give than an equal law:
   Give us this day our daily bread.
   What when the poor begin to take
   hold on the laws that their masters make?
   Give us this day our daily bread.
   Then the lords begin to pray,
   then the lawyers hastily say:
   Give us this day our daily bread.
   And lest they should call on Messias in vain,
   they seize it before they pray again:
   Give us this day our daily bread.

A crowd of poor people have gathered. A PRIEST *enters*

THE FIRST MAN. Father, must we pay tax when we need bread?
A WOMAN. Bread, father!
ANOTHER WOMAN. Father, bread.
THE SECOND MAN. I heard an abbot once, preaching in his abbey
   say a man had a right to his meed of food:
   having none, if he took it, he were no thief!
THE FIRST MAN. Nay, I heard the Bishop of Rochester say

JUDGEMENT AT CHELMSFORD

the King owed all his liegemen relief
from their burdens; why then should we pay tax?
A WOMAN. Father, food is scant; we want succour.
THE PRIEST. Alas, children, I have no more than you.
I cannot help it; I have lived long among you
and you know I have never thrived when you needed
nor wassailed when you wanted. My lords are away
in great towns, busy with much trouble
of foreign crowns and lands, politics and the like.
A MAN. Does the King himself know the pains of his people?
A WOMAN. Has the King blood in his veins? does he sleep?
THE PRIEST. Alas, the King is young and deep in business,
consulting with the Emperor and many great dukes,
propounding the boundaries of the Turk beyond Danube
perhaps, or how to save Constantinople.
Be patient, children.
THE WOMAN. We have been patient since the world began,
Let them leave the Danube and save us,
as they could have saved my man who died in the famine,
gnawing a few leaves. I lay all night
saying what they said God wills us to say:
Give us this day our daily bread. He is dead.
Where was his bread? did the King or the armed lords
or the merchants or the lawyers or the fat furred foreigners
who ride so fast down the roads to London help?
Father, if God meant to us to live decently
there is knavery in the air; his goodness is stolen somewhere.
THE PRIEST. Be patient and mild, daughter. God sends
tribulation as a means of testing his friends;
no resting if no running; trust,
trust him to give you back more than you lost,
and a purchase so great that the payment is little cost.

JUDGEMENT AT CHELMSFORD

A MAN. Empty bellies are bad believers;
give us a crust or two; we shall trust better.
Enter another PRIEST

THE SECOND PRIEST. Essex is up! they have met at Brentwood all.
Thomas the baker at Fobbing refused the taxes,
and my lord Chief Justice who had come down with commissions
has galloped back to London; we missed *him*
but the heads of his clerks hurry after him on poles.
[Cheering
Kent is up too. Wat Tyler leads,
Essex-born, though has lived in Kent long,
We met his fellows at Barking. Up, all!
THE FIRST PRIEST. Folly!
THE SECOND PRIEST. No, folly. We have a fine watchword:
'Who holds with King Richard and the true commons?'
Who of you are true men?
THE CROWD: All! all!
God save King Richard and the true commons!
Another man runs in
THE MAN. Ho, news for Everyman! a message for Everyman!
Thus says John Ball the preacher:
John Sheep-herd, priest of Colchester, greets well John
Nameless and John the Miller, and John Carter, and bids
them be ware of guilefulness in the towns; and bids them
stand together in God his name, and bids Piers Ploughman
go to his work, and chastise well Hob the Robber;
and take with you John Trueman and all his fellows and
none other, and have you one head and no more.
John Miller, John Carter, John Trueman, John Nameless,
all true Johns, all true Nameless,
come to the King!
SHOUTS. All the Nameless to the King!

JUDGEMENT AT CHELMSFORD

More men throng in. JOHN BALL *enters. There is loud cheering*

JOHN BALL. Hear, men and women! To be poor,
when all are poor, is a trick of the bad weather;
or to have, when all honest folk stand together,
some a little richer, some a little poorer,
must be as may be; God's clay are all,
and Christ send his Christmas merrily to all.
But now is a new thing which is very old—
that the rich make themselves richer and not poorer,
which is the true Gospel, for the poor's sake.
Do you know what Holy Church says? Holy Church
says when you need food you have a right to take it,
and no sin; it is within her law
that no man has any right to rob his brother,
and a man may use arms to preserve his own.
Many bishops and learned clerks say
this is God's truth: I tell you what Holy Church
teaches; now is the time we followed the teaching—
to the King! to the King! down with false clerics!
down with all lawyers! the King of England
shall save the English yet: nameless men,
come you all to the bounty of God and the King.
This is how we know the Kingdom of God,
that the rich make themselves poorer and not richer.
It is our business to see that his kingdom comes—
quickly.

[*Cheering*

No man who is not in grace can own property;
he has no place in God's household, no right,
be his might or his rank what they may, to be steward
of Christ's furnishings for Christ's folk: say,
can churls and cheats be chosen for God's stand-bys?
churls though lords, cheats because lawyers? I,

JUDGEMENT AT CHELMSFORD

John Ball, John Nameless, tell you all,
and will tell the King or the Pope in Rome to his face,
no man not in grace can own property;
through all creation salvation is the root of dominion;
title-deeds are nothing unless the Lamb signs them;
they damn a man deeper. Who dare deny—
who?—that the devil can only own the devil,
and the devil's children can possess nothing but themselves.
Therefore up, follow to London! swear—
and you shall see the foreigners flee before you—
to be faithful to God and the King and the true Commons!

ALL. God and the King and the true Commons! On.
[*They pour out*

THE CHORUS. Babylon now sits quiet on Tiber and Thames,
sleepy with drunkenness; over her the many jewels
are little licking flames confined in beauty;
the scarlet of martyrs' blood stains her purple
and drains down to the sound of instruments of music.
Count the kinds of merchandise she buys—

VARIOUS VOICES. Gold
    silver
       precious stones
           silks
   scents
     ointments
        frankincense
            cinnamon
              oil.
   All manners of vessels of iron
          brass
            marble
   wood

JUDGEMENT AT CHELMSFORD

    ivory.
        All manner of food
  fine flour
     wheat
       wines.
         All manner of riches
    bulls
      sheep
        horses
          dogs
            cats
  ships
     trumpets
         music
           great arts
  cities
     slaves
       women
           and souls of men.

THE CHORUS. Alas, alas, that great city London!
 The merchants of earth shall weep and mourn over her,
 for no man shall buy their merchandise any more;
 there shall be no eyes to see or hands to finger
 or ears to linger at all for sweet sounds:
 deaf and blind and half-paralytic
 she shall stumble into the judgement away from God.
 to feed evermore on the chaff she proffered the poor.
CHELMSFORD. I have said it! I have kept the faith! Cedd,
 witness that no year has gone by
 that somewhere—at Thaxted or else—I have not cried
 that the people must be saved in earth as in Heaven
 and the angels dash pride into the pit.
ST. CEDD. It is so; since God let his heavenly wit
 dwell on earth, hell has never quite

battened the hatches down to make all tight
and the sentries set where its ship floats on the sea.
Hell has met always with windy weather.
THE ACCUSER. I do not deny it; but let the commons try
to put into action what the common doctrine says
and back they are driven down the old ways
by the wall of gold, iron and steel. See—
it is not altogether your fault, sister, I agree.
Man finds the doctrine of exchange hard and strange—
see how your rebels fared once with King Richard.
> [*Some of the rebels are driven in by a wall of armed
> men, all in steel with faces covered by steel. They
> move like automata. The rebels are scattered or
> slain or taken*

THE CAPTAIN OF THE ARMED MEN [*in a booming metallic voice*].
Take the chief of the rebels to execution.
It is good that a few men should die for the State.
THE ACCUSER. He is right, is he? or is he not? God
ignored the argument; he merely died.
> [*The armed men move out, conveying the rebels*

CHELMSFORD. With each childbirth the struggle begins again;
no sooner have a few men known their sins
than they die, and the old easy grudge stirs
in the hearts of the new age; it prefers
bestiality of pomp to the peace of blessing.
How long, O Master of heaven? Lord, how long?
THE ACCUSER. I do not say you are wrong, sister; your task
is hard. Heaven may ask for impossibilities,
but it rarely gets them. That perhaps is as much
its own fault as yours; I may say so—but you,
rue and repent: that is what you have to do.
ANTIOCH. Nor you alone, little sister; all we
lament for the quailing and the failing. Here

JUDGEMENT AT CHELMSFORD

in heaven repentance itself is a wonderful laughter,
a beauty of God's devising; but recall we now,
lords and brothers, the bitter moments below
when we knew how we went the way we would not go.

[*All the* SEES *and* CHELMSFORD *kneel*

ALL THE SEES AND CHELMSFORD.

Have mercy upon me, O God, after thy great goodness: according to the multitude of thy mercies do away mine offences.

Wash me thoroughly from my wickedness: and cleanse me from my sin.

For I acknowledge my faults: and my sin is ever before me.

Against thee only have I sinned, and done this evil in thy sight: that thou mightest be justified in thy saying, and clear when thou art judged.

Behold, I was shapen in wickedness: and in sin hath my mother conceived me.

But lo, thou requirest truth in the inward parts: and shalt make me to understand wisdom secretly.

Thou shalt purge me with hyssop, and I shall be clean: thou shalt wash me, and I shall be whiter than snow.

Thou shalt make me hear of joy and gladness: that the bones which thou hast broken may rejoice.

Turn thy face from my sins: and put out all my misdeeds.

Make me a clean heart, O God: and renew a right spirit within me.

Cast me not away from thy presence: and take not thy holy Spirit from me.

O give me the comfort of thy help again: and 'stablish me with thy free Spirit.

ST. CEDD. And the blessing of the Mercy be on you all.

The SEES *rise*

EPISODE VI

It is always the same and yet it is not the same.
Brothers, the Faith has done something, since
first our great Prince allied himself
to men on the side of their right instincts. Much
is tattered and torn; and long forlorn
amid barbarous angers and desires may men be,
as when from the sea came plunging the Danish fires
on Catholic Christendom, but he always there
ran up and down the stair of heaven. See,
this is how it all went out, and how still
it may go out again, if the shout of the pirate crews
bursts from the cold clustered woods—the moods
and melancholy hungers of men are always piratical.
Call Osyth, my lords: did she die when she died?
Her instinct was Christ's and deeper than theirs,
since she knew, as we know, that Love can love and be
 loved.
What else but the Faith has shown that truth to be true?
THE CHORUS. Osyth, Osyth, Osyth!
Show from beatitude! appear out of grace!
show again the time and the place
when the axe was the sign of the high heart's warmest
 embrace.
Blessed one, show!

Celestial music. The NUNS *and* ST. OSYTH *enter from Heaven. They descend to the lower stage, and group themselves*

ST. OSYTH. Daughter and wife was I amid the East Saxons;
God called me at last to a third vocation—
to a separation from all for his name's sake:

blessedly my husband permitted it; because he fitted
his heart to my peace he shall never cease to know
the goodness of God's will. I took the vows
with God's authority and my husband's, presently I ruled
a house of nuns peaceably here in Essex,
where we went about the business of understanding
after our proper manner the expanding circles of Love.
Remained that he deigned me yet a fourth calling,
installing me in a martyrdom—holy and happy is he.
I left father for husband, husband for grace,
grace for himself: the Danes took the islands
on the Essex shore, and began from those forts to pour
over the land, killing for pleasure, their leisure
filled with savage torments. Christ be merciful
to them and to us and to all; Christ befall
now and ever all men and all men's neighbours.

THE DANES [*without*]. Harou! harou!

                They come in

ST. CEDD. These are the two great instincts of man;
that is his state to be for ever torn
between love and hate of love. Look, brother,
our Lord took flesh to save the one from the other.
Is it a wonder that some years must pass
before wholly the dust of sin is changed
to the manner of holiness everywhere?

THE ACCUSER. God made me just.
I have admitted that he and you both
have a hard labour in man's slow-witted heart.
I can praise Osyth as well as you all.

                             [*He calls down*
Now, Osyth, now—for the vow and the veiling!
    [*The flight and massacre of the* NUNS. OSYTH *is
    taken. She is set kneeling among the* DANES

JUDGEMENT AT CHELMSFORD

THE DANES [*gathering round*]. Harou! harou!
ST. OSYTH. What shall I say? am I to say that Love
 does not love and cannot be loved?
THE DANES. Harou!
THE DANISH CHIEFTAIN [*holding his axe over her*].
 Say the axe is the only certain thing!
 Say the axe is your father and husband; say
 the axe and the blood on the axe is your only lover.
 Say the blood on the axe is your only love!
ST. OSYTH. The blood on the cross is come again to its
  living:
 Love has no loss anywhere at all.
THE CHIEFTAIN. Harou!
      [*He swings the axe down close to her head*
 Say you are frightened of this axe.
ST. OSYTH. Of course I am frightened
 as I used first to be as a child when it lightened—
 but I laughed too! as I laugh now at this,
 and at you, friend, if you will not think it unkind.
THE CHIEFTAIN. Feel the wind of Odin, and the Ravens
   flying! [*He swings the axe on her other side*
ST. OSYTH. I have felt a winter frost much colder,
 when I knelt before the altar of Love that loves.
THE CHIEFTAIN. Say the axe is your father and mother and
   husband.
ST. OSYTH. I will attend to it rather, if my Lord wishes,
 for a sweet friend and task, as a cook to his dishes,
 an actor to his part, or the heart of man to his pleasant
 loves, till the present Christ take them all.
 Now is his name.
ST. CEDD. His name is Now.
ALL THE HEAVENLY PERSONS. Now!
      [*The* DANES *strike* OSYTH *down*
THE DANES. Harou!

THE CHIEF. Ravens, what temples stand against Odin?
  death out of the sea takes them;
  and the sea pours over and breaks them,
  and the Ravens hover above the cities;
  they peck the eyes of the Romans flying,
  the falling consuls, the lictors dying;
  Harou, harou, the Ravens hover.
  Rome is over the pit of the falling,
  Odin, send us the Ravens calling;
  the axe is man's father and sister and brother,
  the blood on the axe is the mother of men.
THE DANES. The axe!

[*The* DANES *pour out*

THE CHORUS. Osyth, Osyth, Osyth!
  rise to beatitude; take again place
  in the Glory apparent; show how the Grace
  lifts to the life: blessed one, show!

[OSYTH *half-rises*

CHELMSFORD. No: delay . . . .
  What did you see, Osyth, as you died?
ST. OSYTH. I saw the City where Love loves and is loved.
  It was striking out of earth; all the liking
  of man for man, woman for woman, man for woman
  opened outward into a glory; it ran
  out of the hidden points of the flesh and the soul
  into the whole pattern of exchange of beauty,
  and Fate free, and all luck good.
CHELMSFORD. How then?
ST. OSYTH.   For all men
  are man in him, and his two natures gather
  all loves of all creatures to the love of the Father.
CHELMSFORD. Do not go, Osyth; heaven is in you;
  you do not lack heaven, wherever you are.
  Do not go back; stay with me a little here.

JUDGEMENT AT CHELMSFORD

ST. OSYTH. I were well willing to do this, if our Lord chose.
CHELMSFORD. Would he not? entreat him for me: Patriarchs,
  entreat him for me—
  that Osyth and the blessed dead may tread my roads,
  as at Bishop's Stortford and by Good and High Easter,
  more perhaps at Pleshey where still
  the bells ring triune to the enclosure of prayer.
JERUSALEM.   Nay, never
  has our courteous Lord forbidden any to tread
  earth, if her will be so: the blessed dead
  are free everywhere through all the City—
THE ACCUSER. And indeed I am he who shows them to you.
  I talk with them often by Brentwood and Dagenham,
  down by Tilbury or away by Dunmow and the Baddows
  and many places else on many evenings.
  The more you know me, sweet, the more you know them.
CHELMSFORD. I begin to believe it, my lord; only smile,
  when you are harsh—and be as harsh as you will.
  I shall believe in love the whole while.
  I am a little afraid still—
THE ACCUSER.   Princess,
  your eyes are as lovely in penitence as were the Magdalen's.
JERUSALEM. Let Osyth do her will; she is in the Unity.
ST. OSYTH. I will go at once; I will find my old homes
  and many others—how, brother, did you name them?
  Brentwood, Dagenham, Tilbury, Dunmow, the Baddows.
  O sweet! I will go, I will go quickly.
        [*She runs out.* CHELMSFORD *begins to cry from sheer
        relief. The* ACCUSER *passes behind her and speaks,
        without her knowing certainly who it is*
THE ACCUSER. A little, a little; wait a little, sweet.

EPISODE VII

THE CHORUS. Messias that made man
  wishing him extravagance of love and great generosity
  began with as much of his own delight
  as ever to hold in his heart that figure had might.

  He began with himself for a plan:
  he formed an image of his joy and called it man;
  he breathed therein everlasting desire for the bright
  clear intellectual vision of his own delight;
  he sealed in the pure field of that lesser nature
  this that for ever he had in common with his creature.
  Man with man, woman with woman, man with woman,
  knows the lovely extravagance of joy,
  and, haste though they have and wild though it run to waste,
  since Eve's hand thrust through the torn leaves,
  there is no other end in any his plight,
  in hell that deceives or heaven that justifies,
  than the candid wise vision of continual delight.
  He that is bone in man's bone and blood in man's blood,
  he that alone in the desert and sorrowful stood,
  he is feast in the feast and song in the song,
  strong in exercise, long in the laughter,
  maker of sensation, master of neighbourhood,
  mayor of the City of the Good in the blood and the bone.

CONSTANTINOPLE. Daughter, this is common knowledge
  in the low degrees of the heavenly college:
  even in your world, even made with heavy hands,
  the image of the joyous City stands.
  What, since your time began, holds this in common?

JUDGEMENT AT CHELMSFORD

CHELMSFORD. Man with man, woman with woman, man with woman;
God's grace has kept those joys in me, and I
witness before all devils that man's heart
is still more Christian than his wrangling will;
legends and tales, and now to sound and sight
truth in our awful wonder of delight.
THE ACCUSER. Be humble, sweet; delight is apt to lead
into bleak tombs of the spiritual dead.
CHELMSFORD. Cannot bones live? what charnel place was left
uncleft when he ascended out of hell?
Tell, songs of feasting! love of woman, tell!
                              [*The music of* OLD KING COLE
THE CHORUS. Old King Cole and he called for his bowl
and he called for his fiddlers three,
and there was fiddle, fiddle, fiddle, and
                              —twice fiddle fiddle,
for 'twas my Lady's birthday,
and therefore keep we holiday
and a merry merry merry day.

    KING COLE *of Colchester enters, with his attendants.*
                    Wine is poured out

KING COLE. Blessed be peace now [*they drink*], and you, my men,
betake yourselves well to drink's happiness, and the harp's;
these things flank fellowship. Sit all down,
make good cheer and be jolly; harvest
is in the barns, and the Twin Stars kind.
The Roman peace builds the barns, and the British
wheat fills it. Picts and pirates lose
their hold on the land: go we now cheerfully

about our business in quiet. Sit all down
and break voices in singing. Who begins?
THE FIRST MAN. Marcus, begin.
THE SECOND MAN. What shall I begin?
KING COLE. What?
'Bald-headed Caesar'—what else? Chorus, all.

Song

Bald-headed Caesar went to Britain
to sell his father's cast-off shoes:
Chorus. Wow, wow, wow and a fig for their fighting;
Colchester cackled and could not choose.
Down the dirt ways, lump and thump,
the by-blows of bald-headed Caesar stump.

Hook-nosed Caesar went to Egypt
to find a girl of Ptolemy's kind;
Chorus. Wow, wow, wow and a fig for their flirting;
back he brought her and had to be blind.
Down the dirt ways, lump and thump,
the by-blows of hook-nosed Caesar stump.

Bald-headed Caesar went to the Senate;
there the rich men stuck him with knives:
Chorus. Wow, wow, wow and a fig for their fumbling;
Caesar had more than a dozen lives.
Down the dirt ways, lump and thump,
the by-blows of bald-headed Caesar stump.

[*Loud cheering. They all drink*
KING COLE [*pouring out the libation*].
To the Fortune of the Divine Emperor.
ALL [*shouting and pouring*].
To the Fortune of the Divine Emperor.
THE FIRST MAN. They say the Fortune of the Divine
Emperor

JUDGEMENT AT CHELMSFORD

may make him divine long before he wishes.
He has pains in his inside.
ALL. Sacrilege! sacrilege!
THE SECOND MAN. The Sacred Emperor has no inside.
THE THIRD MAN. Or if he has, he has no pains there.
THE SECOND MAN. Or if he has, they are growing pains.—
  Who
  said once, when he felt death on him,
  'I think I am on the point of becoming a god'?
KING COLE. Hush, fellows: you may talk so here,
  but when you are in Rome—do as the Romans do.
THE FIRST MAN. Our lord and god Diocletian has an eye on them.
THE SECOND MAN. He has held the Empire together; he and his Caesars.
THE THIRD MAN. And our own Constantius Chlorus not least.
KING COLE. Some of you were with him in—
        A MESSENGER *runs in*
THE MESSENGER. Sir, the excellent Caesar Constantius is here.
KING COLE. What?
THE MESSENGER. He has just ridden through the gates.
  He has left the legions to march north; himself
  ridden here. In a moment he will be in the house.
KING COLE. Let us show well to Caesar.
        [*They put on behaviour. Trumpets.* CONSTANTIUS
        *enters, with the eagles and a few officers. The
        formal reception in silence*
CONSTANTIUS CHLORUS. We are very glad to know you, sir.
  Your town
  has been a security to us now some years,
  in a time when our legions have had sweaty work
  on our frontiers, and within them sometimes. Sir,

we are Rome; it is Rome who thanks you now in us,
and do not think because you hear occasionally
of losses, defeats, massacres even, that Rome
is lost easily, for all the lavish raids
of the barbarians. Sir, the Empire—
say rather the City, it is the greater name—
is more than all the noisy peoples, the races
shouting against each other from Persia to the Wall.
Tribal and national warcries sound everywhere
but Rome is settled beyond all nations and tribes.
If it went down—luck rules all—
you would have with some trouble to invent it again.
He is a wise nationalist who knows that his nation
is only half the truth; the other half
he can only find by getting outside his nation.
That, sir, is the use of the City; there
all the nations can know themselves through others;
these must do so; you, sir, know
that unless you live in the love of your neighbours you
    are nothing
but a silly noise, however loud. So the peoples—
your British, for example—must learn to obey
Europe, Rome, the City.

KING COLE.   My lord,
because the City is beyond all tribes
and all lives, even our dukedom of Colchester,
I have believed in it and kept my people
as a street in the City rather than a village of their own.
I have been called disloyal and unpatriotic,
no Briton; better, they say, to run
tribally howling, as free as the wolves in the woods,
than to be only a gate to the great City.
I have not thought so.

CONSTANTIUS. No. If Rome lacks anything

it is a soul worthy her; a dream, a myth,
a wonder of vision as much mightier than she
as she than all the screaming animals of the races.
The gods are old and tired; only the sublime
providence of our lord Diocletian sustains all things.
The City, and a little friendship within the City—
that is man's total sum of good.
You can rest us here to-night?
KING COLE. Sir, willingly.
It may please your Highness that I present my child,
my only one, a daughter, and a loyal friend of Rome.
CONSTANTIUS. We are debtors everywhere to all such; call her.
And hark, privately a moment.
> [*Several go out.* CONSTANTIUS *and the* KING *come down together*

Because you are a friend
I will say this—do not answer me—if there be
any of a sect called Christians among you,
bid them not show while we are here.
The divinity of the Emperor will have them cut off:
that is one thing in Italy, but here quite another.
I cannot afford the men to kill or be killed
because of godheads. Besides . . . but leave it there.
I have had one man executed at Verulam
who put himself in the way of it. No more; pass.
> [*He turns and sees* HELENA *entering. He stands quite still*

KING COLE. I present, sir, my daughter and your Highness' servant.   [*They stare at each other.* HELENA *genuflects*
CONSTANTIUS [*mechanically*]. We are very glad to see you.
HELENA [*genuflecting again*]. Sir and my lord.
CONSTANTIUS. I did not know that I was looking for anything . . .

KING COLE. My lord?
CONSTANTIUS. . . . and now suddenly I have found it. Sir,
to let the princess wear such jewels in her hair
is to be reckless of riches.
KING COLE. My daughter wears
no jewels, sir.
CONSTANTIUS. I did not think so, and yet
I would not believe that her forehead was so bright.
'Tis, yourself, sir, gives us permission. You, gentlemen,
leave us.

[*All but* HELENA *go out*
It seems that I am still somebody;
a world or two moves when I speak, but I do not know
why that should be. Who are you?
HELENA. Sir, my father
told you: I am Helena of Colchester.
CONSTANTIUS. I
was Constantius Chlorus the western Caesar; now
I am only the perception in a flash of love—
HELENA. A peremptory phenomenon of love,
fiercer than your eagles.
CONSTANTIUS. All my eagles together
have never frightened the Picts so much as I
am frightened by the mere eyes of you.
Is Love the only untired god that is left?
Do you believe, augustitude, in the gods?
It does not matter, only—we must say something
lest we should go away or they come back.
Speak to me then.
HELENA. Sir, I have been taught
that God is love and have heartily believed it,
but now I know that when our Lord took flesh
he made flesh so lordly that no God of Rome
was ever divinitized into such a glory.

JUDGEMENT AT CHELMSFORD

CONSTANTIUS. Helena!
HELENA. Caesar!
CONSTANTIUS. I am Caesar again, now
you have given me back my function in the City.
What did you mean by what you said about God . . .
Helena?
HELENA. Caesar . . . God has made flesh
part of his infinite and adorable redemption,
and when I say Caesar, it is all clear
because this is the very image of redemption.
CONSTANTIUS. Blessed one, what you say is as difficult
as to believe that your voice is able to exist
being so beautiful. But . . . are you a Christian?
Do not say. I think that both Rome and I are come
into possession of a soul. Vision of glory,
I adore you, I love you; my heart breaks with you.
HELENA. Caesar, most blessed and adorable Caesar!
　　　　　　　　　　　　　　　　　　[*Their hands touch*
CONSTANTIUS. If there should be something that had my power
and your spirit, he should alter the world. Rome
needed but such a redemption to be both
in earth and heaven; it was heaven she lacked. O City,
O most adorable and most glorious City,
Rome in Love is something Rome has not known.
You are the mother of love. [*He kisses her*
HELENA. Love . . . love . . . O Caesar.
　　　　　　　　　　　[*She faints in his arms. He catches her*
CONSTANTIUS. Golden beatitude of beauty, a new City
shall rise from you and me; our two hearts
making a future from this quality of greatness
shall strew time with a fresh order of perfection,
a holy wisdom, sprung from Colchester and Rome,
redeemed flesh blazing with primordial glory—

JUDGEMENT AT CHELMSFORD

Love our first child, and our second child
the tiaraed Augustus, woman and man in Victory.

[HELENA *recovers herself*

HELENA. Sweet my lord, let me go now.
CONSTANTIUS. Must you? go then; and if you are a Christian,
which yet I must not know, but if you are,
commend me to the God who made you lovely
and set such lucid powers within your flesh
as half would make me think he lived within you.
Good-night, my Colchester.
HELENA.   Good-night, my Caesar.

[*She withdraws*

CONSTANTIUS. Love is our first child; if we have a second,
I dedicate him to this hour. He shall
draw a new doctrine into the heart of Rome,
even if, to do so, he change the place of Rome.
Gentlemen!

The KING, *&c., return*

Sir, we must alter our intention. Now—
to-night—we must be gone. Command our horses.

[*To a servant*

KING COLE. My lord—
CONSTANTIUS.   No evil: good, all good. Hark,
I will say no more than—pardon and expect us.
Sir, men take joy in men and women in women,
friendship and delight of love, but this—a Christian?
What do the Christians believe?—No, do not say.
It is not time yet; wait. Good-night: our horses!

[*They go out*

THE ACCUSER. You do not, my lord Constantinople, smile
to see the beginning of your greatness? This man died
at York: his son was Constantine, and a Christian—
no one knows why.
CONSTANTINOPLE.   Indeed no one knows why.

JUDGEMENT AT CHELMSFORD

But in some exchange between the Omnipotence
and man, in some such ravishing hour as this,
when our incarnate and most courteous lord
exhibits the actual unveiled beauty of flesh
to eyes of love; making the love and the loving,
the lover and the beloved, the beloved and the lover,
into a glorious mystery of himself—
might that not be an obscure reason in God?
Brother, our lord is incarnate; you forget—
and not a mirage in a desert of piety.
The infidel has walled up Holy Wisdom,
which this man's son first built, but a million lovers
circulate Holy Wisdom through the world,
to be spiritual sees of Christendom. There is
an apostolic tradition in the blood
when the flood of the spirit takes it, as the water
mingles with the precious and original blood.
Speak, brothers.

CANTERBURY.   Man's room of earth and air
  is often gay through his gloom with miracles of sweet play;
he hears the birds or the poets, he sights
the sea or architectural lines; he loves
great designs; his rhythms turn holy rites:
sense is one great defence against the Fall.
It has pleased God to throw a light thence
(as one of your poets said) on a world of greatness,
an invisible world, a world of absolute power.
For Eden wall is low and man's eyes look over
to see where the doves of Pentecost hover
through and about the giant tree of life,
rife with its twelve kinds of fruits; Paradise
shoots rumours through his flesh and heavenly humours
through his soul. Who witnesses thus?

CHELMSFORD.   Brother and lord,

JUDGEMENT AT CHELMSFORD

    ask my fields and towns; it is so still
    as it was ere the first tribesmen found the ford
    over Thames upwards.
CANTERBURY.   Shrill is the call, shrill,
    as then in the forests so now among the machines,
    man hears in his working at a smile or a sunset or a song.
    Who hears sows; where reaps he or where gleans?
JERUSALEM. In me; in the other gloom,
    the long blank of the tomb that is no tomb
    when all happiness parts from the broken hearts
    when the insolent and inflamed horror sweeps
    over man's Christendom of flesh, and leaps
    teeth and claws on his heart; the Lord Diocletian's beasts
    are but an image of this, when hell's persecution
    rages everywhere and always through all peace—
    pain along the nerves and along the lives
    drives: everything is but a vision of pain:
    who witnesses thus?
CHELMSFORD.   I again,
    down through the docks of the fields and the docks of the towns
    till the heart rocks with the threat of the terror. Yet
    I have set, holy ones, my will and my word beyond
    all earthly words; I bid my Christ to his bond.
    Could he, if he wanted, rid himself of me for ever?
    Never; it is mine to command and his to obey.
    Pray, shall I? this I say when I pray:
    Be quick, be quick; it is I; you love me; come.
THE ACCUSER. Ha, sweet, have I driven you to ground at last?
CHELMSFORD. Come, come; lord and my love, come.
    JERUSALEM *comes down to the lower stage. Two seraphs*
        carry in front of him a covered burden

EPISODE VIII

The Chorus

Sing, my tongue, the glorious battle,
    Sing the ending of the fray;
Now above the Cross, the trophy,
    Sound the loud triumphant lay:
Tell how Christ, the world's redeemer,
    As a victim won the day.

Faithful Cross, above all other
    One and only noble Tree!
None in foliage, none in blossom,
    None in fruit thy peer may be;
Sweetest wood, and sweetest iron!
    Sweetest weight is hung on thee.

JERUSALEM. Christ our City, have pity on all barbarians,
all tribal shriekings beyond the City,
Docetists or Arians, denials of the Man or the God,
the earth or the heaven, made one in one birth,
one Passion, one Resurrection: make election,
daughter.

CHELMSFORD. I made it long since; I will not leave anything out; now I bring all to all.

JERUSALEM. Yet let some voice of yours speak while we show
that the tale of the mystical legend may have its meaning,
and Helena Empress be shown for all souls' queening.
Shall it be Cedd?

ST. CEDD. Not I; choose rather
some other worker who spread the news,
one of your saints and children, a son
of your district, your diocese—any; name him.

CHELMSFORD. Light in the dim ways, flame in the heart's home,
I call one who later was a bishop himself,
but young gave tongue in me for a blessing,
confessing in Little Easton the Christhood.
Thomas Ken, come! . . . and hear you him preach,
as teaching his people on a May Day of festival.

> KEN *enters and speaks as if from his pulpit to his parishioners*

KEN. You are to consider, good people, that all the things that are said about our blessed Lord in Holy Scripture are said also about his way with the soul. For his work is threefold: what he did on earth, and what he does in the Church, and what he does in every soul which desires him to work upon it; and these three manners of working, agree in one. So that when we say that he is the Way, we mean it in these three kinds. And this I have very often expounded to you.

But this is true too of those tales and legends which the Church recommends to her children, as is said concerning the Apocryphal Books in the articles of our own Church of England: 'and these the Church doth read for instruction of manners, though she doth not account them canonical.' Days of holy men are celebrated among us that we may remember them as examples to us. There are, besides these, certain days of observation—which are meant for our profit; and this very Sunday on which we are met here is one of them. It is called in our Kalendar the Invention of the Cross, by which is meant the Discovery or Finding of that Cross on which our holy Saviour died. We have been told that this very Cross, which was preserved by, as it were, miracle for many hundreds of years, was brought again to light by a pious woman, the Empress Helena, who was the mother of the first Christian Emperor Constantine. It was said once that she was an English woman and came from this very country of yours now called Essex, or the land of the East Saxons, but I think learned men say that this is not so and that she came first from certain parts beyond the Danube. But whatever this truth may be, still she was married to the Roman Caesar of Britain, and it is becoming, because of that old tale, and because of her place here, and because of her son who brought peace to the Church, and because of the grace that was shown her in the Discovery of the Holy Cross—it is proper, I say, good people of Essex, that you should consider what this Finding of the Cross means.

For first consider that she lived in great love and pleasantness with her husband the Caesar Constantius as long as God allowed them, and that after he died at York she did all that was in her power to guard and cherish and teach her son who was to be the great Emperor of all the world. But after this was done, and he gone to his own wars, she gave herself wholly up to God. And consider now with yourselves by how many pleasantnesses God has shown his meaning to you also, and by how many proper strictnesses he has shown you that he will have you come to himself only. Consider this a little, I pray you.

> [*He pauses. The* EMPRESS HELENA *enters, in the robes of an imperial widow, attended by several women and priests. She kneels in prayer*

JERUSALEM. Helena . . . Helena.
THE CHORUS. Helena!
> [*She listens, rises, and seems to speak to her attendants*

KEN. Now it was so that our good Lord, having determined

to show grace to this holy matron, put it into her mind that she should make a journey through all the Empire of Rome until she came to Jerusalem; which was very possible for her because she was a great lady, but is not at all so possible for you and me who are not the parents of Emperors. But are we not all called to take our journey to another Jerusalem, which is above? and can we find any other way but by much care and spiritual travelling? such as that holy lady had done in her heart before ever she began to understand the will of God towards her. And consider you now for a space the many toils and vexations that she endured on her journey, and we on ours, and the whole Church of God upon its own— of which we here in Essex are a small part.

> [*He pauses.* HELENA, *in some state, begins her passage round the stage, moving round with the sun, and passing by* ROME *and* CONSTANTINOPLE

ROME. Lady of old Rome, pass to old Jerusalem.
CONSTANTINOPLE. Mother of new Rome, pass to new Jerusalem.   [*She comes near* JERUSALEM *and stands still*
KEN. But it is one thing to come where the Cross is and another thing to find the Cross. Trials and vexations are God's way of bringing us to God's holy place, that is to say, to the Jerusalem that is within our souls. But he brought Caiaphas to Jerusalem, and Pilate; yes, they lived in it and were familiar with it. You may come to this Church where we are and know it, yes, kneel and stand up in it, and say thanks to God for it; and all the while you shall be as far from that other Jerusalem as Judas was from Christ when he shouldered him in the crowd. That holy lady had found a Calvary in her heart before ever she came near it on earth. Consider therefore what speed you should be making now.

> [*He pauses.* HELENA *comes up to* JERUSALEM *and*

JUDGEMENT AT CHELMSFORD

kneels. He blesses her. She stands up, and moves towards the hidden Cross. A pace or two away she stops. The whole tableau is rigid

KEN. But, O good people, how blessed are you if, having come to that Jerusalem, you do indeed find, by God's grace, the secret and hidden thing. For find you the Cross without you, as did that blessed lady, you shall find a precious, an inestimable treasure, the wood on which our Saviour rested without resting, the bloody, bloody wood he bedewed. But find you the Cross within you, as that blessed Empress also did, and you shall find Christ himself, Christ that is the Cross, and so holy, so sweet, so fresh and fragrant a Cross that you shall laugh to find how you have mistook him. For this Cross—but consider you this a little moment.

[HELENA *signs. The* SERAPHS *throw back the cover.*
HELENA *and her attendants kneel*

KEN. This Cross is no longer an unwilling sacrifice, no, nor a difficult sacrifice; it is not a slow duty, no, nor a quick duty; nor anything at all but our most sweet and courteous Lord being to us a justification and a sanctification, and our very life itself; and this is in all of you to be found as surely, O much more surely, than the Empress of Rome found the wood of the beams in Jerusalem. And it is this which saves, justifies, sanctifies the Church of God—all of you, and I, and that fortunate Helena, and her son, and her husband, and any and all men in all districts and dioceses; and the Church and all mankind has good cheer by this. And we in this land that was of the East Saxons and is now Essex, and belonged once to old Rome under Caesar and now to new Jerusalem in Christ; and especially you, my own people of Little Easton, rejoice we all to-day for the great and wonderful Invention of the Holy Cross, that Christ found for all us and we in him, and all souls that be by his most sweet manhood and foundation bound fast to him; and afterwards by his grace doubly born to him: and go we all forth thinking of this and praising him, without whom nothing had been at all for ever and ever. Amen.

>[*He goes out*, HELENA *withdrawing to the side. The* SERAPHS *support the Cross*

EPILOGUE

THE WHOLE CHORUS.
>Bend thy boughs, O Tree of Glory!
>>Thy relaxing sinews bend;
>>For awhile the ancient rigour
>>That thy birth bestowed, suspend;
>>And the King of Heavenly Beauty
>>>On thy bosom gently tend!

JERUSALEM. Bend, Christian soul, the hard branches,
slowly loosen the rigid sinews; flow
into the vital Christ-of-the-Cross. Where
have you been all this time but only here?
this is at once indictment, judgement, and release,
when your Peace awakes through all moments at once.
This is that which is you.

CHELMSFORD.   I know, as I knew
from Cedd's mouth first, and afterwards spoken
by others: I too have had children who said so
in emblems and images. Heavenly kinsmen, sound
some song of theirs, while I bound myself in his frame.
My Lord heard me call; quickly he came.

ST. CEDD. Choose Francis Quarles, a chronologer of peace.

THE CHORUS. Ev'n like two little bank-dividing brooks,
That wash the pebbles with their wanton streams,
And having rang'd and search'd a thousand hooks,
Meet both at length in silver-breasted Thames,
Where in a greater current they conjoin:
So I my best-beloved's am; so he is mine.

Ev'n so we met and after long pursuit,
Ev'n so we join'd; we both became entire;

No need for either to renew a suit,
for I was flax and he was flames of fire:
Our firm-united souls did more than twine;
So I my best-beloved's am; so he is mine.

He is my Altar; I, his Holy Place;
I am his guest; and he, my living food;
I'm his by penitence; he mine by grace;
I'm his by purchase; he is mine, by blood;
He's my supporting elm; and I his vine:
Thus I my best-beloved's am; thus he is mine.

CHELMSFORD [*leaning happily on the Cross*].
 O Grief, I take the Joy your grief brings;
 Joy, what is Grief while that Joy lives?
THE ACCUSER. Sweet lady, this is the answer to all.
JERUSALEM. Fair daughter, this is the truth of all.
CHELMSFORD. Blessed master, now I can love you right.
[*To the* ACCUSER
Blessed father, now I can see you right.
[*To* JERUSALEM
 Call them, all those that are I.
 Call them, to be one pattern here with me.
THE CHORUS. Adeste, fideles, laetantes, triumphantes.
All the persons enter
CHELMSFORD [*aspiring forward from the Cross*].
 Are you all here?
ALL THE PERSONS. All; all.
CHELMSFORD. Answer then, I for you and you for me—
 all you my past, all you my present, all
 you invisible powers that shall be yet my future.
 Say, shall I name the glory, in you and for you?
ALL. Lady, we name the glory, in you and for you.
CHELMSFORD. Say, shall I take the Cross, in you and for you?
ALL. Lady, we take the Cross, in you and for you.

JUDGEMENT AT CHELMSFORD

CHELMSFORD. Say, shall I melt to the Love, in you and for you?

ALL. Lady, we melt to the Love, in you and for you.

JERUSALEM. Brother, finish your work. [*He re-ascends*

THE ACCUSER [*laughing*]. Do *I* shirk the Joy,
I who am God's true knowledge of all things made?
Come, beloved. [*He takes her from the Cross*

CHELMSFORD. Dearest of all lovers!

[*They embrace passionately*

THE ACCUSER. Most sweet lady,
I have waited an hour, and yet an hour for this;
now I will lift you where we have willed: on,
on to the City, the Love between all lovers.

        [*He takes her up the steps. As she comes near the height she pauses and leans over*

CHELMSFORD [*calling to those below*].
Now, children of miracle, in you and for you!

ALL [*including the heavenly persons and the Chorus*].
Now, lady of miracle, in you and for you!

        [*She reaches the height. The whole company begin the* TE DEUM. *During the first five verses,* CHELMSFORD *meets and embraces the* SEES

THE WHOLE COMPANY. We praise thee, O God: we acknowledge thee to be the Lord.

All the earth doth worship thee: the Father everlasting.

To thee all Angels cry aloud: the Heavens, and all the Powers therein.

To thee Cherubin, and Seraphin: continually do cry,

Holy, Holy, Holy: Lord God of Sabaoth;

        [*She turns back to the* ACCUSER *and gives him her hand*

Heaven and earth are full of the Majesty: of thy Glory.

        [*The* ACCUSER *takes her to the centre; the* SEES *group round the two of them*

The glorious company of the Apostles: praise thee.
The goodly fellowship of the Prophets: praise thee.
The noble army of Martyrs: praise thee.
The holy Church throughout all the world: doth acknowledge thee;
The Father: of an infinite Majesty;
Thine honourable, true: and only Son;
Also the Holy Ghost: the Comforter.

> [CHELMSFORD *takes a step forward, the* ACCUSER *close behind her, on her right*

Thou art the King of Glory: O Christ.

SEED OF ADAM

A Nativity Play

CHARACTERS

THE TSAR OF CAUCASIA (*King of Gold*)

HIS CHORUS

THE SULTAN OF BAGDAD (*King of Frankincense*)

HIS CHORUS

ADAM

EVE

JOSEPH

MARY

THE ARCHANGEL

TWO ROMAN SOLDIERS

THE THIRD KING (*King of Myrrh*), a Negro

MOTHER MYRRH (*Hell*), a Negress

The scene is before the house of Adam; to the right of it are the stables; on the left, at the front, the stump of a tree or a high stone

NOTE

THE only existing manuscript is that of the first version, printed in *Christendom*, September 1937. Of the second version, slightly expanded from the first, there are many typescripts which vary in accuracy, but after some difficulty I have identified the one which contains the author's own faint corrections. This is reproduced here, except that (*a*) the literal corrections necessary to all the scripts have been made; (*b*) two stage directions, added by the producer but approved by the author in performance, have been included on p. 9; and (*c*) the capitalization has been altered in one or two places to conform with the style of the other plays. The list of characters is compiled from the programmes used at the Brentwood and Oxford performances (1937 and 1939), both of which were approved by the author. It seemed best to combine the two, since I was uncertain which would have had his final approval. I should add, that in performance one alteration was required by the Censor.

RAYMOND HUNT

SEED OF ADAM

The TSAR *enters with some of the* CHORUS

CERTAIN VOICES. Juggle, sir; throw up the golden slivers.
OTHER VOICES. Sir, no; show rather the rivers,
  molten and golden streams; fertilizing, barricading,
  cities and nations, from stations of earth-edging Esquimaux
  to the hanging gardens of tropical sense:
  and there the high ships sailing, the deep ships unlading.
FIRST VOICES. Necklaces, bracelets, ear-rings; gaudies and gew-gaws!
OTHER VOICES. Purse rather and pocket of outer commerce; mind
  finding after kind, and all traffic its own.
THE TSAR. I am Gaspar,[1] Tsar of Caucasia;
  I sprang from our father Adam's loins
  in a bright emission of coins; Eve's need
  of gilded adornment nourished me to dig and dive.
  Pearls I brought up; springs I let forth: who
  will be beautiful now? who profitable then?
  Men thrive and I take my fee.
  Tricked out in riches half the world follow me;
  who fall, crawl or are kicked into dry ditches.
      The SULTAN *enters, with the rest of the* CHORUS
CERTAIN VOICES. Sir, play; throw up the notes of gold,
  or stir into silver smoke the rich incense.
OTHER VOICES. Sir, no; our old throats are tired.
  Show rather the philosophical plan,
  chess-playing, brick-laying, sooth-saying;
  the design of line, point, and curve.
FIRST VOICES. Titillate the brain by ear and eye!
OTHER VOICES. Build the austere academies to show why.

[1] Traditionally, Melchior is the King whose gift is gold. C. W. has reversed Melchior and Gaspar, here and in an early poem. [*Ed.*]

SEED OF ADAM

THE SULTAN. I am Melchior, Sultan of Bagdad.
  Adam my father and Eve my mother
  construed me aloof from sister and brother
  through a post-paradisal afternoon.
  I build my mosques under a philosophical moon;
  I ride on the body's curves through spirals of air
  to the bare and rare domes of Bagdad my see.
  I give to whoever serves with me
  gnomic patterns of diagrammatic thrills.
  Half the world live in my train;
  who refrain, bereft of brain, are left to common ills.
SEMI-CHORUS. Give us the golden matter,
SEMI-CHORUS.   and the golden chatter,
THE CHORUS. for to-morrow everything begins again.
          [*They gather about the* KINGS, *some sitting or lying*
ADAM [*coming out of the house*]. Dullards of darkness, light's lazy-bones,
  poor primitives of our natural bareness,
  where's your awareness? will moans and groans
  for gold of brawn or brain regain
  the way to the entry of Paradise? up!
  shut your eyes, will you? or make a play
  for your leisure, and a treasure of your idleness? You,
  have you nothing better to do
  in our world but play hide and seek with oblivion?
  Say, say something, say
  who are you? I will tell you, tell you what you knew,
  I am Adam.
SEMI-CHORUS. Father Adam, the pasture is thin,
  the sheep and the hogs are thin, our coats
  button thinly about our throats
  thrawn with wind and thirsty for wine.
  Exchanges—his and mine—help us
  to bear with the bitterness of having nothing.

SEED OF ADAM

What should *we* do, feeling for Paradise?
Better to suck at the heel of the Tsar.
SEMI-CHORUS. Father Adam, if we go looking and snooping round
corners,
we see terrible shapes trooping,
things eagle-beaked, giants with scimitars.
In Eden you found them friendly; here
what should we do but hide while they stride and deride
the bitterness of our having nothing?
Have you seen us slinking from those neighbourly taunts?
Better to go drinking the rhythms of the Sultan.
ADAM. If you found Paradise, you would find everything.
THE CHORUS. Call with the old bluster to muster by masses,
and seek!
SOLO.   Speak civilly, father!
                         Where
shall we go? climb invisible cords into the air?
for road, river, and lane
are searched; it is not to be found.
THE CHORUS. And to-morrow everything begins again!
SOLO. What is this way? behind what sight or sound?
SOLO. He lost it, and he cannot say.
SOLO. There is not any.
SOLO.   Yes; it is bought for a penny
and slept off.
SOLO.   No; wise men have recognized
it is only our mothers' forms rationalized.
SOLO. The Tsar declares it is hope learning to grope.
SOLO. The Sultan says it is sensation living in negation.
SOLO. It is the loss of the one thing prized
masochistically advertized;
SOLO. or adolescence flushed with immature sense.
ADAM. Babies!
THE CHORUS. Who lost it?

SEED OF ADAM

ADAM.   I. What do you know,
children, of what living on this earth is like then?

THE SULTAN. Father, you must not think you are everyone.

THE TSAR. Your children are men and women, and not you.

THE SULTAN. Individualized essence of you, perhaps;

THE TSAR. with each his particular Paradise in a nutshell.

THE SULTAN [*touching his lyre*]. Nuts! nuts!

THE TSAR [*throwing gold pieces*]. Nuts! nuts!

BOTH.   Nuts for the men-monkeys!
Monkey-nuts! follow, follow, monkey-nuts!
scratch and snatch for a portion of monkey-nuts!
grab and grizzle for a ration of monkey-nuts!
houp-la!

> [*The* CHORUS, *chattering and fighting, run about like monkeys. They gradually become involved in a general fierce battle and drift off, following the* KINGS, *with high shrieks*

ADAM. I must set my law upon them; one thing first.

> [*He turns, meeting* EVE, *who has come out of the house at the noise*

EVE. Are they fighting again?

ADAM.   What else?
They have not the pain that in us stops us fighting.

EVE. Have they found anything?

ADAM.   Nothing, my Eve.
They cannot find the centre, the core of the fruit
where the root of return is. I dropped it; it is gone.
Where is Mary?

EVE.   Mary has gone to the fair.

ADAM. Under the Mercy! . . . what is she doing there?

EVE. Watching mountebanks, laughing at clowns,
applauding jugglers and tightrope walkers,
listening to talkers, admiring lovers,

riding with children on the roundabout,
everywhere in the middle of the rout,
being, by her nature, all things to all men.
ADAM. Will she never discover any preference? any partial
liking for this where or that when?
Will she never care to marshal phenomena?
Cows, clowns, and crowns are alike to her—
has she not a trick of nursing the sick,
and as agile through all as the honey-plucking bee,
catching as much sweet there as from booths at the fair?
She must follow now another mind than mine.
I am set. Call Joseph; they shall be married.
EVE. Married! Mary? but why? and why Joseph?
ADAM. Lest I should die. She shall be wedded
lest our youngest born should be a prey
in her simplicity to her sisters and brothers.
I will not have her a scullion and a scorn
in the huts of Caucasia or the harems of Bagdad.
Joseph is a warlike and dutiful lad.
Call him.
EVE. What is he, where is he, now?
ADAM. Lieutenant-general of the Sultan's horse,
an Islamite, a genius in cavalry tactics!
To see swung whole squadrons in the charge,
and—in a wild clatter of words breaking—flung
down the speaking of a poem, when the matter is sprung
to the flashing and slashing of a steel line
at the throat's blood. Hafiz taught him
and Omar; he outgenerals them; call him.
EVE. Will Mary have him?
ADAM. As soon as any.
O pest on her for a zany of goodwill!
EVE. Husband!
ADAM. Be easy. I am petulant. My want

worries at my throat, while she wants nothing,
nor ever sighs for nor even denies Paradise.
EVE. Paradise perhaps is hers and here.
ADAM. Among the sick or at the fair?—
Look, there she comes: call Joseph, I say.
He is in Bagdad's train. I must go again
to quieten their brawls. I will give them peace.
I will show them if I am Adam for nothing.

JOSEPH *and* MARY *enter*

ADAM. Joseph, am I your lord?
JOSEPH. In all things, sir,
under the justice of God.
ADAM. Your father, Mary?
MARY. Sir, by the Direction.
ADAM. It is well; hear me.
I do and undo; I am Adam. Paradise
shuts its last mouth upon us, and I am afraid.
It may be, after I have conquered yonder apes,
and shaped them to placabilities, that I shall find
by counting them some form unguessed,
some archangel disguised, some person or place
where is the grace of the Return. If, well;
if not, the thing this world must soon become
catches us up. Whether this be or not
I am determined you two shall be married.
A heart of purity and a mind of justice
to be integrity. What say you?
JOSEPH. Sir,
I am of no more worth to the princess Mary
than the fly-flick of her mule's tail.
MARY. But as much, Joseph, indeed.
JOSEPH. You hear, my lord?
ADAM. Never mind her.
Since she loves all, she loves you. What of you?

SEED OF ADAM

JOSEPH. She is the manifest measurement of God's glory
correcting time.
ADAM [*motioning them before him*]. You are both my best of
children.
> [JOSEPH *and* MARY *kneel;* ADAM *raises his right arm*

By the single indecipherable Name
I swear you, Joseph and Mary, to betrothal.
> [JOSEPH *and* MARY *rise and face each other. The upraised
> palms of their right hands touch. They turn to face* ADAM

When I return from conquering the world, be ready,
as then shall be, in time and space, convenient.
Come, Eve.
> [ADAM *and* EVE *go out*

JOSEPH.   Am I appointed for your husband? . . .
Answer, princess . . . no? no then, do not speak,
do not break through such an outgoing stress of light,
as is the sovereign blessedness of the world,
there indivisible, all ways else divisible.
Do not with descent, O altitude, even of mercy,
sweeten the enhancèd glance of those still eyes
which to my lord's house, and to me the least,
illumine earth with heaven, our only mortal
imagination of eternity,
and the glory of the protonotary Gabriel.
> [MARY *stretches out her hand to him; he kneels and kisses it*

MARY [*murmuring the name*]. Gabriel, Gabriel: well spoken is the
name.
As I came from the fair I looked back; there
I saw it all in a sheath and a shape of flame,
having an eagle's head that turned each way
as if it were guarding something and looking for something.
Its eyes burned at me; the noise
of the hurly-burlies and the hurdy-gurdies,
the ball-spinners, the silk-sellers, the rum-peddlers,

the swings, and the songs, rose to a whirring voice,
the air was a hum of sound; I heard it come
as if the fair all rose in the air and flew
on eagle's wings after me; I ran
through the fear and the laughter and the great joys.
I came by the vineyards to my father's roof;
there it held aloof a little.
I saw you; I gave you my hand, Joseph,
at my father's will. It has still power,
this hand of Adam's daughter, on all creatures of heaven.
JOSEPH [*as he kneels*]. O princess,
your hand is the fact of God's compact of light.
MARY. I have heard such talk among the lovers at the fair.
Bless you for telling me, Joseph.

> [*He releases her hand. The* ARCHANGEL *appears at the back, as it were casting sleep towards* JOSEPH, *who sinks slowly forward, and lies still*

MARY. Joseph!

> [*A pause*

Joseph!

> [*She sees him lying*

THE ANGELIC CHORUS [*without*]. Adonai Elohim! Adonai Elohim![1]
THE ARCHANGEL [*standing behind* MARY]. Adonai hu ha-elohim!
THE CHORUS [*as the angelic army without*]. Shalom lach eschet-chen, Adonai immach beruchah at bannashim.

Al-tiri Miryam ki-matsat chen lifne ha-elohim.

Vehinnach harah veyoladt ben vekaret et-shemo Yeshua.
MARY. How shall these things be, seeing I know not a man?
THE CHORUS. Ruach hakkodesh tavo alayieh ugevurat elyon tatsel alayich: al ken Kadosh yeamer layyillod ben-ha-elohim.

---

[1] The Hebrew is written phonetically, as for the Sephardi pronunciation (vowel sounds as in Italian, all *r*'s distinctly sounded, *ch* as in *loch*). The Ashkenazi pronunciation can be used if desired.

SEED OF ADAM

MARY. Behold the handmaid of the Lord; be it unto me
according to thy word.

> [*The* ARCHANGEL *passes round and enters the stables.* MARY
> *remains rapt*

JOSEPH [*he rises to his knees, as before, and wakes*]. Under the
Protection! Mary . . . Mary . . .
MARY.   Yes, Joseph?
JOSEPH. Mary, you are changed; you are in love.
MARY.   Yes, Joseph.
JOSEPH [*starting up*]. Ah, ah! but who . . . ?
MARY.   No one, Joseph.
Only in love.
JOSEPH.   It must be then with someone.
MARY. Dearest, you did not hear: we said *in love*.
Why must, how can, one be in love with someone?
JOSEPH. Because . . . but that is what *in love* means;
one is, and can only be, in love with someone.
MARY. Dearest, to be in love is to be in love,
no more, no less. Love is only itself,
everywhere, at all times, and to all objects.
My soul has magnified that lord; my spirit
rejoiced in God my saviour; he has regarded
the nothingness of his handmaid. He has thrust
into this matter his pattern of bones, as Eve's
towers of cheeks and arrogant torches of eyes
edify red earth into a pattern of manhood.
JOSEPH. But it must be at some time and in some place.
MARY. When you look at me, dear Joseph, do you think so?
JOSEPH. Babylonia and Britain are only boroughs of you.
Your look dimensions the world. I took once
a northward journey to find fables for the Sultan
and heard a lad on the hill of Faesulae syllabling
a girl of Faesulae who nodded good-morning at him,
and that her form timed the untimed light.

SEED OF ADAM

Place must be because grace must be,
and you because of glory. O blessing,
the light in you is more than you in the light.
MARY. The glory is eternal, and not I,
and I am only one diagram of the glory:
will you believe in me or in the glory?
JOSEPH. It is the vision of the Mercy.
MARY.   Hold to that.
But for salvation—even of those who believe
that time and place and the one are the whole of love—
Love—O the Mercy! the Protection!—
shall make his flesh as one in time and place.
It shall come in the time of Augustus Caesar,
in the place of Bethlehem of the Holy Ghost,
in the coast of Judaea: not quite Jerusalem,
but not far from Jerusalem, not far but not quite.
O Thou Mercy, is this the secret of Thy might?
When Thou showest Thyself, that Thou art not there
to be found? we find Thee where Thou art not shown.
Thou art flown all ways from Thyself to Thyself,
and Thy ways are our days, and the moment is Thou.
O Thou Mercy, is this the thing to know?
Joseph, come, take me to Bethlehem;
there the apparition and the presence are one,
and Adam's children are one in them;
there is the way of Paradise begun.

    [*They move round the stage to the stone. As they go, the*
    CHORUS *re-enter on all sides*

THE CHORUS. In Thule, in Britain, in Gaul, in Rome,
among the slim pillars of Bagdad, in round mounds of Caucasia,
we heard the maxim that rules the schools of prophets:
this also is Thou; neither is this Thou.

With double hands and single tongues
the prophets climb the rungs of heaven,

in the might of a maxim gained and given:
this also is Thou; neither is this Thou.

But we who wander outside the rules and schools
compromise and complain,
before the clot in the blood has shot to the heart or brain:
this is not quite Thou and not quite not.

Sister, sister, did you dream?

What did you see on the banks of the body's stream,
in Thule, in Britain, in Gaul, in Rome,
under Bagdad's dome, by the mounds of Caucasia?
SOLO. One came walking over the sand,
one and a shadow from a desert land;
I saw a knife flash in a black hand.

At daybreak a child is born to the woman;
he grows through the noon to his full stature;
she devours him under the moon; then at morn—
THE CHORUS. Save us, Father Adam, or we perish!—
SOLO. or in a mirage of morn the child is reborn.
And to-morrow everything begins again.
THE CHORUS. From bone, from brain, from breasts, from hands,
from the mind's pillars and the body's mounds,
the skies rise and roll in black shadows
inward over the imperial soul:
over our sighs in the moon of dusty sorrow—
O, O, could everything begin before to-morrow;
over the creak of rusty grief—
to-morrow will be soon enough for belief;
over the kitchens of a pot neither cold nor hot,
and the thin broth, and the forming of the clot—
not quite Thou and not quite not.

Father Adam, save us or we perish.

[MARY *sits on the stone*, JOSEPH *stands behind her. From*

opposite sides two ROMAN SOLDIERS *run in, turn to the front, and come to the salute*

FIRST SOLDIER. Octavianus Caesar Augustus,
SECOND SOLDIER. filius Julii divi Augustus,
BOTH SOLDIERS. orders the world in the orbit of Rome.
FIRST SOLDIER. Oaths and service to the lord Augustus;
SECOND SOLDIER. incense and glory to the god Augustus:
BOTH SOLDIERS. to the god Augustus and the Fortune of Rome.

[*They wheel inwards, and fall back on either side.* ADAM *re-enters as* AUGUSTUS, *accompanied by* EVE *and the two* KINGS

ADAM. I was Julius, and I am Octavianus,
Augustus, Adam, the first citizen,
the power in the world, from brow to anus,
in commerce of the bones and bowels of men;
sinews' pull, blood's circulation,
Britain to Bagdad. I in brawn and brain
set knot by knot and station by station.
I drive on the morrow all things to begin again.
Look, children, I bring you peace;
I bring you good luck; I am the State; I am Caesar.
Now your wars cease; what will you say?

THE TSAR. Hail, Caesar; I am your occupation for the days.
THE SULTAN. I am your sleeping-draught for the nights: hail, Caesar.
THE CHORUS. Hail, Caesar; we who are about to die salute you!
ADAM. I will take now a census of the whole world,
the nations and generations of the living and dead,
to find whether anywhere it has been said
what place or person Paradise lies behind,
even among the prophets who made a formula for the mind.
Each man shall answer, on or under earth,
from Cain and Abel, who were first to explore
womb and tomb, and all whom women bore,

to the pack that died at Alexandria yesterday.
Answer, children, and say, if you can. I know
the thing that was threatened comes; there is still time.
Go!

> [*The* SOLDIERS *run out; there is a deep and confused noise.*[1]
> *Presently they return, bearing papers*

FIRST SOLDIER. All these millions dead

SECOND SOLDIER.   and dying; these thousands
dying or dead;

FIRST SOLDIER.   these hundreds, and sixteen—

> [*He drops his spear towards the nearest of the* CHORUS *on his side, who answers as from a sepulchre*

ONE OF THE CHORUS. and seventeen

ANOTHER.   and eighteen

ANOTHER.   and nineteen

> [*All answer in turn, as the* FIRST SOLDIER, *and then the* SECOND, *pass, pointing their spears. The* SECOND *comes to* JOSEPH

JOSEPH [*answering according to the number of the* CHORUS]. and thirty-six

> [*The* SOLDIER *points to* MARY

JOSEPH [*answering for her*]. and thirty-seven.
Shall I add one more for the child that slumbers in your womb?

---

[1] The producer suggested that something should be added here, and used to prepare for the entrance of the Third King shortly afterwards. C. W. had begun to write this additional matter, but the following fragment is all that we have:

TSAR. When the Archangel spoke to you in the true Paradise
and your heart broke—what did he say, there
under the trees? something you could not hear
about not-dying

SULTAN.   When you ran and pushed
your way through hedge and river, when you rushed
down the ledge of rock between the abounding foliage
near the water rounding Paradise and the world outside—
a few leaves of the hedge clung to your coats

TSAR. a few drops of water hung on your skins.
That was the beginning.

SULTAN.   Twinning what was one

SEED OF ADAM

MARY. O no, Joseph; he is something different from all numbers;
you cannot tell how or whom. The people are reckoned,
but the child that comes through me
holds infinity in him, and hides in a split second.

[*The* SOLDIERS *return to* ADAM

FIRST SOLDIER. Hail, Caesar; those who are dead
SECOND SOLDIER.   and those about to die
BOTH SOLDIERS. salute you.
Octavianus Caesar Augustus;
filius Julii divi Augustus;
gubernator, imperator, salvator, Augustus.

A VOICE [*off*]. What is this difference between the dying and the dead?

The THIRD KING *enters, followed by a* NEGRESS, *carrying a scimitar*

ALL [*except* JOSEPH *and* MARY, *in a general moan*]. Ah!

THIRD KING [*looking round*]. What provincial talk is this? what academic
pedantic dichotomy? O la, brothers!

[*Seeing the* KINGS *left, right*

THE TWO KINGS. Ah, brother, how did you find us?

THIRD KING. Indeed I might not have done;
but my mother here has eyes and a nose,
and with each sun recognized more strongly
gold's glint and censer's smell.
As the wind of infinity blows
earth is always leaving clues for hell,
and hell has only to follow that news of earth.
[*To the* CHORUS]
No wonder you talk so if you have them here
talking of distinctions and differences, smells and savours,
sight of gold, sniff of incense, flavours
of this or that differing degree of corruption.

[*To the* KINGS]
   You left me away in a stony land,
   brothers; I was lonely without you.
   I came to find this mind of Rome,
   this concept, this Augustus, this new Adam.
   Why, father! The old Adam, after all!

ADAM. It is you, is it?

THIRD KING.   I. You saw me
   when you breathlessly slid down the smooth threshold
   of Paradise gate? and saw the things that were hid
   as God warned you you would? did you know
   I was the core of the fruit you ate?
   Did you remember, ungrateful that you are,
   how you threw me away, with such a swing
   I flew over Eden wall, dropped,
   and stuck between two stones?
   You did not see; you did not look after me!
   Smell and taste for you; let the core go to hell.
   But God looks after the sparrows.
   Presently the sun split the core,
   and out grew I, the King of the core.
   I have travelled to get back to you ever since.

EVE. And who is she?

THIRD KING.   Ah, she!
   At the heart of the core, in the core of me,
   lived a small worm you could not see.
   The sun is a generous sun; he set us both free.
   She lives by me, and I by her.
   I call her my little mother Myrrh,
   because of her immortal embalming. We two
   have come, my other mother, to live with you—
   if you can call it living.

ADAM.   What else?

SEED OF ADAM

THIRD KING. O well! She has her own idea of food.

                                                          [*He indicates the scimitar*

The nearer the relation, the better the dish.
But you will not *die*; no, I do not think you will *die*.
I did not, and I have been eaten often,
you may imagine; it was a long way from here,
and a long time ago, that we made our start,
and angels on the way delayed us,
with exhortations of earnest heavenly evangels:
but what can angels do against decaying matter?
Matter can only be corrected by matter,
flesh by flesh; we came through and came on,
and I everlastingly perishing. The worm
of that fruit, father, has a great need to feed
on living form. But I do not think you will die.

ADAM [*to the* SOLDIERS]: Seize her.

        [*They rush forward. She laughs at them, and they fall back
        on their knees*

THIRD KING.   Whom are you seeking?
Are you come out with swords and staves to take us?
We were often with you in your temples: now—
Father Adam, you were always a fool,
and it seems at the top of your Roman school
no better; will you arrest the itch
with your great hands? will your bands pitch
their javelins against the diabetes of the damned?
The belly is empty in hell though the mouth is crammed:
a monotonous place!

THE CHORUS.   Father Adam, lord Augustus!

THIRD KING. Among the stones and locusts she lived on me;
it is your turn—this is my refrigerium.

        [*He draws back. The* TWO KINGS *drop their gold and lute.*
        EVE *covers her face. The* NEGRESS *walks slowly round, the*

SEED OF ADAM

CHORUS *falling on their knees as she passes. At last she comes to* MARY. *Meanwhile the* CHORUS

THE CHORUS. Call the kings!
   saints! poets!
            prophets! priests!
  Call the gospels and the households!
  those of Aquino and Assisi!
            Stratford! Chalfont St. Giles!
     caskets of Caucasia!
            censers of Bagdad!
ALL. Help us and save us!
THE TWO KINGS. Balthazar our brother is stronger than we.
THE CHORUS. Call on the households!
            harp-stringer of David!
     hewer of wood for Joseph!
            ink-maker for Virgil!
     galley-captain of Caesar!
            armour-bearer of Taliessin!
ALL. Come to your defences! all heavenly lords,
  stand about us with swords.
THIRD KING. Election is made, capital rather than coast:
  she thrives most on the dear titbits of perfection.
  Sister, you are lovelier than all the rest,
  and like the busy blest. She shall eat you alive
  for her great hunger; take pity on her appetite.
       [JOSEPH, *drawing his own scimitar, thrusts himself between them*
JOSEPH [*crying out*]. Ha, ha! to me, my household!
  There is no God but God: in the name of God!
       [*The scimitars clash; the* THIRD KING *touches* JOSEPH *in the thigh; he stumbles and is beaten down*
THIRD KING [*dragging him away*]. Little man, martyrs and confessors
  are no good here, nor are poets any good.

167

They are all a part of the same venomous blood.
Come away, come away, and wait your turn quietly.

                    [MARY *takes a step or two forward*

MARY. Dearest, you will find me very indigestible.
The stomach of the everlasting worm
is not omnivorous; it is a poor weak thing:
nor does the fire of Gehenna do more than redden
the pure asbestos of the holy children; if mine,
is for the fire and your dangerous appetite to find.

      [*The* NEGRESS *attacks* MARY *with her scimitar.* MARY *goes
      back before her, at first slowly, moving round the stage*

MARY. Sister, how slowly you carve your meat!

THIRD KING. Be easy, sister; you will not get away from us.

MARY. Nor she from me, brother, which is more important.

      [*The movement of the two women quickens and becomes a
      dance; the scimitar flashing round them in a white fire.
      The* CHORUS *sway to the movement,* ADAM *only remaining
      motionless*

MARY [*suddenly breaking into song*]. Parturition is upon me: blessed be He!
Sing, brothers; sing, sisters; sing, Father Adam.
My soul magnifies the Lord.

THE CHORUS [*hesitatingly*]. My spirit hath rejoiced in God my saviour.

MARY [*dancing and singing*]. For he hath regarded the low estate of his handmaid:

THE CHORUS [*gathering strength*]. behold, from henceforth all generations shall call thee blessed.

      [MARY *at the door of the stable, where the* ARCHANGEL *is
      seen, catches the uplifted wrist of the* NEGRESS *in her right
      hand. They stand rigid, foot to foot*

MARY [*singing joyously through a profound suspense*]. For he that is mighty hath done to me great things;

SEED OF ADAM

THE NEGRESS [*in a shriek of pain and joy*]. and holy is his Name.
                           [*She faints at* MARY's *feet*
MARY [*leaning towards* JOSEPH]. Joseph!
My son calls to his foster-father: come!
prince of maidens, hasten to the master of maidenhoods,
and the pillar of maternity.
JOSEPH [*half-rising*].   O mother of the world's brightness,
I sought uprightness, and yet it failed in the end!
MARY. Most dear friend, my lord, it delayed the scimitar
but till my son took flesh under its flash:
the heavens constrain me to glory: Joseph!
         [*He springs up and to her, and takes her into the stable*
ADAM [*in a strong voice*]. His mercy is on them that fear him from
generation to generation.
         [*The* CHORUS, *singing, gather about the* TWO KINGS, *as at
         first*
FIRST CHORUS. He hath showed strength with his arm;
SECOND CHORUS. he hath scattered the proud in the imagination
of their hearts.
FIRST CHORUS. He hath put down the mighty from their seats;
SECOND CHORUS. and exalted them of low degree.
FIRST CHORUS. He hath filled the hungry with good things;
SECOND CHORUS. and the rich he hath sent empty away.
THIRD KING [*stretching out his hand towards the* CHORUS]. Are you
now so gay?
              [*As his hand sinks down, they fall on their knees*
And you, lord Adam,
do not speak too soon; you desired the boon of salvation—
have it! You desired twice—me and not me,
the turn and the Return; the Return is here,
take care that you do not now prefer me.
JOSEPH [*coming from the stable*]. Sir, send a midwife to your
daughter.

SEED OF ADAM

All things are rigid; only Mary and I
move, and the glory lies even between us.
The Return is at point to issue; befriend salvation.

> [*All the figures are rigid, except* JOSEPH *and the* THIRD
> KING. ADAM *speaks with difficulty and without moving*

ADAM. Whom shall I send? whom?

THIRD KING. We, call we you father, are not yours;
we are the things thought of before you, brought
into Eden while men were not, when
in the Days hunger was created, and lives
with a need always to feed on each other. This
was felt in the first kiss of man and woman.
Mother, there is a good cake for you now
to take everlastingly; go, kiss her, love
hungers: deliver her and she shall deliver you.

> [*The* NEGRESS *leaps up and turns on him*

The eaten are on your left hand, the uneaten on your right;
go—there is no thing living so dextrous as you.

> [*The* NEGRESS *and* JOSEPH *go into the stable*

THE ARCHANGEL. Adonai hu ha-elohim!

THIRD KING. What do you see, man? but I see.
Flesh is become that firmament of terrible crystal
your prophet saw: within it wreathed amber
and fire sheathed in the amber; now
the fire and the amber and the crystal are mingled into form;
what do you hear, man? [*He pauses*] but I hear
the terrible sound of the crystal singing as it spins
round the amber where the fire is hidden, and now the amber
is hidden in the crystal, and the crystal spinning into flesh,
twining into flesh: it slows, it stops, it sinks—
what do you know, man? but I know—
it drops into the stretched hands of my mother;
my mother has fetched a child from the womb of its mother;

SEED OF ADAM

my mother has taken the taste of the new bread.
Adonai Elohim!

[JOSEPH *comes from the stable*

JOSEPH. Father Adam, come in; here is your child,
here is the Son of Man, here is Paradise.
To-day everything begins again.

[ADAM *goes down to the door of the stable*

MARY [*meeting him and genuflecting*]. Bless me, father: see how
to-morrow is also now.

ADAM [*making the sign of the Cross*]. Under the Protection!
peace to you, and to all; goodwill to men.

[*They go into the stable*

JOSEPH. Our father Adam is gone in to adore.
THE TSAR. Blessed be he who is the earth's core
THE SULTAN. and splits it all ways with intelligible light.
THE CHORUS. Christ bring us all to the sight
of the pattern of glory which is only he.
THE ARCHANGEL. Yeshua!
THE TSAR. Blessed be he whose intelligence came to save
man from the gripping of the grave: blessed be he.
THE SULTAN. Blessed be he who, because he does all things well,
harries hell by his mercy: blessed be he.
THIRD KING. Blessed be he who is the only Necessity
and his necessity in himself alone.
EVE. Blessed be he who is sown in our flesh, grown
among us for our salvation: blessed be he.
THE CHORUS. Christ bring us, by his clean pact,
into the act which is only he.
THE ARCHANGEL. Yeshua!
THIRD KING. He consumes and is consumed.
THE SULTAN. He is the womb's prophecy and the tomb's.
THE TSAR. He creates, redeems, glorifies: blessed be he.
EVE. He is all our heart finds or lacks.
JOSEPH. He frees our souls from hell's cracks.

THE CHORUS. Christ bring us, by his true birth,
  into a new heaven and earth.
JOSEPH. Blessed be he whose love is the knowledge of good
  and its motion the willing of good: blessed be he.
THE CHORUS. Adore, adore: blessed for evermore
  be the Lord God Sabaoth: blessed be He.

APPENDIX

SEED OF ADAM

Charles Williams's synopsis, written for the programme; and his notes for an address delivered after a performance at Colchester, October 1937

SYNOPSIS

THIS Nativity is not so much a presentation of the historic facts as of their spiritual value. The persons of the play, besides being dramatic characters, stand for some capacity or activity of man.

Adam, after leaving Paradise, is seeking the Way of Return. His many children, descendants who form all mankind, are tired of the search, and prefer the occupations offered by the Tsar of Caucasia and the Sultan of Bagdad: one calling them to outer things such as trade, exploration, &c.; the other to inner, such as art or philosophy. All these are temporary diversions, and Adam attempts to recall them to their proper business. He fails. In order to save his youngest daughter Mary from their persecution, he determines to marry her to her young lover Joseph. Mary is characterized by a love of people and things in themselves, and has gone beyond the tiresomeness of personal preference. The Archangel appears to her, and declares the Incarnation; she talks to Joseph of the nature of Love, and they go on their journey to Bethlehem.

The Chorus meanwhile exhibit their fear of the coming of some terror upon them out of the ends of time and space.

At this point Adam (or Man) returns in the shape of Augustus Caesar. He has conquered and quietened the world, and he takes a census of all mankind, dead or living, in order to discover, if he can, any knowledge of the Way of Return. The census is completed, but Adam-Augustus is the only known saviour. A voice interrupts, and there appears the Third King. The Third King represents the experience of man when man thinks he has gone beyond all hope of restoration to joy, and is accompanied by a negress, who is, briefly, Hell. The two are come at last to destroy and consume all mankind; they come to Mary first. The play ends with the overthrow of the destructive cannibal nature of man at the moment of the Nativity, and with the adoration of the Omnipotence.

NOTES

ADAM and Dullards of darkness, light's lazybones ... but this did not take me far.

The shepherds and the Wise men (kings)—the poor and others. The poem on the kings—the imaginations. Original idea of the poor [*i.e. for the Shepherds*]: and in a few fragments I toyed with this notion. But it did not produce anything very interesting; and anyhow it was not a true contrast, unless I made the kings the rich, i.e. the great capitalists, which I was very ill-disposed to do (i) because I did not wish to save the capitalists easily in view of Christ's remark about the rich—at the Crucifixion perhaps but not just at the Nativity, (ii) because then I lost my Imaginations, especially my myrrh and Third King. And then Miss Potter wanted a Chorus, and the Chorus and the Shepherds would have been too alike. So the Shepherds disappeared into the Chorus. Mr. Eliot has made choruses a little difficult. I know all about the Greeks, but they do not prevent one being told one is copying Mr. Eliot.

Well, I went on brooding, and the Kings increased. But there remained the awful difficulty of how to make the thing interesting. Which do you find most *interesting*—I don't say which do you think most important—the Nativity or the latest murder? Well, *if* you found the Nativity most interesting you would be reading theology. And do you? No. I am like you. And as I considered this my attention hung about the Third K. I had originally intended each K. to have a female slave—partly to use up Miss Potter's females, partly to give opportunity for dress—or the opposite, partly to combine both sexes in each imagination. A K. with a dancing girl, a K. with a geometrician or a scribe, a K. with something more dangerous than himself—darker, a Negress. There was my first Negress.

Meanwhile I had, in my usual way, abolished Time and Space. I was prepared to bring in anyone. After all, the Nativity was a local event, besides being universal. Augustus and so on. How did we, if we did, bring in Augustus? How did we keep in Adam and keep out Aug.? Now remark this is a real technical difficulty. There are ways of doing it—one might make Adam unnoticeable, or one might ... I don't know. But as I saw Adam he was important; I did not wish him to get to be the Chorus Leader; the Chorus were rapidly becoming imperialistic. And then one of those admirable clicks happened, and I said to anybody: 'Good God! Adam-Augustus, Augustus-Adam.' Admirable—*if* it could be done.

Well, then there was Joseph—and the Blessed Virgin. I was quite clear that the old man leading a devout girl on a donkey was not for this play. There are profound and awful possibilities in it, and one day I will do it. But there is something of it in the later plays of Shakespeare, and as a rule it is safer *not* to go trying to reap what He left. I will put S. into a novel when I want him but I will not chase after him. Besides, was there not a Mahommedan tradition that he was young? I hope there is; I thought there was —good: let us have a young Mahommedan Joseph, and let us (incidentally) make the second King a Sultan. The captain of horse I threw in as a picturesque extra, though it fitted so well with poetry that I have done it over again in my Taliessin poems.

And a just man? This theme is not much in. But it exemplifies [the] difference. The B.V.M. and her characteristics: love of God—before [the] coming of God (as such) to her: what state? Love. The romantic pressure of the individual.

THE DEATH OF GOOD FORTUNE

A CHRISTMAS PLAY

CHARACTERS

MARY
GOOD FORTUNE
THE KING
THE LOVER
THE MAGICIAN
THE OLD WOMAN
THE YOUTH
THE GIRL

The scene is an open place in a city

THE DEATH OF GOOD FORTUNE

MARY. Incipit vita nova: substance is love,
  love substance. Begins substance to move
  through everywhere the sensuality of earth and air.
  I was its mother in its beginning: I taught
  the royal soothsayers to follow a moving star,
  and brought them to their primal, far, and hierarchical Head.
  I am Wisdom whose name is Mary. I wept by the Dead.
  I arose with the Arisen. I see now
  where terribly through all spheres of gods and men
  pulse his ambiguous life and death dealing vibrations.
  His are all the alterations: and here shall be ours.
  There is on earth a being called Good Luck;
  he has spun much joy; his nature is heavenly,
  but when men fell, he was half-blinded;
  he does not know himself nor do men know him.
  I have determined that in this town this very day
  this gay popular lord shall come to his change
  and a strange new vision of himself; for now
  my lord my Son has made this clear—
  that all luck is good luck. And I,
  I struck by seven swords, witness too
  that all substance is love, all luck is good.
  Nor anywhere, for any flood of shed blood,
  sharp single anguish, or long languish of grief,
  shall any deny my word, or the great cry
  to every man upon earth of my lord your Son—
  all chance is heavenly, all luck is good.
  Let us see Good Fortune come now to his trance.
  She seats herself. The OLD WOMAN *enters with a* YOUTH
THE OLD WOMAN. This is where the king will come; stay here.
THE YOUTH. Everything is gay this morning; see how the fair

THE DEATH OF GOOD FORTUNE

glows in the market: the tumblers calling and springing
and the jugglers flinging their quoits. I will go there
when we have seen the king. I will wrestle or cast
a hammer as fast and as far as their own champions.
I will be no puny challenger. Hey,
the blood runs quick this fair morning.
Will you speak to the king yourself, great aunt?
THE OLD WOMAN.   Yes.
They say that since his new guest came
the king will do all he is asked. I will task him little.
He could give me a house without hurting himself,
and will, I hope: there is good luck in the air.
THE YOUTH. And then I will go to the fair; I would fain see
the humped long-necked beast they call a camel
or a man fight, as they say he does naked,
with the wild long-toothed tiger from Seringapatam.
THE OLD WOMAN. Whatever you like.
THE YOUTH.   So I will. Who
is the king's new friend, to please him so?
THE OLD WOMAN. People like us do not know the lords' names,
only their acts. He came walking one day
into the city, under a bright sky,
himself as light and gay as that morning or this;
he was clearly a noble prince. Where he went
every event seemed better, every chance the happier.
That day I added to my store a piece of gold,
and all my neighbours told like good luck.

Enter the LOVER *and the* MAGICIAN
THE LOVER. O but since he came, this king's friend,
this lord, this miracle-worker, even my fortune
seems to have grown greater. I love more,
and there is more joy in my more love.
There is a neat trick about the moments
that brings me to my sweet at any odd time

THE DEATH OF GOOD FORTUNE

   when my heart is like to break not to see her.
THE MAGICIAN. It may well be: he says his name is Good Fortune.
THE LOVER. I can believe it indeed: he is all aerial.
   O Good Fortune, be my god, and bless
   me with her, and both of us with you.
THE MAGICIAN. He is like the full profession of my best art
   gone out of itself into mankind.
   We find too often the last prophecies are lost
   at their end in a mist of faint knowledge. He,
   this god—call you him so—at least this star,
   came to the city in a dazzle. That I foresaw:
   the law of the planets foretold a great event—
   which must be he: unless beyond the bound
   of all sidereal traffic, there were something more—
   but that no astrology has ever found.
THE OLD WOMAN. Sir, will the king come soon?
THE LOVER.   Soon.
THE MAGICIAN. Nay, it seems no one even waits now:
   lo, the king, and—do we say a star?
THE LOVER. Star or daemon—call him our god Good Fortune.

     The KING *enters with* GOOD FORTUNE, *the* MAGICIAN's
                         daughter attending

THE KING. This city, that holds all our lives,
   thrives well; but now you are come,
   our lord Good Fortune, it has a spell within it
   to be fortunate for ever; strangers shall see and say
   how our devotion praises in the phases of its passage
   only you; to you is all our homage.
   Here we rule best and love best;
   here knowledge finds wisdom and age rest.
   Happy are you, Good Fortune, and we in you.
   Deign only to maintain your grace in this place.
GOOD FORTUNE. I am Good Fortune, satisfaction, the action of the
   heart

THE DEATH OF GOOD FORTUNE

when all goes well. I have made this your city
my divine choice; mine while I care to stay—
and I think now I shall not leave you; I
have a power of fidelity too, and it may be true
that I shall stay here and enjoy you; your town
shall be known everywhere for a nest of young delight,
a camp of successful joys, and a rest for the old.
I am always young, a giver of good things,
and you here, by my mere arbitrary choice,
I deign to gratify; cry then my praise;
no god is stronger than I except Pan,
and Pan and I have divided the world between us.

MARY. It is known everywhere that Pan is already dying,
for the substance of love takes him with great shocks;
and you too, fair lord, shall find what locks
were broken for ever when my Son strode through hell.

THE KING. It is true; my armies, since you came, win
on all my frontiers; where my enemies entered in,
they are thrown back; victory is mine alone.
I have good chance now to reward good service.

THE OLD WOMAN. My husband's blood being shed then for you
in one of your fights, and he dead, great sir,
grant me the reward of his service; grant me a house
for old bones to lie securely. No alms;
only my own roof. I have saved; it lies
hidden in my lodging, but the lodging is dank and rank
with the smells of the butchers' quarter. I would rather live
in the new houses you, my king, have built
beyond the river: besides, now I live
with my son and his wife; we cannot get on together.
She is young and bitter and I am old and tired.
My husband died for you; give me now
a proper lodging where I can live on my savings.

THE KING. Willingly; take which you choose: our lord here

smiles on all petitions, and I allow,
I would do also anything for my friends here
but they do not need it; their ends are beyond me:
yours is in your maid and yours in your art.
Yet my heart is apt to give: is there none?
and you?
THE GIRL. Nothing.
THE MAGICIAN. Nothing?
THE GIRL. What else?
Can you, father, or your new god Good Luck
help me in a world where despair only is true?
No; if that is a god, I am an atheist.
I will wait a little to see if your god will die.
GOOD FORTUNE. Do you say, girl, that I am bound to die?
THE GIRL. I say I do not believe in you; nothing more.
GOOD FORTUNE. Look round; see them happy; will not you be?
Worship me, and see what I can do.
THE GIRL. I have lived long enough on earth to know
that earth has no new birth of good luck.
GOOD FORTUNE. But I am not of earth; I am aerial,
born in the mid heavens, a prince of the zodiac,
heir to fine fantasies, lacking nothing.
Will you take them as a gift?
THE GIRL. No; they exist nowhere.
They are the twist of man's heart to defend itself.
You may come from the middle air, but you are deceit
if you do; your feet have no print on our soil.
MARY. He is deceit indeed, but only because
he does not know how great a prince he is.
Since my Son died, all things are good luck,
and fate and good luck and heaven are one name.
GOOD FORTUNE. Am I defrauded in my chosen town?
ALL THE OTHER PERSONS. No.
Lord, she is obstinate, false, heretical;

THE DEATH OF GOOD FORTUNE

 she will stick at nothing to make herself great:
 abate displeasure; treasure us instead.
THE KING. Cense we now, in divine ritual, this godhead.
THE LOVER. Tread we the circle; beat we the solemn vow.
THE YOUTH [*to the* OLD WOMAN]. Shall we go?
THE OLD WOMAN.   We cannot.
THE YOUTH.   Why? the fair waits.
 Must we stand by while the king ceremonializes?
 let's to the prizes! let's to the loud noise!
THE OLD WOMAN. Hist! you will do better if you worship the god.
        [*The ceremony of censing; during which—*
MARY. Before the advent of the necromantic kings
 in the beginning, I saw a star sliding,
 shining, guiding their god-divining caravan.
 Its name was called *TYXH*, its flame was fortune,
 its messenger and shape on earth was this lord here,
 whose sphere above attended my Son's birth;
 but he, being blinded by cloud, is half-minded
 to glorify himself for only half his worth;
 I must teach him all: it is time that he should die.
GOOD FORTUNE. Ah! . . . rocks the earth, or was it I?
THE KING. God, what frightened you?
GOOD FORTUNE.   What lightened then
 or did my eyes dazzle?
           [*He leans on the* LOVER
THE LOVER.   Your hand is cold!
 what is the matter, our God?
GOOD FORTUNE.   My head splits!
THE OLD WOMAN. You have cramp in the stomach, or else the
  damp airs
 of the valley have given you a chill.
GOOD FORTUNE.   My spirit is flung
 into fits of terror!

THE DEATH OF GOOD FORTUNE

THE MAGICIAN. He is rigid in a seizure.
GOOD FORTUNE. Ah!

[*He falls*

THE KING. You—look! what ails him?
THE MAGICIAN. I did not dare
even to fear this—
THE GIRL. But I—I knew.
THE YOUTH. Come; you promised; let us get to the fair.
Our lords die; are we to cry their wake?
Take we a quiet—
THE OLD WOMAN. I am afraid! hush!
Be quiet yourself, you fool!
THE MAGICIAN. Must I look?
Must I think that this god can die?
Must I think that a secretly-sliding star
that the gods neglect has struck this lord of Good Luck?
When that hiding opens—

[*He kneels by him and stands up*

He is dead.
THE OLD WOMAN. Dead?
THE KING. He—*he* dead?
THE YOUTH. All the fair has stopped! what has happened?
THE LOVER. This god cannot die.
THE MAGICIAN. So? And yet he is dead.

[*They all stare at* GOOD FORTUNE; *then they look at each other*

And what will happen now?
THE GIRL. O woe!
I did not quite believe it!
THE LOVER. But if Good Fortune
is dead . . .
THE OLD WOMAN. The money! the money I hid away
to spend on my own living, and save my head
from having at last to lie in a bed lent

THE DEATH OF GOOD FORTUNE

by my son's wife grudgingly till I died. . . .
Come!
THE YOUTH. But the fair?
THE OLD WOMAN. Curse the fair! Come.

[She hurries him out

THE LOVER. If Good Fortune is dead, what will happen to love?
THE MAGICIAN. What indeed?
THE KING. To the Kingdom?
THE MAGICIAN. What indeed?
THE LOVER. The city, he said, is a place of youth; if
Good Fortune . . . and how much is truth a part of Good
Fortune?
THE GIRL. Not at all: that I do know: not at all.

[He stares at her and rushes out

THE MAGICIAN. Sir, will you not also hurry to see
about the frontiers? are no fears growing in you?
THE KING. Yes.

[He begins to go, and returns

Do you try first: can you spy
by your tables of magic the truth of this? Try.
THE MAGICIAN. My art was my heart, as her savings and his love
and your royalty were hearts' realms too; it is sped
if this lord of fortunate chances is indeed dead.
THE GIRL. Father—
THE MAGICIAN. Hush! If your atheism was right,
plight yourself to it, but do not now speak.
THE KING. Try.
THE MAGICIAN. I will try—to please you, and to satisfy
myself that what I feared might come has come.

[He lifts his wand

I lift the hazel rod in the banishing pentagram
against the god of illusion, against Lilith the accurst:
depart, incubi and succubi! depart, phantoms;
I call on the stars of heaven in their even rule,

THE DEATH OF GOOD FORTUNE

exact powers, to show me the fact happening.
Show me the measured fate of this kingdom: show!

                                  [He speaks to the KING

Your enemies move on your borders; in the front line
your orders are frustrated; one of your towns is on fire;
your reserves are belated in the forest. This god
shall be waited on soon by many men,
and your kingdom be past and your crown given to another,
because the curse of the death of Good Luck is come, and . . .

                                               [He tries to see

THE KING. Look; look forward but a month!
THE MAGICIAN. Good Luck is dead: I can see nothing
  beyond this moment, the moment of his death.
THE KING. A week—nay, a day; see but a day;
  see if I can hold them back but so many hours—
THE MAGICIAN. Do you think that your powers of war are to be the only
  sons of luck? is the haft of your kingdom more
  than the craft of my mind? I see nothing; do you hear?
  I who beheld—what did I then behold?
  infinity? yes, except for one star
  that was always moving there, and never where
  my art expected. Here are your other friends—
  back so soon? It seems something ends
  their plenilunary content.

            The OLD WOMAN *returns; she is crying*

THE OLD WOMAN. Thieves! thieves!
  My house was broken open and my floor dug up—
  my money was gone: send, sir, some guard
  to take the thieves. I am a poor woman
  and had hoped to have peace in my last days.
  Send someone to hunt the thieves, my king.
THE KING. You are not like to have peace, nor I neither.
  Something more will be here soon to strike.

THE DEATH OF GOOD FORTUNE

THE OLD WOMAN. What do I care if your enemies share your
  crown?
 I shall wait until they pass; the grass that grows
 in a palace gate finds soil too poor at a hut's.
 All that I need is freedom from my son's wife.
     The LOVER *enters*
THE MAGICIAN. And your life, young man?
          [*The* LOVER *looks at him terribly*
         It began well.
 Who would have thought the death of a god could change
 what (it seemed) fell beyond the gods?
THE LOVER. Be still: he said right; this is a city of youth.
THE MAGICIAN. Love is kind to youth.
THE LOVER.   Love is . . . old man,
 take care; the heir of love is a torn heart.
THE GIRL. Were you happy?
THE LOVER. Happy? We were fortunate and therefore happy.
 But you knew better.
THE GIRL.   Are you sure of that?
THE KING. If indeed Good Fortune is now dead,
 our god, our only hope, behoves all
 to put away our loves, and what may fall
 take nobly, to make a nucleus of hearts
 resigned with one mind against Fate
 to share what we have, and in natural honour brave
 all else. Resign yourselves; be strong.
THE LOVER. Sir, that is nonsense; that is the talk
 of men who believed once that loss might occur.
 Never was I of those. Woes might be,
 but this is more than grief, and yet belief
 rages in me, delirious but unable to die.
 Good Fortune may be dead for you, but for me
 his spirit roars here, demanding godhead,
 nay, having it: I will not be resigned.

THE DEATH OF GOOD FORTUNE

THE KING. What will you do then?
THE LOVER.   I do not know what I will do.
  But I will not be content; it is all untrue,
  this content, this resignation: love must live,
  and if a woman coils up in another's heart
  and spoils love's accidents, love's substance must gather head,
  I do not see how, but somehow: love must live.
THE KING. That he could do while Good Fortune lived.
  But I must lose my crown now, and why
  should you show less content? all the earth
  is resigned: why should a lover's mind escape?
THE LOVER. Because his love is more substantial than yours.
                                                [*To the* MAGICIAN
  Master, though your knowledge fails, you are not unwise.
  Which of us two is true?
THE MAGICIAN. Either; go you
  living in death and he dying in life.
  Toss for your choice.
THE KING.   Which did the stars say
  was the wiser? which is the power in your own mind?
THE MAGICIAN. Give me your hands; there is much power in the
    hand.
  My predecessors say that all enchantment
  is summed in the free hand; therefore a priest
  fetches blessing out of the air with his,
  or a woman stretches hers to love and be loved
  with the palm's inward: give them; if the gods die,
  let us see, wherever rage and resignation endure,
  what cure there may be.
                                                  [*He takes their hands*
                        Now the shrouded battle
  in my brain halts; I see the unclouded stars
  sitting still, as if they were the will of Nature,
  of substance the creature. I see, between two skies,

THE DEATH OF GOOD FORTUNE

the great stars, the million hints of perfection,
stretching far away, and I see the moving star,
spending its glory everywhere, and not losing,
descending: is it devising to earth—and here?
It is coming down; the earth is drenched with it;
blenched on high, its great companions sit,
fit to be watchers of fate, but not fate;
fate is the stolen gold and the false love
and the lost battle, in the death of all good fortune.
Hold yourselves; veil yourselves; the core
of the moving star shoots at my back; who
waits in this city to be clothed with the star?

                              [*He whirls round on* MARY

Woman, by the star that glides into your frame,
by the path that Nature hides from all wizards,
by the wrath and the resignation of death, speak!

                                     [MARY *remains silent*

Mother of the only moving star, speak!
Mother of disaster, mother of destiny, speak!
Mother, if you are a mother at all, speak!

                                     [*He falls on his knees*

MARY. I will speak because you know of what I speak:
you, wizard, though you do not reach it, know.
But tell me first what you think you wish to know.
THE MAGICIAN. It can only be spoken under great veils,
since it is we who must be what we wish to know:
when all fails, what is the right thing to be?
MARY. You must be as you can. I say only, when all fails,
then is the time, brother, to work a little.
THE OLD WOMAN. No work will fetch me my warm room
where I can be alone or ask who I like.
I worked once; now I want to rest;
how can I rest in my son's wife's house?
MARY. My own Son sent me to live in another's.

THE DEATH OF GOOD FORTUNE

  I have no mother's word for any woman,
  sister, beyond this terrible biting word.
THE KING. Tell us this difficult biting word.
MARY.   No;
  biting but not difficult; quite simple.
  When your god Good Fortune dies, the only thing
  is to bid your god Good Fortune rise again.
THE OLD WOMAN. That is silly.
THE KING.   That is impossible.
THE LOVER.   That is true.
THE GIRL. O do not say so, do not say so; I know it is true.
THE MAGICIAN. Do it.
MARY.   It is a great risk you run.
  You may not, when it is done, much believe it.
THE THREE MEN. If it can be done, we can believe it.
MARY.   Can you?
  We shall see; I will do it anywhere for any who ask—
  on seas or in cities; wherever Good Fortune dies,
  there am I to bid him rise, if you will,
  after his proper manner.
        [*She goes to the body and touches it; then she stretches her
           hand over it*
  Good Fortune, god Good Fortune, do you hear?
                                                        [*She pauses*
  Good Fortune, dead Good Fortune, do you hear?
GOOD FORTUNE [*in a dead voice*]. I hear; all the dead shake before
    you.
MARY. Where are you?
GOOD FORTUNE.   In a dry place, between two skies.
MARY. Go forward. . . . Where are you?
GOOD FORTUNE. Among millions of stars;
  it is difficult here even for the ghost of a god
  to move forward, as my substance makes me move.

MARY. Sparks of perfection, shining hints of perfection;
between the hints, sparks, and slivers of perfection,
go forward.... Where are you?
GOOD FORTUNE. Dying in death.
THE LOVER [*murmuring*]. That is it! that is it! that is where I am
now.
MARY. Where are you?
GOOD FORTUNE. Under a shape crucified and burning.
MARY. Go forward.... Where are you?
GOOD FORTUNE. Your voice is behind and before me.
I am before you; you are on a throne.
A child is standing on your knee; a small hand
blesses everything, though nothing but I am there.
It is marked with a dark ring of dried blood.
MARY. What does he say?
GOOD FORTUNE. He says: 'Live, Good Fortune'—
woman, woman on earth, tell me to die.
MARY. What is he doing?
GOOD FORTUNE. He has taken my heart from my side,
and is twisting it in his hands.
MARY. Untwisting.

[*She pauses*

Live; do not sleep; tell us what he says.
GOOD FORTUNE [*moaning*]. O... he says: 'Good Fortune, you have
your fortune;
yours is the only fortune; all luck is good.'
THE LOVER. That is it! that is it! all luck is good.
Why did you tell me to be resigned? Fool!
Why did no one tell me?—all luck is good.
THE GIRL. Dare you say it?
THE LOVER. Dare you not believe it? up!
bear up with me and say that luck is blessed.
THE MAGICIAN. This is the track of the single moving star,
between motionless stars: all luck is blessed.

THE DEATH OF GOOD FORTUNE

THE KING. How is it true there is no evil fortune?
  it is evil fortune to lose my crown and my head.
THE OLD WOMAN. To be bullied by my own son and nagged by his
    wife;
  it is silly to call that kind of luck good.
MARY. It is done; you must make your own choice now
  and show as you will. Live, Good Fortune, live.
  Live and return and tell us what you know.
GOOD FORTUNE. How shall I be able to tell you what I know?
  I found myself riding through the heavens; below,
  on earth, wise men were riding to a Birth,
  to a lonely, difficult, universal gospel
  of the nature, its nature and all things' nature.
  The star in which I stood was moving to a loving
  between the Mother and the Child, and as I saw
  I became other than I was and a new creature;
  I was the master of all chances; all chances
  made the multiple star in which I rode.
  Therefore it shone, and now I take a new name
  that came when the Child smiled for the sake of its Mother:
  I will be called Blessed Luck for ever;
  the temples fall; and all kinds of fate:
  blessed is the Nature and the Fortune in the minds of men.
  Who among you all has professed me now?
  who moves with me to welcome all chances that may come?
THE MAGICIAN. This I know, if I do not believe: here am I.
THE LOVER [*to the* GIRL]. Say.
THE GIRL.   Say for me.
THE LOVER.   I will say for both—
  this we believe, if we do not know: here are we.
THE OLD WOMAN [*to the* KING]. Will you agree?
THE KING. Why should I agree?
  I think it makes sense and I think it does not;

THE DEATH OF GOOD FORTUNE
if I have found defeat is there no defence
less wild than this?
THE OLD WOMAN.   And how can I agree
when I think my child hates to have me there,
my own son, and I nowhere else to go?

[She screams out

You! Stop! what do you say it all means?
I only ask common honesty in the gods.
Do you say, you fellow who pretended to die,
that whatever happens to me is equal good fortune?
GOOD FORTUNE. Yes.
THE OLD WOMAN.   It means nothing to me.
THE KING.   Something
perhaps, but nothing I have any hope to be.

[They turn to go

MARY. Sister, only those whose hearts are broken
might at a pinch blame you, but not here.
Brother, if you will not push to the last inch
your knowledge of defeat, you must keep your heart unspoken.
But these here, they have to make the choice
or to know, at the very least, that the choice exists.
You have chosen your ways; be blessed; go with God.
[*To the others*]
And you, great ones, you must always make your choice,
or always, at least, know that the choice exists—
all luck is good—or not; even when the ninth
step is nine times as difficult as the first.
[*To the audience*]
And you—this has been sung a long time
among you, as among the cities your companions—
Antioch, Alexandria, Bologna, Paris, Oxford.
Substance moves in you; my lord your Son
loves you; choose your ways. Go with God.

[They go out

THE HOUSE
BY THE STABLE

A CHRISTMAS PLAY

CHARACTERS

MAN
PRIDE
HELL
GABRIEL
JOSEPH
MARY

*The Scene is in Man's house on the one side
and in its stable on the other*

THE HOUSE BY THE STABLE

Enter MAN *and* PRIDE.

PRIDE. What, are you not tired? will you still walk?
  will you still talk of me and of us and of you?
MAN. I desire nothing better now, and nothing new.[1]
  It was a high and happy day when we met.
  Will you never forget it? and love me always?
PRIDE.   Yes:
  I will love you always.
MAN.   So I believe indeed,
  and feed on the thought—to be everlastingly loved.
  Tell me, how did this surprise come true?
PRIDE. It is no surprise—if you think what you are.
  Indeed, it were stranger if I adored you less.
  You are Man, the lord of this great house Earth,
  or (as its name is called in my country) Sin;
  you are its god and mine; since you first smiled
  and stretched your hand to me and brought me in,
  since our tenderness began, I have loved you, Man,
  and will—do not doubt; kiss me again.
MAN. You are my worshipful sweet Pride; will you be
  so arrogant always to others and humble to me?
  Will you always make me believe in myself? I am Man,
  but before you came, Pride, I was half-afraid
  that someone or something had been before me, and made
  me and my house, and could ruin or cast aside.
  But when I look in your dove's eyes, Pride,
  and see myself there, I know I am quite alone
  in my greatness, and all that I have is quite my own.
PRIDE. So this wonderful house where moon and sun

---

[1] These first three lines may be omitted when a curtain is available.

run with lights, and all kinds of creatures crawl
to be your servants, and your only business is to take
delight in your own might—it is yours and mine,
a shrine for your godhead, and for me because I am yours.
MAN. Thus endures my love for my own Pride.
To thrust you out were to doubt myself; that
is a bygone folly now—I will do so no more.
PRIDE. No; do not: be content to love me.
See, to teach you (let me pretend awhile
that I can add something to your style—I
who am also and only your creature) I have brought here
my brother, born of one nature with me, my twin,
or a moment younger: let me call him in,
and he shall tell you more of what I have planned.

Enter HELL

MAN. Are you my Pride's brother? give me your hand.
We must be friends; tell me, what is your name?
HELL. I am called Hell.
MAN.   And where, Hell, do you live?
HELL. Why, as to that, it is not easy to give
a clear definition of the place; it is not far
as your journeys go, and no bar to finding,
but the minding of the way is best found by going,
and that (of all means) best at my sister's showing.
MAN. We will go there some time.
PRIDE.   O soon, sweet Man, soon—
for, I must tell you, I have begged of my brother a boon,
first because you are my sweetheart, and next
because the laws you have made everywhere mean
you should have all the best. This is a brave
house you live in—and let me call it Sin,
because my tongue trips if I name it Earth—
but my brother in his country has a house braver still
and has promised it to us, of his own kind will.

THE HOUSE BY THE STABLE

MAN. Aye, has he? that is noble, and yet he knows
perhaps I would take it from him, would he not,
and I saw it one day and chose to have it for mine.
PRIDE. O love, how I love to hear you talk so!
but for my sake do not be harsh to my brother;
for your Pride's sake, smile at her brother Hell,
and treat him well.
MAN.   Why, that I will do.
How now, Hell, shall I have a house from you?
Tell me of it.
HELL.   It is strong and very old,
but (by a burning I have made there) never cold,
and dry—the only damp would be your tears
if Man could ever weep. The air provokes
hunger often—you are so sharp-set
you could almost eat yourself. The view is wide—
heavenly, as men say in your tongue, to the other side
of the sky at least, so far it seems away,
and whatever is there will never interfere;
that is quite certain. Because my sister desires
I will give you this house if you choose.
MAN.   And because my thews
are strong enough to take it too perhaps?
HELL. That also, no doubt.
MAN.   Well, let that be.
You are a good fellow, Hell; you shall live there
whenever you like, even if you give it to me.
The three of us could be royal in such a house.
We will have a drink on it first.
            [*He goes to fetch wine*
HELL [*to* PRIDE]. Have you seen the jewel yet?
PRIDE [*to* HELL].   No chance;
I think he has forgotten where it is himself.
HELL [*to* PRIDE]. What have you been doing all this while?

PRIDE [*to* HELL].   Hush!
  I have a trick now; play to my lead.
MAN [*pouring out the wine*]. This is good wine; I have had it in
    store
  more than I could guess; it improves with every flask.
  None could ask better. I must have tended the vines
  when I was young; there are no vines now
  or few: I have sometimes thought—were it not for my smile
  over it—the land would be more sterile than it was.
  Here; drink. You must need that.
PRIDE [*to* MAN].   Sweet,
  for Pride's sake throw him something in return,
  some trifle; I would not have my lord
  seem under an obligation even to Hell
  my brother—though indeed I meant well enough
  in persuading him.
MAN.   You are always right; no kindness
  but I am always just to pay it back.
  Now, brother, you must take something—yes,
  no words; I say you must. What will you have?
  Pride, what shall I give him?
PRIDE.   If you would be
  kind, play a game of dice—the best of three:
  it would please him; he loves a gamble.
MAN.   Dice? good.
  What shall we play for?
PRIDE.   Something quite small,
  or even nothing at all; the game is the thing.
MAN. No; something I will chance in return for a house.
  What?
                                              [*He drinks*
PRIDE. A handful of dust of your own—Earth;
  or—if you want, as becomes you, to risk more—
  say that old jewel your servant talks

often of—more often than becomes him.
Soul, he calls it, I think.
MAN.   Soul? yes;
truly he does talk thus; but if
ever such a thing was, it has been tossed
one day away in a corner of the house and lost.
Besides, I have heard him sing sometimes of a bird
that sat in the leaves of paradise and sang,
and in his song he calls that bird Soul.
I do not know; my paradise is I,
and any soul that sings in me I will try
on the dice any time.

                                                        [*He drinks*

                Look at me, Pride; you will be
always faithful, will you not?
PRIDE.   Always, by my will.
MAN. I would kill you else.
PRIDE.   I am not easy to kill
by any who have loved me. Sweet, we forget my brother.
Come, let us risk this lost jewel your soul
on the dice, let Hell have his chance of finding.

                    Enter GABRIEL

GABRIEL. Sir, by permission; there are poor people outside
seeking shelter.
PRIDE.   Insolence!
MAN.   Who?
GABRIEL.   One
from these parts, a youngish working man,
and has his heart's love with him, his wife,
a fair-faced girl, and (I think) near her time.
It is a harsh night; if I may suggest
she needs immediate rest—a room, and a bed.
PRIDE. Man, this servant of yours clacks his tongue
more freely than mine should do; must you keep

rooms where any riff-raff tramps may sleep—
and have supper too, I suppose? you, sir,
I am speaking to you.
GABRIEL. And supper, madam, you suppose.
HELL. Hey, you, speak well to your lord's guest,
my sister, or. . . .
GABRIEL [*angelically*]. Or. . . ?
MAN. Rest quiet, Hell:
I have had this fellow for servant a long time,
ever since before I came hither, wherever
I was before I came hither; he suits.
He is neat and quick and keeps out of the way,
and looks after my accounts—at least someone does,
and it isn't I; let him alone.

[*He drinks*

GABRIEL. Will you choose, sir, to speak to them yourself?
MAN. Why . . . it were wrong to turn a mother away
and pity to turn a woman, on a hard night,
in a plight of that kind; but tramps in my rooms . . . yet
one should be tender when one is comfortable, sweet,
tender to the poor, yes?
PRIDE. I confess, dear Man,
I cannot see why; one cannot do what one would—
no, not you even, my bountiful god—
and (as things go) they are only encouraged to expect
more than anyone can do. My darling, have a care.
MAN. Well, there is that . . .
GABRIEL. I think, sir,
you should see them now.
MAN. Do you? Well . . . well,
just for a moment then; let them come in.
You are always ready to beguile me. And as for you,
Hell and my sweet Pride, be merry the while.

[GABRIEL *goes out.* MAN *drinks*

THE HOUSE BY THE STABLE

HELL [*to* PRIDE]. Surely that is Gabriel, that old gossip of heaven?
PRIDE [*to* HELL]. He? I cannot tell; angels and I
  never met much, not for me to recognize.
HELL [*to* PRIDE]. Your dove's eyes are not so sharp as mine.
  I have peered more deeps than you; besides, sleep
  takes you sometimes; it never takes me,
  and after a while he who wakes for ever
  finds the tingling and aching make sight the sharper
  in the land where the heart-breaking troubles the light.
  I am sure it is Gabriel; wait; show no sign—
  only be ready to whisper Man a little
  and keep your eye on the door.
PRIDE [*to* HELL]. Why, what can he do?
HELL [*to* PRIDE]. I do not know; nothing, I hope; if Man
  chooses to play, it is his affair and mine.
  But keep close; we may win the jewel yet,
  and Man get clear with us to my nice house.

[*He sniggers*

PRIDE. Come, if you will see them, let us drink first!
MAN. Gabriel might have brought me more wine first.
  The curst fellow! he must be taught his job,
  and not to rob me of time for wandering tramps.
  Well, I have promised this time. Here, now
  let us drink to our union—
HELL.   Eternal, eternal!

GABRIEL *brings in* JOSEPH *and* MARY
GABRIEL. Here, sir, they are.
MAN.   What do you want?
JOSEPH. Sir, shelter for one night, by your permission.
  Our mule has gone lame; the dark overtook us
  and all but shook our hearts with perils of the road.
  My wife is in no condition to go on.
  To-morrow we will be gone.

MAN. Poor wretch!
  She needs a fetch of care.
PRIDE. Beware, sweet.
  It is easier to let them in than to get them out.
  You are too kind. Besides, if you have a mind
  to go on this journey with our brother Hell,
  you do not want strangers to rack your house
  when your back is turned: anyone as great as you
  must be true to his glory.
MAN. She is a poor lass.
PRIDE. That is why; if she were of our class—
  not yours; you are non-pareil—but my brother's and mine ...
  but do as you think best!
MAN. For a night's rest ...
PRIDE. To have people like these in the house—imagine!
  But you, I know, are their master—and mine.
  I am only thinking of your glory.
MAN. Well, yes;
  I see that ... Gabriel!
GABRIEL. Sir!
MAN. Think:
  is there no shed near where these could be stored
  for a night in reasonable comfort? I can't afford
  to have them inside; my Pride will not stomach it,
  and yet I am loth to push them both outside
  till their plight is a little better.
GABRIEL. The stable, sir:
  it is empty since you chose to dispose of your stud.
MAN. Good: give them a shake-down of straw there:
  [*Half-aside to* GABRIEL] and hark! if you care to hand them a hunch of bread
  I shall look the other way.

                    [*He drinks*

THE HOUSE BY THE STABLE

GABRIEL.   Sir, it is God's bread.
I will do as you say.

MAN.   O God, God!
Why must you always bring your fairy-tales in?
Did God build this great house Sin?
Did God send this pleasant leman Pride?
What has God ever done for Man?

GABRIEL. He gave that jewel your soul.

MAN.   O soul!
This is your old clack, Gabriel. In the whole
of my vast property I never found it anywhere—
with flesh, fish, or fowl. It must needs be some old
hidaway rubbish. And what is God doing,
if God is, being bounteous to me?
For anything I can see, I had neither God
nor father on earth: I was always just Man
since the world began. You tire me; go,
get them away.

GABRIEL.   Sir, just as you say.

JOSEPH. Sir, a blessing on you for this grace!
Thank him, Mary.

MARY.   Sir, God will bless you;
nor will my Son, when he comes, forget
what you gave nor with what spirit. If
he can be ever of use to you, I vow
now, in his name, he will be well content to be.

MAN. You are heartily welcome. Gabriel, have them away.
                          [GABRIEL *takes them across to the stable*
There, they are gone: now we can drink again.
Pour it out, Hell. Pride, give me your hand;
am I not a grand fellow?

PRIDE.   Sir, just as you say!
Nay, I love you, dear Man, for being so fine,

so full of your own importance. Do you not find
me more to your mind than a girl like that?

> [*While they dally*, GABRIEL *covers the Nativity, and the three sing the Magnificat, which* PRIDE *interrupts at the following points*

MARY. My soul doth magnify the Lord, and my spirit hath rejoiced in God my Saviour, for he hath regarded the low estate of his handmaiden: for, behold, from henceforth all generations shall call me blessed.

PRIDE. Henceforth, we shall be the only blessed ones on earth; and no generations of anything except our joy.

MARY. For he that is mighty hath done to me great things; and holy is his name. And his mercy is on them that fear him from generation to generation. He hath showed strength with his arm; . . .

PRIDE. Be my arm of strength, Man.

MARY. . . . he hath scattered the proud in the imagination of their hearts.

PRIDE. Imagine me in your heart.

MARY. He hath put down the mighty from their seats, and exalted them of low degree.

PRIDE. Be mighty on me; exalt me to your great degree.

MARY. He hath filled the hungry with good things; and the rich he hath sent empty away.

PRIDE. O rich, rich!—bear off, my dear;
no, my brother is here. Tower—will you?—
over me in your power? O but fling him too
your glory's world's wealth! let all my house
go down before your head's crown of splendour.
Tender us all our desires out of your greatness:
to him his gambling moment, his catch of chance;
then snatch me to yourself for ever.
Then, at the gate of your house, when we go

THE HOUSE BY THE STABLE

I will kiss you so ... do you know? wait, my sweet!
Hell, have you the dice?

MAN. I have dice here.
I used them often enough when I played with my friends,
but since I met you I have forgotten my friends.
Love of you tends to that.

HELL. Do we play for a stake?
I do not mind; the game is enough.

PRIDE. Yes:
but a stake, all the same, makes the game more amusing.
And, brother, you forget—you play for that jewel
called soul.

MAN. Why, it does not exist, or if,
you will never find it.

PRIDE. It will do; it is in my mind
that to play for the chance to find it is well enough.
What do you say, Hell?

HELL. Aye; if I have his will
to lay hold of it, if I can, by my own skill—
nothing unfair, no force; but if it is found,
I take it in free exchange for the house and ground.

MAN. You shall, brother, for your sister's sake and yours.

HELL. However precious?

MAN. Though it were worth my all.

[*He drinks*

I am no miser; I was always open-handed—
was I not, Pride my lass? give me a kiss
and I shall win the game and my soul as well.
Two out of three; throw.

[*They play*

HELL. Five.
MAN. Six. Ha,
that is my gain. Kiss me again, Pride.

PRIDE [*to* HELL]. Quick now, while he is blind with me.

[*While they kiss* HELL *changes the dice*

MAN. Well tossed, Hell; you have a knack, but my luck
is in now, and I back my luck to win.

[*He drinks*

GABRIEL. Man, where are you?
MAN. Who was that called?
PRIDE. No one.
HELL. The wind.
MAN. It was a voice of some kind.

[*He looks out*

The rain is over; the stars are out; one
over the stable is more sun than star.
PRIDE. How slow you are! Man, your Pride is waiting.
MAN [*he is now rather drunk*]. Waiting, is she? let her wait then.
Why, you hussy, you are a part of me.
I am not to be called in as if I were Gabriel
to be scolded at pleasure.
PRIDE. No; it was but that leisure
of ours, in Hell's house, I was wanting ... but so,
just as you say.
MAN. Ha, yes: again.
To it again.

[*He throws*

Five.

[HELL *throws*

HELL. Six.
MAN. What tricks ...? let me see. Six: it is—you have won.

[*He roars with laughter*

Ho, this is a fine thing we have done—
drawn the game.
HELL. No; one throw more.
MAN. More? how many times have we thrown?

THE HOUSE BY THE STABLE

HELL. Twice.
Hurry!
MAN. What, hurry? what do you mean?
you are as saucy as this quean herself.
HELL. Throw; I am impatient for you to go.
MAN. Do you hear that, Pride? he wants us to go.
He wants to hunt for my soul.
[*He roars again with laughter*
PRIDE. No.
I do not think he will long hunt for that.
MAN. Well, kiss me—a kiss hearty and strong,
better than before; give me the winning throw.
[*She leans over and kisses him lazily*
JOSEPH. Man, Man, where are you?
MAN. Aye! . . . here.
Who wants Man?
PRIDE *and* HELL. No one; no one; throw.
MAN. Someone wanted; someone called; who?
PRIDE [*seizing his hand*]. Throw—with me, thus; and I with you.
MAN. Let me go. I am Man; I will not be forced.
I will have you horsed on your brother's back, my girl,
and take such a cudgel to you as will crack
some of those pretty bones.
PRIDE [*to* HELL]. Throw first,
and he afterwards; or at the very worst
we will persuade him he threw and lost the game.
HELL [*throwing*]. Six.
MARY. Man, where are you?
MAN. That was the girl;
that was the pretty wife—hey, now
I am coming, Man is coming.
PRIDE *and* HELL [*seizing him*]. No; throw.
MAN. What is this? what is happening? How
do I hear a voice I have not chosen to hear

outside my house? Who made my house?
There was no one, was there?
PRIDE. No.
HELL. No.
MAN. Then how
do I hear the voice of something outside me?
Or is one of you playing a trick on me? Pride,
if I thought ... I am caught ... my mind is twined in a voice ...
it isn't yours ... whose is it? Ho, you,
Gabriel!
HELL. No; leave Gabriel alone.
PRIDE. Sweet, sweet Man, leave Gabriel alone.
MAN. No; Gabriel is my fellow; he will help.
He was here before I came hither; he suits.
He will tell me the voices. Gabriel, Gabriel, I say!
GABRIEL [*coming across in his magnificence*]. Here!
Sir, God made me and bade me wait
on this moment in your life: what do you need?
MAN. You are a good fellow: come here: listen.
My brother Hell and my leman Pride mean
to have me finish ... that was not it neither;
there was something else ... the girl, Gabriel, the girl.
I heard her call out: where is she?
Is she in danger?
GABRIEL. No; she is quite safe.
This is the game, sir, is it?
[*He picks up one of the dice and looks at it*
PRIDE [*to* HELL]. Fool, you have tried too many ways to get him.
HELL [*to* PRIDE]. Damn him, who would have thought grace was so near
as to hear that small squeak of a drunken voice?
MAN [*sleepily*]. The game, yes—but I don't know where we were.
Throw for me ... the girl is safe, is she?
and her baby ... hadn't she got a baby?

THE HOUSE BY THE STABLE

GABRIEL. She has.
  Now.
MAN. Yes . . . to be sure. . . . Pride . . . Pride,
  where are you?

[He dozes off

PRIDE. Here, darling, here.
GABRIEL [*catching her by the hair and pulling her back*]. Peace:
  let the poor fellow sleep a little; you
  would never be caught by anything as natural as drink.
HELL. Let her go. What are you doing there with my dice?
GABRIEL [*tossing the dice in the air and catching it*]. Dice—ha! So:
    that is better.
  It seems now to have only one six:
  and now we can play the last throw again.
HELL [*whining*]. I won't! I tell you I won't! I won't play.
PRIDE [*snarling*]. Don't you, Hell: the nasty-minded scut,
  pretending we cheated.

    [GABRIEL *takes each of them by an ear, and knocks their
    heads lightly together*

PRIDE. Oo! don't—you hurt!
    [*She drops to the floor, moaning and rubbing her head*
GABRIEL. You wanted the game; you shall win or lose on the game
  by the luck of the game, but all luck is good.
  Toil and spoil as you will, still in the end
  the flick of every chance must fall right.
  Throw.
HELL. I don't . . .
GABRIEL [*terribly*]. Throw.

[HELL *throws*

     Five.

[GABRIEL *throws*

     Speak—

  what is it?
HELL [*cowering*]. Six.

P   211

THE HOUSE BY THE STABLE

GABRIEL.　　　　　　You have had a long run,
you and all your tricks, but to-morrow's sun
rises on a world where untruth is always untrue.
That is simple enough but too difficult for you.
Get to your house and the burning you made—and not even
that is your own; the fire is borrowed from heaven.

　　　　　　　　　　　　　　　　　　　[HELL *goes*

And as for you, sister, you poor cheap
cowardly shrew; you . . .

　　　　　　　[*With an awful angelic effort he restrains himself*
I will teach you one lesson; kneel up; say after me:

　　　　　　　　　　　　　　[*She obeys. He puts on his glory*
Glory to God in the highest, and on earth peace:
goodwill to men.

　　　　　　　　　　　　　[PRIDE *repeats the words, snivelling*
And now go.

　　　　　　　　　　　　　　　　　　[*She begins to get up*
　　　　　　No; on your knees: go.

　　　　　　　　　　　　　　　　　　　　[*She shuffles away*
MAN [*waking*]. I dreamt my Pride had gone.

　　　　　　　　　　　　　　　　　　　　　[*He stares round*
Where is she? what has been happening? call her, you,
Gabriel.
GABRIEL. Sir, soon, if you tell me to.
They will wait, I know, by the gate you call Death,
which is the usual way to Hell's house.
You may catch them there or yourself call them back.
But there is a thing to do before you go.
MAN. What? do you bully me? I want my Pride;
I want to be a god; she made a vow
never to leave me.
GABRIEL.　　　　　　Nor did she—to be just.
It was I—for this single night—made her go.
MAN. You are above yourself.

THE HOUSE BY THE STABLE

GABRIEL.   Above or beside—
  distinct enough at least to deal with Pride.
  There is a thing that you must see to-night
  of your own sight, without Pride's arms round you
  or Hell's hand in yours. This one hour
  out of all time is given you to see it yourself.
  To-morrow things may change. The woman you saved
  half by your will from a little chill in the night,
  and from blistered feet, has a word to say. Come.
MAN. It seems I made her a poor offer, yet
  she was better in the straw than in the street:
  do you not think so? You look grander than you used.
GABRIEL. Sir, it is only that you give me more attention.
  When Pride is about, no one can see straight.
  You shall see more than I. Come when I call.

                              [*He goes to the stable*

JOSEPH. Blessed one, what is your will now?
MARY. Dearest lord, to show Man my child;
  lest in some testy humour the rumour should fade.
  If he sees, his heart may radically move to love,
  whatever he forgets, wherever he sets his eyes.
JOSEPH. He who with all this Earth offered us the straw?
MARY. Did we deserve, dearest, under the law,
  this birth that I kiss? Nothing at all is given
  till all is given, I know; that is heaven.
  But then also it is heaven to know that all
  is given at once in the smallest free gift—
  even sometimes when only half-given. O my Son
  reckons as no arithmetician has done;
  he checks his amounts by the least and the greatest at once.
  O my Own, there are no, no accounts like yours!
JOSEPH. Blessed is he in his sole free choice!
GABRIEL. Lady, Man is a little drunk, and a little
  sleepy, with a little hankering after hell,

but yet also he has a faint hurt
at having offered as he did; if it pleased you now
to expose the Holy Thing—
MARY. O let him come!
let him come quickly!
GABRIEL. Man! Man!

[MAN *stumbles across*

MAN. It is almost too bright here to see. Where
is the lady? I did give her a hunch of bread
and a place to lie; she might else have been dead.
JOSEPH. Do not talk nonsense.
GABRIEL. Do not talk at all.
MAN. No, but I am trying to understand: why
should I who had one house, and another beyond
promised, have been so fond as to offer straw
in a stable? and yet ...
GABRIEL. Do not trouble your brain;
gain is as difficult to understand as grace.
JOSEPH. Do not talk, I say, lest the Divine One sleep.
MARY. Nay, let him talk as he will; he is mine; come,
Man my friend; it is true that but for you
I might have come to an end—here, at least.

[*She gives him her hand*

Look, my Son thanks you.
MAN. Was he born here?
MARY. This very night, in your stable; therefore, dear Man,
you, if you choose, shall be his god-father.
MAN. What will you call him, lady?
MARY Jesus, because
he shall presently save his people from their sins—
and Hell shall play no trick on them more.
MAN. I did not quite refuse you, did I? or did I?
I cannot tell; Hell has made me stupid.
Did I deny you all or did I not?

THE HOUSE BY THE STABLE

Look now, he must have something to please him.
The house is full of things, and none right.
Stop; I remember something out of sight,
out of thought, but always I have had round my neck.
> [*He fumbles at his breast and pulls out a jewel*

There; it was once bright; it might serve.
I do not know what it is at all.
But if you should want a bed for the rest of the night,
there is my room the best.
GABRIEL. But this is your soul
I have searched for all this time!
MARY [*laughing up at him*]. Great Hierarch, even
the angels desire to understand these things,
and a mortal hand does more than the Domination.
Leave Man and my Son and me our mystery;
let us think our own way and not yours.
Look, I will breathe on it—so, and see
how it dances, and how my Beloved's glances follow.
Take it again, Man, a little while;
we will go up to your room.
> [GABRIEL *and* JOSEPH *help her to rise*

Now be the gloom
of earth split, and be this house blest
and no more professed by poor Pride to be Sin,
for the joys of love hereafter shall over-ride
boasting and bragging and the heavy lagging of Hell
after delight that outstrips him—step and sight.
> [*She makes the sign of the Cross towards the house*

Take us, O exchange of hearts! this we know—
substance is love, love substance. Let us go.

> *They go out*

GRAB AND GRACE
OR
IT'S THE SECOND STEP

(Companion and sequel to
THE HOUSE BY THE STABLE)

CHARACTERS

PRIDE
HELL
GABRIEL
FAITH
MAN
GRACE

GRAB AND GRACE

The scene as before. Enter HELL *and* PRIDE, *bedraggled and tired;*
HELL *carrying a large bundle*

PRIDE. No rest? no comfortable house?
　These lands are as empty of homes as our bag of food—
　yet I should know this place!
HELL. 　　　　　　　　　　Why surely this—
　yes, look, in this crook of the hills,
　look, here is Man's house once more!
　After this hundred years we have been wandering
　through the malignant lands, to think we have come
　again to your old home. What think you, Pride?
　Might it not be possible to find a rest here?
PRIDE. Why, it would be worth while to try; I
　and you too were so beshouted and bevenomed
　by that slug-slimy Gabriel that we lost our heads
　and ran too soon. Man cannot have forgotten;
　few do; their faithfulness to me is astonishing.
　Shall we knock, do you think?
HELL. 　　　　　　　　　　Prink yourself first.
PRIDE. This accurst mud!
HELL. 　　　　　　　That dress will not provoke him
　under your yoke again.
PRIDE. 　　　　　Look and see
　if we have anything better in our odds and ends.
　　　　[HELL *opens the bundle, and they poke about: fragments*
　　　　　fall out
PRIDE. I cannot think why we carry all this.
　What is this red stuff?
HELL. 　　　　　　　A little of Abel's blood.
　A drop of that in a drink gives a man heartburn.

PRIDE. And this?
HELL. Take care; a bit of Adam's tooth
that he broke on the first fruit out of Paradise.
He has had neuralgia in his jaws ever since.
PRIDE. And this—thistledown?
HELL. The kiss of Judas.
PRIDE. Judas?
HELL. You were sick of malignant plague when it happened—
but the child whom Man sheltered when we had gone
grew, and grew spoiled, and Judas, one of his friends,
encouraged Man to kill him in a sudden brawl.
There is no time now to tell you all.
PRIDE. All
meaning that when Man had got rid of me
things did not go so well as Gabriel thought?
You fool, Hell, why did you not tell me
all this sooner?
HELL. I had forgotten; my fits
make me dull. We are not what we were;
neither you nor I have ever been the same
since the great earthquake and the talking flame.
PRIDE. Hell,
did we not hear that Man had a changed heart?
I am sure that some antipodean rumour
reached us of his altered humour; that he likes now
prayer and servile monochromatic designs.
Draggled decency might better suit us?
HELL. I will say, looking at our bag, it would be easier.
May not you be converted as well as he?
Try that style: [*He grabbles about*] look, what of this?
[*He holds up a dirty rough cloak*
How of this for a man's earthenware embrace
and a chaste kiss? [*She puts it on*] Your very face looks holy.
PRIDE. What is it?

HELL. Devil knows; the original figleaves, I should think.
You will need a belt. [*He holds one up*] Jezebel's?
PRIDE. My dear, too bright.
What's that?
HELL. The cord with which Judas hanged himself,
afterwards used to tie Peter to his cross.
PRIDE. That is the very thing; give it here.

[*She looks at herself*

I don't know who Peter was, but if
he was crucified, it is something anyone might be proud of.
Pride in a nutshell! [*She wriggles*] with the shell of the nut inside.
Hist, someone is coming!
HELL [*throwing the things in the bag*]. Is it Man?
PRIDE. No; it's a woman; what the devil—
HELL. Chut!
There's Gabriel! Out of sight till we find out more!

They hide. Enter FAITH, *meeting* GABRIEL. *She is dressed
as brightly and sophisticatedly as is possible*

FAITH. Good-morning, Gabriel: where is my lord?
GABRIEL. Madam,
he was in the stables just now, but I think he has gone
back with Grace to the house.
FAITH. The stables?
GABRIEL. Yes.
He has not been there much since the Holy One died,
but this morning something stirred.
FAITH. A word in a song!
O to-day is such a morning as I love,
cloudy and cool; one feels rather than sees
the sun heavenly: he is distilled in the air,
and my heart filled with his future; in the dawn
I made a new song, and would fain sing it,
if Man my lord were free to hear.

GABRIEL.   Madam,
could he do better than listen to Faith's songs?
FAITH. Well, to be frank, that depends; but thank you
for the kind thought. I will go and find him out.
O loveliness, to feel day in the dawn!

                                                                                   [*Exit*

PRIDE [*aside to* HELL]. And will you tell me who Faith is, and what
Faith, in that dress, is doing in Man's house,
and I in this—shroud?
HELL [*aside*].   Not so loud; hush!
GABRIEL [*looking round*]. You need not trouble yourselves to hush; your smell
would give you away; surely it is Hell and Pride?
The old obscene graveyard stink; I think
honest anger and brutal lust smell pure
beside you.
PRIDE.   Stew-faced bully!
HELL.   Sister, be at ease.
Once he had power even over us for an hour,
but not twice thus, not twice.
Abuse you he may; he cannot turn you away.
He must let Man choose now for himself.
PRIDE. Are you sure you are right?
HELL.   Of course——
GABRIEL.   Of course he is right.
I could be, were angels ever other than glad,
a little sad to see you with more tricks.
But now Man has friends if he will,
and if you can cheat him, why, you must.
I can do no more than tell him who you are.
PRIDE. I will tell him that myself.
GABRIEL.   So do.
You seem perhaps more true than most

sins to their nature—and so catch more.
Double temptation when a sin pretends to be truthful.
HELL. No, sir. We need not trouble you to announce us.
GABRIEL. No need; here is Man.

      MAN *enters with* GRACE

HELL.   Now!
PRIDE.   Get away!
 Much better for me to be alone. Man!
MAN [*to* GRACE]. We will build then; I have decided that.
 The cottages are clammy; we need several more
 and more to the mind of those likely to live there.
 First, we must find an architect.
GRACE.   O sir,
 I know a fine one, in design and execution
 better than any; all the worlds praise
 his work these many days.
MAN.   Who then is he?
GRACE. He is called the Spirit; those who know his degree
 add a worshipful title and say the Holy Spirit:
 that as you choose.
MAN.   The Holy Spirit? good.
 We will ask him to come while I am in the mood,
 which passes so quickly and then all is so dull.
GRACE. Sir, purposes last.
MAN.   Yes, but heavily.
 Madam?
PRIDE. Man!
MAN. Do I—ought I—to know...? I have met few
 of your veiled kind; yet——
PRIDE.   Man!
MAN. By my soul, it is Pride.
PRIDE.   Yes. [*A pause*] Do you grieve?
 Would you have me leave, without a word changed?
 I will, if you say go.

MAN. No; stay.
Where have you been? I have not seen you since——
PRIDE. Since your servant told—yes; they *were* lies.
Though indeed I was foolish then, now more wise.
But to mistake folly for foul thought,
to drive me out while you slept! Have you sometimes kept
a thought of me?—no; that is folly again.
I am professed now to other vows,
as my dress shows. I have even changed my name
and am called Self-Respect.
MAN. What, you are one
of Immanuel's people?
PRIDE [*drooping*]. He has a use for all.
[*She turns aside and gets near to* HELL; *then aside*
What was her name? quick, the great sinner,
the woman.
HELL. Mary Magdalene.
PRIDE [*returning*]. Even Mary Magdalene—
and so for me, who did not (I may well say)
sin as much as she—and was she more beautiful?
Once, dear Man, you thought me well enough.
MAN. It is astonishing to see you; you have not changed.
The same lovely eyes under that hood.
It is good to see you once more, my own Pride;
no, I must call you my own Self-Respect.
It is what I will try to remember.
[GRACE *whistles.* PRIDE *and* MAN *turn away.* GRACE *and*
GABRIEL *speak to* HELL
GRACE. And here is poor old Hell!
HELL. Little tin trumpet,
how do you know me?
GABRIEL. O we of heaven
know you all. This boy, whom we call Grace—
he is part of Faith's household, and she of Man's—

is older than you. Indeed, he does not look it,
but your travels in the malignant lands have aged you
more than our millenia.
GRACE.   A thousand years
being as a day. Poor Hell, time to you
is a sorry plod-plod; even Man knows better,
but Hell of all pedestrians is the most tired.
And why are you here, little brother?
HELL.   What is that to you?
May we not talk to Man without your leave?
GABRIEL. Unfortunately, yes.
GRACE.   And is she doing it now!
PRIDE. And tell me, dear Man, how you are faring in Religion.
MAN. Well, I am trying to lead the Christian life.
It is not easy, is it, Gabriel?
GABRIEL.   Sir,
I do not think you have found it too difficult.
PRIDE. To lead the Christian life is always difficult.
How we have to work! digging, building,
giving alms, prayer. Do you pray much?
MAN. A good deal. Gabriel, what do you mean?
GABRIEL. Sir, only that you have been constantly helped.
This boy Grace does most of the work.
MAN. I know Grace has been useful, but to say
he does most—I was up as early as he
and as bustling round my property.
PRIDE.   That I am sure.
I know how dextrous and diligent you always are.
MAN. I will give praise where praise is due, but something
is due to me.
PRIDE.   Much, indeed.
GABRIEL.   Sir——
GRACE. Chut, Gabriel; you will never defeat her so.
Do not argue; make her come out with herself

quickly; believe me, it is your only way.
Call Faith; she is better than you at the game,
and can frame a neater trap, woman to woman.

[GABRIEL *goes out*

PRIDE. It is no credit to any cause not to know
if one has kept its laws well. Flaws
will come, but when one has minded laws—why,
then a certain proper pride may grow.
I have taken Self-Respect for my new name
to adjust properly praise and blame, to keep
myself in mind as a true centre for myself.
MAN. True.
One has more belief, so, in what one can do.
PRIDE. That is it: no weakness, no false meekness.
This humility is too much praised.
One may look at oneself, I hope, without sin.
You, my Man, can keep your thought so poised
that any noised silliness does not hurt.
You are pious—good! but it is *you* who are pious.
MAN. I had not thought of that. Faith sings
only about Immanuel and what he does.
That brings a sense of vacancy sometimes.
PRIDE. Yes: one needs at first a kind of defence
against even heaven. Perfection comes slowly;
and we must not be too holy all at once.

Enter FAITH *and* GABRIEL

FAITH. Good-morning, my lord.
MAN. Good-morning, Faith.
PRIDE [*to* MAN]. This
is another friend of yours?
MAN. Her name is Faith.
She was a friend of Immanuel, the child born
the night you went.... O well, Pride—
I beg your pardon; it is old habit in me—

we need not go into all that now.
There was a misunderstanding of what he meant
and a tussle—you, my dear, will understand
there was something to be said on my side;
but anyhow—it was all rather unfortunate—he died.
But he left with me these two friends,
she and the boy Grace. Let me introduce——
PRIDE. She will despise me, Man. I am poor
and of no account, but I have enough respect
for myself not to push in among the elect,
among—look at her clothes!—my ostensible betters.
MAN. Clothes—nonsense. You look very nice—
quiet and . . . becoming.
PRIDE.   Man!
MAN.   Well, I
have you in my mind as you were when . . . but come;
it suits you. You are my own Self-Respect,
and this is my own Faith; you must know each other.

                                          [GRACE *whistles*

Faith, this is an old friend of mine,
called—do I say Sister?
PRIDE.   Yes—I suppose,
Sister.
            [*She clings to his hand and looks deep into his eyes*
MAN. . . . called . . . Sister Self-Respect.
And this, dear friend, is Faith.
PRIDE.   Pleased to meet you.
FAITH [*coldly*]. Good-morning.
PRIDE.   Is it not a good morning?
[*To* MAN] This house was always good in the spring days.
FAITH. You have known Man a long while?
PRIDE.   Very long.
[*To* MAN] Of course, times change; I know now
you have other friends.

FAITH. Yes.
MAN. No.
You must not say so; at least, if I have,
I do not forget my old.
FAITH. It seems not;
especially when they return in a neat religious
habit, and are prettily disposed to public prayer.
PRIDE. What do you mean—public?
FAITH. I do not mean
praying with others present, but rather that sedate
praying to oneself, with oneself too as listener;
a ubiquitous trinity of devotion the temple-Pharisee
practised long and successfully.
PRIDE. At least I
earned my lodging here by a decent return—
by something other than songs; night was my time.
FAITH. Yes; *my* joys encourage sight,
accuracy, and reason.
PRIDE. My kisses were accurate:
Man enjoyed them and himself and me.
I did not confine myself to singing him songs.
MAN. O now, Self-Respect, they are beautiful songs.
Everyone to his own gift ... indeed,
you always had beautiful shoulders.
PRIDE. Have I not?
as beautiful bare as hers bundled on Sundays?

       [GRACE *whistles.* HELL *creeps towards him*

I am sorry, Man. I did not mean to snap.
I had better go.
MAN. O no, you must not go.
We shall all be great friends—I, Man,
and his Self-Respect and his Faith: why not?
FAITH. His Self-Respect and his Faith! No. Man,
you must make up your mind. There is a strong feud

renewed for centuries, from our very making, between
this lady and myself.
PRIDE. There is indeed—
between my pleasure and your procrastination,
you promising what you do not pay,
and I paying what I need not bother to promise.

[GRACE *whistles*

HELL [*to* GRACE]. Stop that noise!
GRACE. Noise yourself;
Adam called the birds on that note
while you were squeaking and squealing among the crocodiles.
O crocodiles' guiles and smiles and wiles,
when Hell styles himself a judge of music.

[HELL *threatens him.* GRACE *trips him.*

Heels up, gossamer!
MAN. Less noise over there!
Grace, keep yourself quiet in your own place.
Now, let us agree here to be friends.
Love puts all ends at one, and spends
much to do it: come, wine for a pledge.
Gabriel!
GABRIEL. Sir, the ladies will never agree.
If you wish to turn Faith out of doors . . .
MAN. What! my friend's friend! Immanuel's friend . . .
why do you remind me? No; I promised; I am firm.
GABRIEL. Then send Pride away.
MAN. O now, Gabriel,
I owe her, after all, a great deal,
and she understands me, she soothes me.
PRIDE. I am not Pride.
Indeed, Gabriel, I have forgotten all that.
I am the old woman on the new way:
look at me, a demure modest Self-Respect;
nothing spectacular or dishonourable about *me*.

Of course, I am not *blind*; I cannot help
noticing where sinners thrive, or where they sin,
or how parasites and amateur prostitutes are dressed.
FAITH. The professional always hates being outclassed—
I agree there: for the word—let it stand.
Our feud, on my side, is too deep
to use abuse. I say I will not sit down
nor eat nor drink nor sleep in the same house
with—Self-Respect. I do not and will not know her.
PRIDE. And I—*I!*—used to be called Pride!
Is this your charity, you over-painted, over-powdered,
verminous haunch of a hag-bone! you snorting porcupine,
pet of a fellow whose hands never kept his head!
Why, you dilly-down doveling, you mincing mosquito——
  [GRACE *whistles.* HELL *runs at him; they dodge out, shouting,*
  while PRIDE *is screaming and* FAITH *speaking*
FAITH. I will not abuse you. I simply will not know you.
MAN [*shouting*]. Silence! Gabriel, keep the house quiet!
See what Grace is doing and tell him not to.
And now, you two, am I to say nothing?
Am I not to have my own way?
You shall behave in this house, both of you,
as if I were someone.
PRIDE.   O Man,
that is right! keep us in order; send us to prayer.
Rebuke us! Have I hurt you? O beat me
if I disturb you! I am only yours—
and of course God's; but I *am* wholly yours
in a new love, if you choose!
MAN.   This fiddle-faddle!
Argument in, argument out. Man
will have his way sometimes; if I choose
you shall both stop with me, stop you shall.
I will tie you up, Pride!

PRIDE. Anything, anything!

[GABRIEL *has been looking out*

GABRIEL. Sir, look!
MAN. What is the matter now?
What are they doing there? who is the fellow?
Why, it is Hell! Was he here too?
GABRIEL. He is throttling Grace!
MAN. He is throwing him into the lake—
he will drown; it has no bottom. Hi!
Hell there, Hell, leave him alone!
Grace, we are coming!

[*He runs out*

GABRIEL. Sir, Grace can swim;
indeed, there is very little Grace cannot do—
for example—get out of a bottomless pit.
Well, it is proper that Man should run fast
when heaven seems in danger; heaven has done
as much for him.

[*He goes leisurely out*

FAITH. O sister, sister, now we may talk sense.
You must find it exhausting always to be
on guard, watching every word. Myself,
help though I have and celestial succour,
I am glad sometimes when my sister Hope
takes my place for a night; and I can speak
right and direct; the muscles in my face
are controlled naturally and not by sheer work
to please Man's variable moods. Poor Man,
he is a sweet darling, but O I wish
he had an adult intelligence.
PRIDE. You can drop this feud
when Man is not here!
FAITH. He is a born mimic,
and therefore I must refuse to have you here,

or you would catch him with one or the other ruse.
Alone, we may leave it to God.

PRIDE. Why are you so bent
to have him? he will never do *you* good.

FAITH. To obey Immanuel is in my blood; and he
chooses so. But how will Man serve *you*?

PRIDE. O yes; when we have him—as we shall;
you will call one day to an empty house;
anything else is not possible; well, then,
while your songs echo and re-echo, none
to mark them, except perhaps the sun in heaven,
think that Man is another vagrant I
and Hell shall sometimes meet where the sky
has no sun, in the clammy malignant lands
that Hell once made.

FAITH. And now finds
everywhere terribly following him; even here.
O I know well wherever you go,
he and you, you sooner or later feel
the air of the cold iceberg or hot oasis
breaking into the same clamminess, the same
disgusting invisible froth against the skin—
ugh! every wind, every rain-drop,
every grateful beam crawling and sticky.

[HELL *creeps in behind her, making signs to* PRIDE

PRIDE [*getting nearer*]. Yes; we shall have a companion then, to bear
the bag over there of the odds and ends
we stole out of his house; in a dim mist
he shall stumble after us, afraid to lose even us,
or sometimes be pricked by me or kicked by Hell
forward before us, among the shallow pools
or the miry grass under the malignant trees
where the baboons sit and scratch and yowl.
There with us tramping and trapesing for ever.

GRAB AND GRACE

FAITH. Poor wretch! but you haven't . . .
                    [HELL *seizes her.* PRIDE *covers her mouth*
HELL. I have thrown Grace into the lake; quick.
  Shove this cloth in her mouth; tie it.
  If we can hide her we may lure Man
  out of his house into the malignant lands.
  Keep him till the sun sets and leave me alone
  to draw him down among the pits and pools.
PRIDE. Twist her arms behind her: use your fist.
            [HELL *strikes at* FAITH; *she dodges; he hits* PRIDE
  Damn! O anyhow: be quick.
HELL. Give me that cord; they will be a few minutes.
  Hang on to her wrists while I tie her legs.
PRIDE [*panting*]. She is so supple.
HELL.   All right. Now—
  in front then—pull! there. Where shall we put her?
  behind that tree?
PRIDE.   No; Hell, the bag!
  the bag! throw our things behind the tree,
  anyhow, in a heap, and then have her in.
HELL. Excellent! empty it. Now—over her head!
                            [FAITH *digs him in the stomach*
  Ouch! Her hands are about as delicate as iron.
  There . . . steady . . . *there*. That settles Faith.
PRIDE. She can have her feud all to herself there,
  and fill her belly with her own gaudiness.
HELL.   Here—
  help tie it under her feet; so.
  I hear them; quick; carry it over here.
      [*They carry the bag to the back.* MAN, GABRIEL, *and* GRACE
         come in
MAN. Hell, this is outrageous. He might have been drowned.
  O yes, I know he is a tiresome boy.

I am sure he provoked me often, his jokes
and his insolence, but to treat him so—
HELL. I would have seen to it he came to no hurt,
had you not been by: since you were—
But I was rash. I agree I did wrong.
I apologize—gentleman to gentleman. As for him—
here, lad, and another time watch your tongue.
Catch!

[*He throws him something*

GABRIEL.   One of the thirty pieces, was it?
Grace will win them all back, one day,
and not by playing dice.
MAN.   Well, now . . .
where is Faith?
PRIDE.   Gone into the house.
She would not even take the air with me;
she preferred her own room to my company.
[*aside to* HELL] For the devil's sake give me a better belt;
I can't keep my things together.
HELL [*aside*].   Jezebel's?
It is all we have.
PRIDE [*aside*].   Any damn thing.
Your friends, dearest Man, are a little difficult.
Faith is rude to me and Grace to my brother—
not that I mind—and I (poor soul!) thought
just for once I would replace the cord
of my habit with a little brightness, my old lightness
of heart took me so to be with you.

[*She puts on the belt*

Does it look silly?
MAN.   No, but more like you.
PRIDE. Of course, I do forgive your friend. You know
that is where Religion helps. One can forgive.
Is it not pleasant, dearest, to forgive others?

It is far sweeter than anger, more satisfying.
Lying in bed at night, I love to think
how many sinners poor little Self-Respect
has forgiven—even in a week or so. To be oneself
is always to find how much better than others
one surprisingly is. I take no credit,
of course, for that, though indeed, Man,
you loved me: did I seem—never mind.
You loved me.

MAN. Yes.
PRIDE. It was something of a joy.
Did you not feel yourself to be noble then?
MAN. Yes.
PRIDE. O come for a little; come!
No, not in the house—out here,
away from all your people. Yes indeed,
I know we now are otherwise turned
and so will be; but an hour—come!
You shall be true to Faith and I to my vows;
only a little walk, a little murmur,
a reverie, a day-dream, a distant noon-glimpse
of our past joy, a thing forgotten but
for just this one companioned glance,
this twy-memoried gleam far below.
Come.
MAN. I have never been able to forget you.
PRIDE. Come.
MAN. O how the blood runs quicker! O—
Pride, Faith's songs are very sweet
but strange, alien with that accent, sweet
terribly, but to be with you is to lose terror,
to lose the beauty that strips me of comfort. Pride,
that is a dull dark dress you are wearing;
your belt shows it up; it is not like you.

PRIDE. We will see if we can find something brighter,
more to my lord's liking; we might. Come.
> [GRACE *has been poking up among* HELL'S *properties. He plays a tune*

Would you not like to see me? no, say,
there is no dress for Pride as beautiful as she,
as you used to. Only for a moment; only for joy
of the memory; then back to Immanuel and Faith.
Kiss me and say so. Kiss me.

MAN. Hark a minute. Who is that playing?
It is that strange distant song
which pricks a point of fire in each joint.
Grace, what have you there?

GRACE.   This, my lord?
I found it hidden in a heap behind a tree.
It is one of the dulcimers Nebuchadnezzar's orchestra
played at the grand show of the Three-in-the-Fire,
who became, unexpectedly, Four.

MAN.   How Four?
Is that the song's name?

GRACE.   O my lord,
the tale is old: it was one of Immanuel's doings.
Faith afterwards made a good song
on the dance of the Four-in-the-Fire. Hear me play,
and see if your heart does not move to the steps of the Fourth.
Sit, my lord; here is something to sit on.
> [*He begins to roll the bag out*

PRIDE *and* HELL. Leave that alone!

PRIDE. Man, make your servants leave untouched
Our few poor belongings. It is my bag
and my brother's dulcimer.

GRACE.   Nebuchadnezzar's dulcimer;
stolen like Abel's blood and Adam's tooth

GRAB AND GRACE

and all the rest, from this very house.
I only recover it.
GABRIEL. Indeed, sir, you have
a right to your own antiques—to give to Hell
if you wish, but even Hell must not steal.
Your museum was unique, but that bag holds much.
Roll it nearer, Grace.
HELL. Leave it alone.
That dulcimer never came from the bag.
PRIDE. Yes; it is mine.
HELL. Yes; but not from the bag.
That is full.
GABRIEL. Ah but what fills it?
Tell me that, Hell. And look at it!
It is moving.
GRACE [*striking an attitude and sepulchrally*]. And where is Faith?
HELL. How do I know?
PRIDE. Back in the house.
MAN. Something is inside the bag.
PRIDE. Dear Man, only my own pet scorpions.
I cannot bear to leave them behind; one day
I will show them to you, but not just now.
MAN. Scorpions! no scorpion ever moved like that.
What have you got there?
GRACE. Aha!
HELL. Man,
We did not come here to be insulted.

[GRACE *whistles*

GABRIEL. The bag, sir, is trying to attract your attention.
I submit that the whole affair is so suspicious
you have a right to open it.
HELL. No!
PRIDE. No!

[*The blade of a knife appears*

GRACE. Ladies and gentlemen, observe the scorpion's sting.
Little sister, your scorpions may stab you yet.
MAN. It is opening all of itself. Nothing like this
has ever happened in my house before.
GRACE. My lord,
nothing like my lady Faith and I
ever happened in anyone's house before.
Adored be the Omnipotence for ever and ever!
> [FAITH's *head appears through the cut.* GABRIEL *and* GRACE
> *run to help her out*

GRACE. Faith in a bag is Faith at her best!
GABRIEL. No;
even Faith must flag when she is stifled,
and Faith with vision is wiser than Faith without.
FAITH. Faith—and Faith may say so—is pretty well smothered.
O this old smell of Man's horrors
clings to the cloth, the beastly evidence
of things unhoped and undesired,
the present substance of things past and unseen.
Pah!
> [*She stands up*

MAN. Faith, who has done this? I vow
I will now do justice. I keep promise—
I? no; I do not see my way
or what to say, but I swear the promise shall be kept
that I made Immanuel when he leapt into heaven—
mocking (O I know it! I know it!) my serious sin.
Tell me, who has done this?
PRIDE. One
who will finish her work!
> [*She snatches a dagger from* HELL's *belt and leaps at* FAITH

HELL. Fool, leave it alone!
She is immortal like us! O imbecile!
> [FAITH *catches* PRIDE *and bends her back, twisting the hand*
> *holding the knife*

MAN. Drop that!
> [*He makes a movement forward*

FAITH. Stop there, Man.
She has challenged me alone and I alone
will take the challenge. Since you will not choose
by honour or love, will you take the mere fact?
Will you believe in the power?
> [HELL *moves;* MAN *seizes him*

MAN. A little else!
There shall be none beside to interfere;
that at least I can do!

FAITH. Blessed Man,
I will swear at the Judgement that you helped me here.
So, Pride, so.
> [MAN *wrestles with* HELL

PRIDE. Ah, beast!
Help me, Hell!

HELL. Pride, help me!

GABRIEL. Grace,
would not your quick touch finish the trick?

GRACE. I have brought them to a clear field! now yield
the weaker! well I know who that will be.
O Man, well thrown! poor Hell!
> [MAN *throws* HELL *and puts his foot on him*

MAN. Well sung, Grace! had you not found
and struck the dulcimer, I should have fallen to folly
deeper and darker, and my Faith died.
O the sight of the knife cured all.
Does she need help?

GABRIEL. Probably not. I have known
Faith live and thrive in odd places
by her own mere valour. Look now.
> [*In the final stress* PRIDE *breaks down; the dagger is twisted
> from her, and she falls*

GRACE. Well done, Faith! well done, Man! So.
> [*He picks up the dagger*

I thought so; Cain's old obsidian knife!
What will you do with them now, my lord?
MAN.   I?
What have I to do with giving sentence?
> [*He moves away.* HELL *rises*

It seems to me that when I say *I*
or when I think myself someone I am always wrong.
GABRIEL. Sir, you have known that all the time
if you let yourself think.
GRACE.   O chut, chut!
Gabriel, you archangels are so stern—
let our sweet lord make his own discoveries:
do not be so severe on his human reason
you with your communicated heavenly intuitions!
GABRIEL. I too have—never mind. You are right, Grace.
This is not the place or the time for rebuke.
Sir, it is true that for ever in this house
you hold the high, the low, and the middle justice
over all things; yet, as Hell said,
they are immortals; they cannot be put to death.
I do not advise perpetual prison here,
not trusting Pride—nor, sir, to be frank,
thinking you would have much chance against her.
We have seen——
GRACE.   Gabriel! Come off your grand angelic
passion for instruction. This is Man's affair;
I would swear (if I could) he would do himself right,
and us.
GABRIEL.   Very well. Sir, what will you do?
MAN. Do? it is they have done their last and worst.
> [GRACE *whistles.* MAN *looks at him*

GRACE [*hastily*]. My lord, I am sorry; that was old habit.

When I am sceptical I always whistle,
and as for doing their *last*—forgive me; speak.
MAN. Let them go then to their own place.
Up and out!
> [PRIDE *rises*; *she and* HELL *look at each other*; *she screams*

PRIDE.   O no, no!
Man, I will repent, I will do better,
I will be good one day—no, to-day.
Do not send me out to the malignant lands;
do not send me out with Hell! Save me!
GABRIEL. Sister, it was your choice.
PRIDE.   No, never;
not with him. O Man, Man——
GABRIEL. Man is not to be asked now; he judged.
The execution is remitted to us. We
are his household; we wear his livery; we do his will.
The Mercy of God takes Man at his word
and enforces it, by us who obey him on earth. Go.
PRIDE. Man, I loved you——
GABRIEL.   Loved! O little sister,
if anything was wanting, that has finished all.
Call Love in and Pride is lost.
HELL. Come, sister; the journey begins again.
PRIDE. No, no! [*She rushes from one to the other;* MAN *hides his face*] Save me! You have not gone,
you have not walked with him among the pools,
beyond the baboons and the crocodiles, beyond all
but the quicksands that never quite swallow us, under a moon
that never quite lights us, in the death that never quite dies,
and *he*——
GABRIEL.   Is this Pride?
PRIDE.   No, no.
No Pride! O if you had carried that bag—

the things we stole from you are beautiful beside
the things he can fill it with.
FAITH. But what does he *do*?
PRIDE. Denatures.
GABRIEL. Denatures!
FAITH. O horrible! O
God, pitiful God, have mercy on all!

[*There is a pause*

PRIDE. Yes. Hell. I am coming to you, Hell.

[*She stumbles towards him*

HELL [*softly*]. The bag, Pride; do not forget the bag.
It will be filled soon down there,
and now it is your turn to carry it—harlot!
PRIDE. Yes, Hell. [*She fetches it*] Here it is, Hell.
HELL. Come then. [*To the others*] We will be back presently.

[*They go out*

GABRIEL. So. That is done. Now——
FAITH and GRACE. Sh-h!
GRACE. Gabriel, there must be many things in the house
waiting for you. The silver needs polishing
perhaps; or the accounts—think of the accounts!
GABRIEL. Grace, if you were not a Divine gift——
GRACE. Yes, but I am——
GABRIEL. You are. If you were not——
GRACE. I know; I know; you said so. The silver, Gabriel,
the accounts! the dinner! We must dine, Gabriel!
While Man is on earth, he must dine;
and I do better myself on a certain nourishment.
Remember Cana of Galilee!
GABRIEL. Cana of Galilee!
Really . . .

[*He goes out*

FAITH. It is the second step that counts.
My lord, I can say nothing now to cheer

GRAB AND GRACE

    a broken heart; only that mine too
broke; we are not adult till then—O
we are not even young; the second step,
the perseverance into the province of death,
is a hard thing; then there is no return.
Most dear lord, if I could do you good,
    I would; as it is——

MAN.   O Faith, Faith, I loved her.
FAITH. Yes.
MAN.   I loved her; God knows how I loved her.
FAITH. Therefore God shall make all things well—
    O agony! O bounteous and fell judgement!— . . .
When you want me, if you want me, I will come
quicker than you can think. The Peace be with you,
and Love which is all substance in all things made.

                                                [*She goes out*

MAN. A second step . . . a second step in love . . .
    What, O almighty Christ, what of the third?

THE HOUSE OF THE OCTOPUS

AUTHOR'S NOTE TO THE FIRST EDITION

THIS play is not meant to have any direct topical relation. The name of P'o-l'u and the title of its Emperor were taken from certain earlier poems published before the outbreak of the Second World War. It is true that they were there referred to the sixth century, but it is unlikely that between the sixth and the twentieth centuries the state of P'o-l'u, within or without, has much changed; and I should regret now an identification with any particular nation or land which would then have been impossible. It is rather a spiritual threat than a mortal dominion.

Neither are the Chorus and its leaders meant to present any particular locality. Certain details of their original worship are taken from Mr. John Layard's fascinating *Stone Men of Malakula*, but 'the Outer Seas' is a sufficient place for them. It may be argued that these natives are too metaphysical. But the effort after simplicity in verse is likely to end in mere silliness; outside lyric, its achievement is on the whole the mark of the greatest poets in their greatest moments. Nor am I wholly convinced that such a simplicity would be any truer to these imagined minds than their present speech. Their hymn is a free translation from a twelfth-century hymn to the Holy Spirit by St. Hildegarde.

The character of the Flame, or the *Lingua Coeli*, is meant to be exactly what he says: that energy which went to the creation and was at Pentecost (as it were) re-delivered in the manner of its own august covenant to the Christian Church. I had some idea that his dress might suggest this by being of a close flame-colour within and of a deep star-sprinkled blue without. When he speaks to the Christians he throws back his outer cloak; when to the others, he gathers it round him. But this is only a suggestion which I do not press. No effort should, I think, be made to distinguish Alayu's appearance in the first two acts from that in the third.

It remains only for me to thank the United Council for Missionary Education for having asked me to write the play, and for their great kindness throughout. And I should like especially to thank Miss Margaret Sinclair, the convener of the Plays Group. It cannot often happen to an author to meet with such understanding of what an author's business is.

CHARLES WILLIAMS

CHARACTERS

LINGUA COELI, in the form of a Flame
ASSANTU
RAIS—his wife
ANTHONY—the missionary priest
SIRU—a deacon
TORNA ⎱ men of the land
TANTULA ⎰
OROYO—from a neighbouring island; a man of the Chorus
ALAYU—a girl of the Chorus
THE CHORUS
THE IMPERIAL PREFECT
THE IMPERIAL MARSHAL
TWO SOLDIERS

The scene is outside a newly built wooden church; against it, a little higher than the roof, is a watcher's platform with a ladder. On the left and right of the church is the jungle, through which on the right a path leads to the village. Through a break at the back the sea can be seen. TORNA *is on the platform*

ACT I

It is full moonlight. The FLAME *comes out swiftly
from the church, pauses, and speaks abruptly*

THE FLAME. Call this a land in the Outer Seas,
   where the ease and joy of our Lord reaches at last;
   as in all the past of his Church, so now here.
   First it was Jerusalem, then Damascus, Rome,
   all the patriarchates; and some of you to-night
   are alive and alight with fire of this same kind.
   O driven in search or dire in mastery, the mind
   of God's Church is the only final subject of song.
   It is the only and universal joy.
   Joy is man's condition and our language.
   We are of those who first came into being
   when the Holy Ghost measured within the waters
   the angle of creation; then in a sudden visibility
   we dropped from his rushing flame-scattering wind,
   to teach the blessed the speech of heaven and of us.
THE CHORUS [*within the church*]. Fire of the Spirit, life of
      the lives of creatures,
   spiral of sanctity, bond of all natures,
   glow of charity, light of clarity, taste
   of sweetness to sinners, be with us and hear us.
THE FLAME. But each among us has his own charge; and I,
   this new congregation of the faithful in a land
   of the Outer Seas, brought to Christ's doom
   by a missionary mouth. Sins flooded away,
   a stay of guilt granted for old faults
   by the joyous equity of heaven, and food given—
   well might they thrive! But now see, how it happens

that an empire of paganry lies within these seas,
called P'o-l'u; it has long stayed quiet,
but now moves. It stretches wide tentacles,
gasps and clutches, and one by one fetches
into its maw these ancient scattered islands.
O now who shall save my young
innocent Church? who but I? and how I—
alas, you too know; do you not?
ask your hearts, my people, ask your hearts!—
heaven's kind of salvation, not at all to the mind
of any except the redeemed, and to theirs hardly.

THE CHORUS [*singing*]. Composer of all things, light of all the risen,
key of salvation, release from the dark prison,
hope of all unions, scope of chastities, joy
in the glory, strong honour, be with us and hear us.

THE FLAME. And—ask your hearts!—there are nearer dangers!
We who since Pentecost were granted by the Holy Ghost
to men's needs—we powers of heaven, we flames of the Spirit,
we seeds of conjunction—are sometimes seen on earth
in uncovenanted shapes, shapes of triumph and terror,
tempting gloom and greed. Ask your hearts, my people,
if you do not mistake your desires for the fires of the Spirit:
mistake, did I say? God send that that be all,
that you do not crawl in a voluntary and besought error;
terror indeed! But here, on this wild shore,
a sorcerer's child has seen me so in the jungle,
and clairvoyantly traces my glow among the trees
by the sea's edge nearest P'o-l'u. He long,
purposing to gain special and spiritual power,
pretended to keep the Faith. That fails;

THE HOUSE OF THE OCTOPUS

he rails upon it and joins himself to my foes.
Now under the moon he comes again
hoping to catch me uncovenanted. I will fill
his heart with me in his manner, be sure. As I will
yours, if you choose; as you wanted, if you insist.
 [*He begins to move among the trees.* ASSANTU *enters
 slowly*
ASSANTU. Stay a little! stay a little! stay!
Stay for me, Flame of the dreadful Father!
You are he, I know, of whom my master
taught me, who go faster than a wind or a wave
and less traceable, in sea and air, than either,
and neither so strange nor so full of death as you.
O you, the dream and dance of feet more fleet
than theirs who beat the sand when the band of initiates,
in the old days when our people were still pious,
span in the house of spirits, below the heads,
smoke-dried and yoke-fitted, of our enemies
that hang under the beams. Spirit, stay;
they did not see you, Fire, but I saw you;
in the angry smoke of the lodge of initiation
I called to you, fire of the lodge, fire of the spirit,
fire of the dead, licking and pricking our hearts
with the hunger of the sea, and the sea beyond the
 sea.
I only adore you, I alone of all our people.
THE FLAME [*over his shoulder*]. I have told you before, you
 will not catch me thus.
Another latch than that of your lodge of initiates
opens upon us of heaven. I have told you before
there is under all heaven one place only
where I am sworn to stay. Go back; go back.
ASSANTU. You look over your shoulder and seem to speak
but my hearing is too weak to catch your words.

The wind in the leaves and the waves on the shore
    deafen me.
They are mild, but their terrible mildness fills my ears
as if I felt the air of that shore
where the Father and Eater watches and waits for the
    dead.

THE FLAME [*dancing*]. Go back, Assantu, go back; turn again.
Do you think I am here? I am not here; I am there
in the church with the holy ones. What you can see here
is only a spark of the furious dance we made
before my companions and I were gathered and thrown
and sealed to the Christian altars and the souls of men.
It is your nature you see, Assantu, not me.

ASSANTU. The moon's rising is not more fixed than I
to pry after you in the jungle night by night.
I am one of the wise souls; turn and speak;
speak loud; there is none as proud as I to hear.

THE FLAME. I speak to the proud only in their own tongue;
there I am loud; otherwhere very soft,
whether in heaven, at the altar, or in the heart.
I am more gentle and cleansing than any water
for those who find fire in water and water in fire.

ASSANTU. I see an edge of you among the trees; my heart
seems to hear you; speak: what shall I do?

THE FLAME. Lay spells on the shining drops that are flung
    from the spray,
or the sparks that ride in the smoke.

ASSANTU.   I hear! I hear!
That I can do.

THE FLAME.   Bid the shark swim
to be harmlessly stroked by your girls.

ASSANTU.   That I can do.

THE FLAME. Command the dead heads in your lodge of
    spirits,

THE HOUSE OF THE OCTOPUS

    the tiny smoked heads of dead foes,
    to swell where they hang from the roof and live and speak,
    and shout as they once shouted when their dusty hands
    clanged their spears together.
ASSANTU.   That I have done.
THE FLAME. Go up to the images that stand along the cliffs
    looking, for ever and ever, out to the sea—
    as old men's stony longings gaze
    out on the ways of the ocean they fish no more—
    and bid them melt into manhood, and bring you safe
    past the great shore of the ghostly island
    where your fabled Father eats the fabled flesh.
ASSANTU. That you must teach me. I cannot do it.
THE FLAME. If you could do all, you were no nearer me.
    I tell you again there is no place but one
    where the air that we—I and my fellows—breathe
    is tolerable to mortal lungs, the tongues that we use
    are audible to mortal ears. The chosen of my Lord,
    the holy ones, are praying in the church; go there.
    There alone are my own, there alone.
                                     [*He hides himself*
ASSANTU. I thought I heard you; now I hear no more,
    and the fire's edge is vanished. Spirit, stay;
    bring me to the other shore, bring me safe
    past the Father who makes his meat of the dead
    among the fiery volcanoes in the waste of the seas.
    Save me from the soul's swallowing, O spirit, O fire!
THE FLAME. I am weary of you, Assantu; this very night
    I am plight to my lord to begin the purging of souls.
    Hark! you hear the sea on the shore; can you hear
    the waves whispering about the transports of P'o-l'u?
    Hark! you have another thought in mind,
    designed to find without me the way of your will.
    I will warn you no more; go on, Assantu, go on.

The voice of your wife is near; do your choice.
I shall see you again presently among the blessèd.
                          [*He goes into the church*
ASSANTU. Voice's echo and fire's edge disappear.
I hear a human foot.   [*He whirls round.* RAIS *enters*
                Ha, Rais!
Why do you follow me so?
RAIS.   Why do you go?
Why do you wander from our hut night by night?
ASSANTU. To know if that whose passage I saw in the jungle
will come out of the jungle.
RAIS.   Twelve nights
you have gone thus, husband, under the moon.
ASSANTU. These nights, till the full of the moon, are thick
with the spirits of jungle, sea and sky. Go.
You are my wife, but a woman: back to bed!
It is dangerous for women to walk in the full moon.
RAIS. Some—but I am the daughter of a wise woman,
and you, husband, less in that learning than she.
When I was a girl, I was not made a woman
with the other maids, but with a hidden rite
before the sacred images—more than yours.
For the sake of that, and being your wife, I come.
ASSANTU. Speak softly, lest the watcher above hear.
RAIS. Why does he watch?
ASSANTU.   To catch, in sea or sky,
sight of the flight of the planes or the sides of the ships
of P'o-l'u—P'o-l'u, the thick-tentacled octopus,
the empire of mastery within the waters.
RAIS.   And you?
do you too wait here for P'o-l'u?
ASSANTU.   Perhaps.
RAIS. You are a Christian.
ASSANTU.   Am I? or am I not?

THE HOUSE OF THE OCTOPUS

RAIS. You have been washed with their sacred waters; you have fed,
   as I will never do, of their sacrosanct meal.
ASSANTU. I have known many rites. Do not you forget,
   for all your talk of magic and your wise mother,
   it was your brother who brought, ten years since,
   in his own boat the white priest here.
   You are the twin of a Christian.
RAIS.   It was my shame
   then, as now to be a Christian's wife,
   if you are a Christian.
ASSANTU.   Their meal is strong magic—
   unearthly, but then I myself am half unearthly,
   and I find in them and their meal no more than I have
   in my own power already. Speak lower;
   do not disturb our watchman lest his gaze
   wander, and he do not see in the moon yonder
   the thickening shapes of the ships when P'o-l'u comes.
RAIS. What do you want? do you want P'o-l'u to come?
ASSANTU. Yes, for then the white priest will flee.
   He will go into the mountains and so hide
   in a secret place, known only to a few
   and there give counsel and care to all his churches.
   It is so determined, and your brother to be his guide,
   your brother Tantula who knows the enskied paths
   between the heights.
RAIS.   If he does this, Assantu,
   though he is my brother and of one birth with me,
   I will call the curse of my mother on him.
ASSANTU.   No.
   Save your breath to ask help of your mother
   when you meet her after death in the ninth wave
   of the spectral tide that beats then on this shore.
   She will come dimly, floating and fleering on the waters.

You know that women do not find canoes
for their spirits, as men do, and never come
to the island where the Father eats men's flesh,
nor have hope of being made eaters themselves.
Yet—if you will go with me in this,
I might take you with me to feel the melting of the images
and come so to what safety lies beyond—
if you are no Christian.

RAIS.   I—Christian! I!
ASSANTU. Hush! I have spoken with P'o-l'u.
RAIS.   Husband!
ASSANTU. Hush! I had a strange thought. If . . .
if we could purge the land of all Christians—
and stand in the hut of initiates, the house of spirits!—
If the price were the sacrifice of your brother to-night—
RAIS. I never had a brother since he was a Christian.
ASSANTU. P'o-l'u has its eyes and ears here;
its mouth too. I have spoken with it in the jungle.
It spewed me a token; look!
                    [*He holds something up in his hand*
RAIS.   The knotted octopus!
                        [*She falls to the ground*
ASSANTU. P'o-l'u has great magic to give; it knows
the language the carved images speak. Now
do you believe that I am greater than you?
RAIS. Lord, my husband, have mercy on me!
THE CHORUS [*within*].   Amen.
ASSANTU. They will be coming presently. Hark, you!
I and not your brother must be his guide;
therefore your brother must have died. Do you see?
RAIS.   Lord,
say what you will have.
ASSANTU.   Stay you here,
hidden among the leaves. If I sign—

throwing my hand up: thus—come you out;
show yourself; call your brother for a last farewell;
draw him aside here for one embrace.
Hold his arms.
RAIS. Yes, lord.
ASSANTU. I have said
I will betray the white man into their hands.
Do you understand?
RAIS. Yes, lord.
ASSANTU. I had thought
to follow into the mountains and strike there.
This, if it may be, is better. If I speak,
if I strike, obey. If not, despair
at the parting a little, and presently let him go.
RAIS. Yes, lord.
ASSANTU. When they have the priest, the land
shall soon be swept of Christians, and the moon see
the house of spirits opened again, and the faces
of the images on the cliffs flicker with fire.
For this deed you and I shall live long
and when we die come speedily and safe
past the tides of the dead and the Ever-hungry
Father of ghosts. P'o-l'u comes to-night.
Rise. Will you spend your brother?
RAIS. I am all yours.
ASSANTU. Go; wait; watch. Now . . . Go. [*She retires*
TORNA. Who is there? Is that you, Assantu?
ASSANTU. Yes;
I myself. I am late because my wife
wept paganly, and I would go christianly.
But we have forgiven each other. Have you seen anything?
TORNA. Nothing.
ASSANTU. Nor heard anything?
TORNA. Nothing.

ASSANTU. Well,
it is likely the priest will not go to-night.
TORNA. He thinks, at dawn. Will you now go in?
ANTHONY [*within*]. . . . and of the Holy Ghost, be with you
now and for evermore.
THE CHORUS [*within*]. Amen.
ASSANTU. They have finished; it is too late.
TORNA. Amen; amen.
Blessed be Jesus Christ, true God and true Man.
> [*The* CHORUS *begin to come out of the church,*
> TANTULA, SIRU, *and* ANTHONY *last*

SIRU. Will you not consider, sir, and go now?
ANTHONY. No, son; let me stay to-night.
To-morrow in early light we will offer the Sacrifice
once more. Till we can see their ships from the shore
I need not think of flight. Tantula, tell me,
can we not reach the mountains in three hours?
TANTULA. The hills indeed, but a day more before
the heights, and as long again to reach a pass.
P'o-l'u may bomb the roads; it were wise to go.
ANTHONY. It is much against my will to go at all.
ASSANTU. O sir, we have talked that out;
do not let us trouble to talk more.
ANTHONY. You were not with us to-night, Assantu.
ASSANTU. No.
I had more charity for my wife than general charity.
ANTHONY. Parity of love between the single and the whole
is a test of the soul's proportion in grace. I
have for all and each of you an equal love,
being in my place but one equal among many . . .
however my place has been appointed chief.
ASSANTU. If for our Father's sake we are willing to lack
your place and direction, do you take the track
and leave us to our Father. He shall direct our lives.

THE HOUSE OF THE OCTOPUS

OROYO. Indeed it is too late now for anything else.
  This afternoon I saw a single plane
  flying westerly; if they do here as elsewhere—
  as in my own island—they will drop men
  from many planes. Hurry, sir, now.
ANTHONY. I think you persuaded me against my own choice.
SIRU. Sir, it is necessary that you should live
  to give still, by God's will, direction to these isles,
  and support between sea and sea the young Churches.
ANTHONY. And I to live, and you perhaps die!
SIRU. Sir, it is the privilege of the Church under God
  in the light of the Spirit—and so we prayed and believed—
  to decide who shall live and who die.
  Have we not all died once? this
  was once your word and now you must obey your word.
  This smallness of death is only an incident
  in the new life; which, since you brought us, we say
  we must have you away to protect in elect hearts.
TORNA [*from above*]. Sir, go; if we may and as we may
  we will let our brothers within the mountains know
  how here it fares with us. Go; take our blessing,
  and leave your blessing with us.
ANTHONY.   How can I go?
  It is not only my own heart's longings
  that grieve to leave you—something of fear too.
  Forgive the fear: let me speak my doubt out.
  I have worked for you, my children, these ten years
  with hopes and rejoicings—a small service to Christ,
  to whom I, priced at nothing, might show
  these pearls—earnest of the debt I ever owe.
  Now, if I go, if I leave you to that enemy
  P'o-l'u, how shall I endure the pains you bear—

the devastation and desolation of heart,
the physical agony, the extreme swallowing of death?
Or how you indeed?—and now I come
to my soul's inward trouble; you are but young
in faith; barely has the tongue of the Holy Ghost
        [*The* FLAME *appears at the door of the church*
uttered your names to Christ or his white dove
touched you with its wings; is it sure of you? When
Christ wept in Gethsemane, it were hideous if then
it were for your apostasy his tears fell!
Hell is so easy. You, by the shining waters
cleansed, then in the shining winds confirmed—
yes, and you, my son Siru, ordained!—
you are children still; your very sins are childish,
unadult. If now an adult evil—

THE FLAME. O peace, peace! there are no adult evils.
Devils can never mature: only our Lord
grew and knew more. Mystery of perfection,
to make a way to grow even in itself!

ANTHONY. —could you be faithful? could you cling to election?
could you be true? If I should go now,
would you swear again, each of you, to hold to his vow?
You, Alayu, our youngest, would you swear?

ALAYU. I? why, yes, of course.

ANTHONY.   Child, are you sure?

ALAYU. O sir, Siru and you taught me love.
And could I ever deny that warm love?
It is so much everywhere on the point of taking form,
to be more sweet than the promise—and that is sweet,
I could never deny the heat and hope of that love.

ANTHONY. Without help! yet so you all say.

THE CHORUS [*softly*]. We are nothing; yet by God's grace we are a few

THE HOUSE OF THE OCTOPUS

new-called. You brought us Christ, and we
in a host of confessors will bring you the Holy Ghost,
if God so please. Do you doubt, father,
that you leave us, everywhere and always, with God Almighty?
THE FLAME. And they say his fatherhood is more efficient
than yours.
ANTHONY. But to dare all these creatures of sea and air
that populate with hate and greed the spiritual world:
the log that within the marshes of a stagnant soul
becomes the crocodile; the shark's tooth that tears
the despairing heart; the negligent body caught
by waving tentacles! the hidden dark surprise
of all the eyed creatures with meaningless eyes!
Can you, children, meet so mighty a test
from which, again and again, the best have quailed?
If you must, can you die as I would have you?
Speak in the Holy Ghost your inmost thought!
THE FLAME. Speak then; being yoked ever to my own,
when I am invoked, I am always at once there.
SIRU. Sir, when in the disaster of paganry
we lay blind, you came to be our master;
you gathered and fathered us; now we are new-born:
little, but you told us the angels of little ones see
the face of the Father—
THE FLAME.   And I tell you so too.
SIRU. What is due to you and God we shall well pay,
if we may: do not fear; you being gone,
we will walk alone; his work must be done in us,
thus, or in some other way: and this
shall not be much amiss. We must be ourselves
to him, if the time comes, and not you.
Young as we are, we shall do as God will have us,
if God give us grace: we must leave it at that.

THE HOUSE OF THE OCTOPUS

THE CHORUS [*softly*]. We take refuge in the Maker of all and
    the Flesh-Taker;
    we believe that his deeds are enough for our needs;
    we believe that we are in him and he is in us.
    Leave us thus, father, and go with God.
THE FLAME. Do quickly, Assantu, what you do.
ASSANTU. Do but go; there is no time to spare,
    and you and we will fare as well as we may.
    Let Tantula but say a word at parting
    to his sister my wife; and rid yourself of delay.
TORNA [*calling*]. Siru, Siru, I see shapes on the sea.
ASSANTU. It is they!   [SIRU *runs up the ladder*
SIRU.   Where?
TORNA.   There! over there! see!
SIRU. Yes. How many do you guess at?
TORNA.   Nine . . . eleven.
    I think, eleven.
SIRU.   I think, eight transports . . .
    those in line, and an escort of three. Small
    ships all—a matter of three thousand men—
    but more than needs for us.
TORNA.   The whole foreshore,
    the possible harbours, the passes behind; besides,
    they may settle here the central garrison of the group.
SIRU. How long?
TORNA.   Two hours; a little more than two hours.
    They mean to be ashore before the setting of the moon.
SIRU. No planes.
TORNA.   No planes yet.
SIRU.   It is certainly they—
    P'o-l'u in force. They have a quiet sea;
    God give us calm minds to meet them.
                          [SIRU *and* TORNU *come down*
SIRU. Now, father: you have here what you need?

ANTHONY. In the sacristy, and the bread and wine in the
church.
SIRU. We will go and fetch it; let us all go—
one last moment of exchanged blessings,
then you on your way and we to wait in our homes.
Are you, too, ready, Tantula?
TANTULA. Yes.
> [*As they turn towards the church,* ASSANTU *throws
> up his arm.* RAIS *comes out*

RAIS. Tantula!
Brother!
SIRU. Who is that?
ASSANTU. Who is that? Rais! . . . My wife.
Why are you here? we have not any time for you.
RAIS. I had a dream. I saw my brother go,
and ran here to say good-bye. One kiss,
Tantula! I am your sister—though no Christian.
TANTULA. Fetch what is to be fetched. Mine is over there.
I shall be ready to start by the time you are back.
THE FLAME. More than ready; gone; gone far.
SIRU. Well . . . come, father. But the bare time!
THE FLAME. The bare time is always and everywhere.
It is all there is, and so much all that all
is in it, everywhere and always. There is only Now
—the accepted time or it may be the unaccepted.
> [SIRU, ANTHONY, *and the* CHORUS *have gone into the
> church; he follows*

ASSANTU [*to* RAIS]. Get him as far as you can among the trees.
ASSANTU [*to* TANTULA]. I will fetch your own bundle for you.
Where?
TANTULA. There—in the cloven tamarisk tree.
ASSANTU. Good.
I will be back as soon as they come. Wife,
when you have taken your parting, go to our house.

RAIS. Yes, husband.   [ASSANTU *goes among the trees*
         Must you go, Tantula?
TANTULA. Yes.
RAIS. Must *you* help this Christian teacher
   to escape? you, our mother's son? might you
   not fear our mother's vengeance—even here?
TANTULA. I was as much our mother's child as you.
   But I have found the Father: I have come now
   out of all these tales of a spectral Father
   on his island which the smoke of many volcanoes veils,
   but beyond them it lies in a spectral light, and he walks
   horrid, gigantic, among spectral flesh
   rotting round him till he makes his choice to eat
   and the poor souls flying in the deadly air
   everywhere, to be themselves swallowed and disgorged—
   nightmare!
RAIS.   Salvation—
TANTULA.   Yes, indeed salvation
   for those who drive before them bulls or swine,
   dead also, to be eaten ghostly instead!
   But now we know that the Father is a true power
   of good, and his Son our food and not we his,
   and there is but one Ghost, and that holy.
   Think, sister, of this God. All the others
   are nothing.
RAIS.   I will think rather of you now
   than of any father: how can I other,
   brother, when you are going on a difficult journey,
   and the flowing of love between us must be staunched?
   You will not return.
TANTULA.   We shall see that. P'o-l'u
   may not always be the proprietor of these isles,
   and Christ is master of all.

THE HOUSE OF THE OCTOPUS

RAIS.   O your Christ!
Is he faster than the shark or more tentacled than the
    octopus?
Come deeper. I would not have your friends
watch a pagan weep at parting from her brother.
Yes; you will go much farther than P'o-l'u.
TANTULA. If they have not closed the passes.
RAIS.   If you should die,
you will have no boar or fat bull
to drive before you along the solitary road
where the dead come dreadfully to the bleak shore
and find an oarless canoe, and drift alone
to disembark—and you without a sacrifice—
on the other shore beyond, where the Father roams
amid putrid flesh and souls chirruping with terror.
Ask me, Tantula, to name a boar for you
that it may there choke and stifle and decay
instead of you.
TANTULA.   This is all nothing.
We who have come to our Lord have only to go
farther with our Lord. Everything that can happen
is only to go a little farther with our Lord.
RAIS. Where will you sleep to-night?
TANTULA.   As high as we may,
but briefly.
RAIS.   Yes, briefly. You will soon wake
to find yourself on the road.

                                    [ASSANTU *re-enters behind*
                            Hold me. I will fold
my arms about yours. Since I was a child
I have never held any but my husband so close.
Good repose to-night, my brother Tantula.
Whatever Father you find in the land of spirits,
you will find him quickly. To-morrow I will kill a boar

in case his spectre may help you on the dolorous way.
Kiss me.
   [*They embrace. As* TANTULA *raises his head,* ASSANTU
   springs on him, strangling him
ASSANTU. Drag his arms down!
         [*They disappear in the struggle*
RAIS [*without*].   Is he dead?
ASSANTU [*without*]. Finished. Under the trees; quick.
        [SIRU *enters from the church*
SIRU. Tantula! ... It is time now ... Tantula!
       [ANTHONY *and the* CHORUS *re-enter*
ANTHONY. Is my guide as ready as I?
SIRU.   He is not here.
ALAYU. He is saying good-bye to his sister among the trees.
OROYO. It is no time to linger over good-byes.
 Where is he?
SIRU.   Tantula!
TORNA.   He is always an exact man.
 Tantula!
SIRU.   Can he have gone with Rais to her hut?
 Up, Torna; look from the platform down the paths.
           [TORNA *runs up*
 Well?
TORNA. I cannot see him.
SIRU.   What of the fleet?
TORNA. The ships are clearer and closer. P'o-l'u comes.
 No time to spare! Father, you must go, you must go!
           [*He comes down*
ANTHONY. Yes, but I cannot of myself reach the pass
 without a guide.
SIRU.   Who now? which of us knows?
       [*The* CHORUS *murmur dispersedly*
TORNA. The foothills, yes; but not the upper roads.
SIRU. Torna, you had better go as far as you can,

and then do as you may. God is over all,
and as much of the way as the wisest of us knows
is as far as he chooses we shall go of our own sight.
The rest he reserves.

TORNA. Assantu! where is Assantu?
Fool I was to forget; he could serve as well.
He can smell the roads almost as surely as Tantula.
Where is Assantu?

SIRU. He gone too!

OROYO. Something evil is on us.

SIRU. You must not wait.
I perhaps know more than Torna.
I will come myself.

ANTHONY. No indeed, Siru.

TORNA. Assantu, Assantu!

ASSANTU [*coming in quickly*]. Here. Quiet, all of you.
[*He seems to listen*
P'o-l'u has landed spies here already,
scattered on the paths: one we met. Tantula
is dead by him—and he by me. Rais
is safe in the village by now, I hope. Enough.
No time for questions.

SIRU. Assantu—

ASSANTU. I heard as I came.
It is true; I know the roads. [*He listens*
Maybe but one,
or maybe the rest have gone to the lower beaches.
I will go, father, if you will trust yourself to me.
I think the spies have not yet climbed as high;
let us at least try. Are you ready? And I.
What do you say, Siru?

SIRU. I say, begone.

ANTHONY. Farewell then, and God have you in his keeping.

SIRU. Sleeping or waking, God keep you for ever.
Farewell.
THE CHORUS. We, confessing the only glorious Name,
we who have died once bid you a blessing;
move where we may, there is only his joy in his giving,
and living or dying we go all in his love.
[ANTHONY *and* ASSANTU *go out*
OROYO. It is strange, Siru, that there should have been no cry,
that a double death, so near, should be so mute.
SIRU. Why? what do you mean?
OROYO. I do not know.
If there were another guide . . . there is not. Well,
God grant all go right.
THE FLAME [*from the church*]. That, Oroyo,
is the only thing past praying for. Prayer
is only that you may enjoy things going all right.
Allow that, and see how simple prayer is.
SIRU. Back to the village now and wait for P'o-l'u.
ALAYU [*as the others go out*]. Siru!
SIRU. Yes?
ALAYU. They will not hurt
us very much, will they?
SIRU. Fear will hurt you much more.
ALAYU. I should not mind being hurt friendly, nor to die without hurt, but . . .
SIRU. Think that our Lord
saw his enemies as his best and fairest friends
coming to do what he could not do for himself,
even he; that is, to die at the will of another,
and could not help loving them for that kindness.
Come and try; it is harder to think than to do; come.
[*They go out*

ACT II

Day. The PREFECT *enters, with a soldier of P'o-l'u*

THE PREFECT. This is their temple, is it? Drive them up.
        [*The* SOLDIER *salutes and goes out. He returns with
        another, driving in the* CHORUS *singing*
THE PREFECT. Stop. You are Christians, are you?
SIRU.   Yes, lord.
THE PREFECT. All of you?
THE CHORUS [*murmuring*]. Yes . . . yes . . . yes.
THE PREFECT. In P'o-l'u we destroy Christians: you know that?
SIRU. Yes, lord.
THE PREFECT.   P'o-l'u is as empty of Christians
  as the sea of pity or the hard rock of compassion
  or the carved images yonder of springing rice.
  What are those images?
SIRU.   They were made so long ago
  that our people's earliest tales do not recall
  how or when; they were meant for likenesses of gods
  worshipped once; perhaps before men were born.
THE PREFECT. There are not and never were gods in P'o-l'u.
  Only huger and hungrier cephalopods—which you
  call octopuses; over them and us and all,
  in a hall quite empty of men and things,
  the infinite nameless Emperor broods. You may choose
  between Emperor and cephalopods; it is all you can.
  It is all any man can who is caught by P'o-l'u.
  You will only be quietly asked which you will choose,
  but there are ways of asking. So you are Christians.
                        [*He begins to walk down the line*
Are you?   [*abruptly to* SIRU

SIRU. Yes, lord.
THE PREFECT. M'm. Are you? [*to* OROYO
OROYO. Yes.
THE PREFECT [*striking him*]. Speak courteously, pig.
SIRU. For Christ, Oroyo!
OROYO. Yes, lord.
THE PREFECT. Again.
OROYO. Yes, lord.
THE PREFECT. So. And you? [*to* TORNA]
TORNA. Yes, lord.
THE PREFECT. Why?
TORNA. I was once a sinner—
THE PREFECT. What do you mean—'sinner'?
Do I know your foolish outlandish words?
Talk intelligibly: what *is* sin?
TORNA. What, unless one is careful, one forgets,
because, if one does not forget it, it is unbearable:
a weight in the heart, a misery; all the wrong—
yes, and along with it all the good—one has done,
run into nothing but a perpetual grief;
no hope, no pause, no relief; then one becomes
dumb and blind and sick, and still goes on.
And then it is no longer so.
THE PREFECT. What do you mean?
TORNA. Lord, I cannot say it; I am a fool.
It is simply not so. O for oneself,
one may be again lost in misery and pain;
one may be stupid or wicked . . . it is not oneself
that matters; it is this. All that goes amiss
cannot at all alter that sweetness of fact.
THE PREFECT. What has this nonsense to do with your Christ-myth?
TORNA. But that—that not so—that *is* Christ;
and Christ is simply the denial of all one was;

he bids let it pass; sorrow perhaps he may allow
for oneself: but still, somewhere and somehow,
for someone—no, for everyone—he is quite certain:
in good and evil, in flesh and soul, not so.
That is our Saviour. I know; how can I deny?
THE PREFECT. Many gods vanish in the wrappings of the cephalopods.
There is only one salvation then that counts,
and that is unreachable. You will be free to say
on that day, if you can: *This is the not so*.
And you? [*to* ALAYU] are you a Christian?
ALAYU [*trembling*]. Yes.
THE PREFECT. Yes?
You mean you prefer the not so of the octopus?
ALAYU. Yes . . . No; no. I never was,
never. O let me go! It is all wrong—
I never did believe; I can't believe . . .
I will believe anything you say I should.
Save me! I will be the lowest slave of P'o-l'u!
Save me from the octopus!
THE PREFECT. P'o-l'u does not want you.
If you are not a Christian, why are you here?
ALAYU. Because Siru talked to me about love,
and I thought love was coming to me in the drink
after the blessings. They said Christ was love,
and I thought love was swimming into my blood.
I did not believe anything at all—only
I was lonely, and this was thrilling. I was a fool.
SIRU. Alayu—
[*The* PREFECT *makes a gesture of silence*
ALAYU. I was willing and the old man talked.
I will love P'o-l'u.
THE PREFECT. P'o-l'u does not want love.
My soldiers sometimes are glad of a woman or so.

THE HOUSE OF THE OCTOPUS

That is all the love I can offer. Will you go
to my soldiers or the octopus?
ALAYU. Anything, anything but that!
I swear I will never speak of love again.
Only save me! I must not die so;
I must not die yet.
THE PREFECT. Must you not? I think
you must finish what you began. If one man
possessed you, the rest would be hungry and jealous.
Besides, a man has only two arms.
An octopus, eight. No; it is too late.
You are officially a Christian.
ALAYU. No, no!
[*She flings herself on her knees before him, clutching at his waist. A* SOLDIER *strikes her away with his rifle. She falls*
THE PREFECT. Dolt! Have you killed her?
THE SOLDIER [*examining her*]. Yes, lord.
THE PREFECT. Fool!
First you are over-slow and then over-clumsy.
You should know your duties better. For what it was worth
I would not have had her die before her time.
Report yourself for double guard duty
until I remember you—the later the better for you.
You are sure she is dead?
THE SOLDIER. Yes, lord.
THE PREFECT. Accurséd fool!
[*The* MARSHAL *enters*
THE MARSHAL [*lightly*]. Dead?
THE SOLDIER. Yes, Excellency.
THE MARSHAL. Ah well!
A Christian?
THE SOLDIER. Yes, Excellency.

THE HOUSE OF THE OCTOPUS

THE MARSHAL. A pity! a pity!
These witty dialogues of yours, Prefect,
embarrass us all. I call on you others to note
that this was against my personal command. The body
shall be put at her co-religionists' disposal.
Meanwhile perhaps, to avoid more difficulty,
you will go, where I sent you, into the church.
I meant peace, and I hope we may have peace.
SIRU. May we carry the girl's body with us, lord?
THE MARSHAL. By all means. Whatever sacrifices are right
offer on my behalf.
> [SIRU *and* TORNA *take up the body, and carry it into
> the church. The* CHORUS *follow*

THE MARSHAL. You two, go with them.
> [*to the* SOLDIERS

They may talk, or sing—quietly—or do what they choose,
so long as you do not lose any of them. Go.
They are all to stay there till I send orders.
> [*The* SOLDIERS *go into the church*

I suppose your examination broke her down?
THE PREFECT. I asked her if she was a Christian.
THE MARSHAL. I know; I know.
You tasked her imagination too highly.
These revival religions are generally thick
with hysterical adolescents.
THE PREFECT. But, Excellency,
sooner or later you will put them all to death,
as your orders are?
THE MARSHAL. My dear Prefect, I will thank you
to leave my orders to me. I am perfectly aware
of the care you devote to your bi-weekly report,
short as, in all this business of invasion,
it too often has to be. But these Christians

are my affair, and mine only. They will die
when I decide—only I. Is that clear?
THE PREFECT. I have cause to suppose the infinite and hidden Majesty
grows slowly more inclined to think our health
cannot allow this sect.
THE MARSHAL.   Do you tell me so?
How kind, Prefect! But I humbly laid, long since,
my poor thoughts on the matter before the Seclusion.
THE PREFECT. For a soldier, Excellency, you are curiously merciful.
THE MARSHAL. No, no. I would not say so. Economical,
you might call me perhaps; more versed in tradition
than, by your permission, you founders of families
by your own genius and boldness can be. I
come, you see, as a mere descendant of a house
for some generations permitted to serve P'o-l'u
in the more intimate dedications. I have, it may be,
a certain hereditary intuition against your . . . daring.
THE PREFECT. The Sacred and Secluded Majesty—
THE MARSHAL.   There, you see!
How bold you are! Now my—shall I say, tentacles?—
quiver warnings to me at the touch of too much
bandying in commonplace talk of the Sacred Name.
Frame your own as you will, but, for your own sake,
I would not mistake what lies behind the mind of the Throne.
Absorb, absorb.
THE PREFECT.   Excellency, I did not mean—
THE MARSHAL. I am sure, Prefect, you meant nothing indecorous.
Absorption, you know, is our central maxim of policy;
absorption—no haste, no rashness;
gentle, slow absorption. Why do you think

THE HOUSE OF THE OCTOPUS

I have gone to such quiet trouble to catch
this missionary, this wandering white priest?
I would throw the Christians to the cephalopods now
if—In these seven-score isles we have seized,
there are Christians everywhere—yes?

THE PREFECT. Yes.

THE MARSHAL. And then
beyond the mountains—when we get beyond the mountains—
there are more Christians—yes?

THE PREFECT. Yes.

THE MARSHAL. And these,
if they become tiresome, we shall have to kill—
yes?

THE PREFECT. Yes.

THE MARSHAL. Your eyes quite goggle.
I do not mesmerize you, I hope. Pray
disagree, if you wish. Do you wish to disagree?

THE PREFECT. No.

THE MARSHAL. How wonderfully sympathetic you are!
Well then, we must kill if they are tiresome.
Now if we kill, they are wasted. But they breed thickly,
these Christians; and you know as well as I that of late
there has been remarked among us a spreading sterility—
as if we were much too intelligent or too powerful
for our own stock, as if we fed on ourselves,
and were everlastingly perishing. It has been said
that, in places which neither you nor I will mention,
this has caused some anxiety. Another fact
is that in the same unmentionable places destruction,
mere physical destruction—even by the suction
of cephalopods—is considered a poor substitution for the
    better
mental and spiritual absorption. Your girl, now,

well—there she is. But if by a small scare
or a small lure, she could have been brought to endure
—and then to enjoy—first the thought of the soldier,
and then the soldier, and then any soldier,
and then . . . men! You see? And all the time
heartily thanking the merciful heart of P'o-l'u.
She, I allow, would have had no children. But
there are others, and other ways for others. You see?
Agree, Prefect.

THE PREFECT. I agree. But then, for that—

THE MARSHAL. For that we must creep deep into their mind,
and swallow them there. The cephalopodic process
does not keep its lair only in the ocean.

THE PREFECT. And what has this to do with the missionary priest?

THE MARSHAL. He has been wandering here these many years,
founding churches, grounding their minds in belief.
He, I hope, is the channel by which now
I may come into them, and embrace them with mental tentacles,
and enlace them into P'o-l'u.

THE PREFECT. But how will you do that?

THE MARSHAL. Ah I cannot yet tell! I cannot yet
at all guess where he may like to be tickled,
where his heart enjoys the thrilling titillation
of a mental indulgence.

THE PREFECT. But are you sure he will?

THE MARSHAL. No; he may have just the necessary skill
to defeat me; he may be one who rejects the sweet
psychic satisfaction. I admit it. But I have studied
all my life, my dear Prefect, the religious mind.
Every pious man—and, of course, woman—
has one—just one—surface where religion and he

THE HOUSE OF THE OCTOPUS

are so delicately mixed in his soul as to be
indistinguishable; he is never quite sure—
and does not (believe me!) ever want to be sure—
whether his religion or he is being soothed
into a lascivious spiritual delight.
All of them, Prefect, are at bottom religious lechers,
fornicating with their fancies. These carved images
long before our time set up along the shore
are popular—like common brothels in the streets of P'o-l'u.
The Christian Church is a much grander affair,
kept with care—one of those rare buildings
(baths, scents, music, aphrodisiacs)
meant for the best of our families. Well, we shall test
this fellow, swallow his children, repopulate P'o-l'u.
If *he* is caught, all the isles will follow.
THE PREFECT. It will take time.
THE MARSHAL.   We have centuries. And you,
you would warn the Sublime Throne—would you?—
I am doing less than my duty! Take care, Prefect!
Our Master's own cephalopods are very old
and very wise; they are known to have taken a month
to squeeze a man slowly out of consciousness,
as he lies the while on the shore and is given food;
unless the Infinite One, watching, took pity
and spoke under his infinite breath, and they finished
the wretch at once. But that is most unlikely.
THE PREFECT. Excellency, I was only curious—
THE MARSHAL.   There is, besides,
behind the vast hall where he dwells by himself,
another hall, of green glass, filled
with giant ferns, and jade images of octopods,
where some, whom the Infinite Mercy after a week
bade the monsters release, wander mindless.
Or (which is worse) almost mindless, remembering,

when they see the jade shapes, their compressed muscles,
dodging among the ferns, hiding their eyes—
their food is dead fish dropped through a skylight,
their drink water from fountains, each fountain
surrounded by a lifelike tentacle. In a gallery above
the ladies of the families make a habit of walking,
small, laughing lightly, talking scandal,
pointing at the mindless men in the hall. Prefect,
this is the green-glassed centre of P'o-l'u.
True is it that the cephalopodic process
is not only physical. Well . . . let us see.
Bid them bring in the traitor first; and pray
stay here yourself. [ASSANTU *is thrust in*
 Yes. You were late.
We said the moon's fall; it was sun's rise
before you reached my men.
ASSANTU. Lord, we were late
 starting; besides, he went sadly and slowly.
THE MARSHAL. Well. What do you expect now?
ASSANTU. Freedom
 to celebrate again the ancient initiation
 and the favour of P'o-l'u for the adoration of the images.
THE MARSHAL. Your people neglect them?
ASSANTU. Since the Christians came.
THE MARSHAL. It may be we shall presently grant you leave.
 First,
 there is something else to do. You are now mine,
 and you will obey me.
ASSANTU. It was promised, lord—
THE MARSHAL. We and you have no common terms;
 therefore, no agreement. P'o-l'u is unique.
 If you need commonalty, you must believe other faiths—
 the Christian and its Incarnation, for all I care.
 Now you will obey us to whom you have given

yourself when you gave the priest. You will go with him
back to the Christians—and whatever he may say
that you will follow and obey.
ASSANTU. But, lord—
THE MARSHAL. No, no, no buts; you belong now to P'o-l'u,
since you served P'o-l'u: be still now and silent.
Our will is upon you, Assantu. Have him in.
[to the PREFECT]
[ANTHONY *is brought in*
Bound? free him—and free that man.
I offer my apologies. You will permit a few questions?
You are the Christian priest in these Outer Seas?
ANTHONY. Yes.
THE MARSHAL. You have been here at least twenty-five years?
Fifteen in the northern parts; but the last ten
passed mostly in this and the neighbouring isles.
ANTHONY. Yes; that is roughly so.
THE MARSHAL. We know, of course,
about your success; equally, we admire your devotion.
It must have been not without distress
you found yourself forced to abandon your folk.
ANTHONY. It was.
Very grave distress.
THE MARSHAL. Yes. The reasons
that forced you to it no doubt seemed good,
as then understood. I have the report somewhere.
ANTHONY. What knowledge or understanding can you possibly have
of me, or my reasons or actions?
THE MARSHAL. Much every way.
We take care, before we approach the tiniest isle,

to be well aware of our . . . I do not wish to say 'foes' . . .
No; by your pardon, I will speak first.
You were caught in the act of . . . let us say, retreat;
not running; beyond the foothills it is difficult to run;
but—

ANTHONY. That is an unworthy taunt.
THE MARSHAL. No taunt.
Think it a clumsy humour. I cannot vaunt
my skill yet in this language. Forgive me. We heard
you loved your people.
ANTHONY. Dearly; dearly.
THE MARSHAL. Yes.
And if you stayed, you expected martyrdom?
ANTHONY. Martyrdom!
Should *I* have run from martyrdom?
THE MARSHAL. See now!
It was not I who then said *run* . . .
Why are we standing? let us sit down in comfort.
Prefect, a stool for our friend! Squat, you.

[*to* ASSANTU

Now, let us talk like gentlemen. You had reasons.
Setting aside the natural fear of pain,
as unworthy you and me and this parley,
what, will you tell me, led you to leave your folk,
dearly loved, at such a dear moment?
I do not ask idly; I too have reasons.
ANTHONY. I need not give account of my reasons to any
but God and the Church.
THE MARSHAL. No, certainly.
ANTHONY. I was forced
by much insistence to go.
THE MARSHAL. I will well believe it.
ANTHONY. There are things my people prize beyond life
and I beyond my seeming reputation.

THE HOUSE OF THE OCTOPUS

THE MARSHAL. Truly: all religions have high secrets.
Why, I could tell you in our tradition—but pass.
You had your mission to preserve—
ANTHONY. Not mine!
THE MARSHAL. Well,
you had your broader duty to do; and you believed
that your people here, you gone, would hold fast
to what they had received?
ANTHONY. I was—I *am* sure they will.
THE MARSHAL. You left them in fact almost for their own
    good? [ANTHONY *rises*
No, please, father. I understood—
no need for protestation. It could be so.
ANTHONY. Could be? Was.
THE MARSHAL. Was then: you did well.
You and I can speak not only as man to man,
and as soldier to soldier, but as general to general. We
of the High Command do not leap in the first boat
or drop from the first plane. We must school the rest
and rule them from a secluded, perhaps a hidden, head-
    quarters.
It cannot be otherwise.
ANTHONY. Make of it what you will.
Kill me if you choose; see if I fear death.
THE MARSHAL. Rid yourself of any such notion.
Our laws forbid; and the Nameless and Infinite Ruler.
We never persecute; indeed, we never execute
even our criminals. In certain extreme cases—
treason, for example, or sacrilege—we do but leave
the sea, and the sea's inhabitants, free to act.
Is not that true, Prefect?
THE PREFECT. Yes, Excellency.
THE MARSHAL. No; all this talk—you have been very kind—
had quite another purpose. I wish to know

if you were a wise man or a foolish; if—
if you understood deeply how another's good
must always come before one's own; if
you could sacrifice yourself in a way perhaps more trying
than martyrdom; if you could indeed give life,
and succeed. Now I think of releasing you.
ANTHONY.   Releasing!
THE MARSHAL. Restoring you to your place. The unstable world needs
every pledge and grace of fidelity, all points
of ordination and relation. The image of the Father—
to borrow a phrase of expression from your own speech—
must not be desecrated in any mode.
ANTHONY. The only image of the Father is the blessed Son.
THE MARSHAL. Say so, and yet the Son himself established
others in his own image—am I not right?
Your people here are in a strange plight
and need you. I would not have them false to you
lest the fidelity that straightens and stiffens the world
somewhat weaken.
ANTHONY.   I am nothing; the Faith all.
THE MARSHAL. You were to them the fatherhood in the Faith.
Losing your fatherhood—I do not say they would lose
the Faith; but the terrible impersonality of faith
is hard for young souls.
ANTHONY.   That is it! that is it!
That is what I fear—that they should not be able to bear
in any crisis the dreadful abstract principles.
THE MARSHAL. You were right to fear.
ANTHONY.   But then, sir, you—
why are you so tender for them?
THE MARSHAL.   I? Why, thus—
my master the Infinite Emperor is a father too,

and will be. Into the sea of his extreme tenderness,
his avid care, must come the peoples Fate
gives him; but then he is no rough lord.
He desires all to be in peace—believe
however they will, so they receive kindly
what kindly he gives. I must a little fear
lest these childlike and rash pupils of yours,
for want of a word of advice, might ill judge,
and suffer then such ill as pure goodwill
would keep from them. You and I would both fill
(might we so) their hearts with such conscience
as would earn much touch of blessing from the lord of
    P'o-l'u.
ANTHONY. But what is it then that you would have me do?
THE MARSHAL. First, go back; be to them again
all you were; be father, pastor and master.
They cannot live unless you live by dying
a daily death for them.
ANTHONY.   It is so, I know.
THE MARSHAL. We of the High Command must be spent so.
ANTHONY. They grow from God's seed in our soil.
THE MARSHAL. And our toil is always to supply their need.
ANTHONY. High as ever they reach, they spring from this.
THE MARSHAL. And go much amiss if they disobey.
ANTHONY. I would cherish and protect them.
THE MARSHAL.   So you may,
in—if I should say a small thing, you would be
on a sharp guard and look at once for deceit.
Well, I would not wake your doubt; yet to spell
one word two ways is no great thing,
nor to separate two meanings in one sound,
if it were found proper.
ANTHONY.   Are you playing with me?
THE MARSHAL. No, by the heart of P'o-l'u! It is one word

by which in our tongue we name the Emperor
and you in yours your God. When you say God
we, as it happens, use the same syllable
for our master in the solemn rites. Syllables to us
are traditional; they have a civil value; the hierarchy
is preserved honourably, generation after generation,
by this care. It is no affair to be altered,
hastily, in a day, for a small, however sincere,
however—let us even allow—perhaps correct
sect—but small, I say, as to-day counts.

ANTHONY. This is hard.

THE MARSHAL. Not so hard, if the way be not barred
by a profane pseudo-religious obstinacy.
But this is clear—you, and you alone,
can discuss it in good sense with us of P'o-l'u.
You, and you alone, can explain all.
You are a father in the fatherhood; do not disown
your duty to your children.

ANTHONY. I must think of this.

THE MARSHAL. Do so.
But first, for all our sakes, be again
their teacher and elder. In all pieties a preacher
or a priest rules—except in such lewd
and crude unwrapping of marvels as this fellow,
retching here, yellow with fear, might devise,
were he not under your eyes. But no priest
nor preacher can rightly initiate conduct unless
the Fatherhood profess in him its original mystery.

ANTHONY. The Fatherhood chooses as it will for that.

THE MARSHAL. True,
and has chosen. It was you whom here first it chose,
and though when these troubles began you might well
   suppose
you should lie hidden, yet now, being bidden out,

to take again your fatherhood were wisely done.
It was you by whom their new life was begun;
let it continue in you.
ANTHONY.   I promise nothing.
THE MARSHAL. When I ask your promise, refuse it if you choose.
Your people are in your church. I had search made
for them particularly along all the shore.
Now I restore them to you and you to them—
one lacking, alas! She was rash, and my men;
and in a flash of temper. . . . Had you been here—
you were not.
ANTHONY.   What has happened?
THE MARSHAL.   Had you been here—
Do not leave these childish folk again.
Let it be;—no; you will hear. My dear Prefect,
will you tell our guards the Christians within are free
to come and talk here—not to wander.
The sentries yonder have been given orders to shoot.

> [*The* PREFECT *goes into the church and in a moment returns with the* SOLDIERS

Here is your guide and fellow-prisoner; he
is free too, to go with you as you will.

> [ASSANTU *rises.* ANTHONY *speaks to him. The* MARSHAL *meets the* PREFECT

I think I may claim the cephalopodic process
is beginning with some success. Gentleness and sweetness
are more entangling tentacles, Prefect, than rifles.
THE PREFECT. It needs your skill, Excellency.
THE MARSHAL.   You are too kind.
I will see you again presently [*to* ANTHONY].

> [*The* MARSHAL *and the* PREFECT *go out*

ASSANTU. Will you come to the church?

ANTHONY. Wait a moment; I must have a moment's prayer
before I meet my children.

[*The* FLAME *comes from the church*

THE FLAME. Prayer? I am there.
ANTHONY. Blessed Spirit, show me what I should do.
THE FLAME. Indeed . . . but most prayer is instruction to
him.
ANTHONY. Since I have been brought back to these again,
it is clear I am more needed here than elsewhere.
THE FLAME. If indeed you can be said to be needed at all.
ANTHONY. Else, our retirement must have succeeded better.
I have more good to do them, more help
to bring—
THE FLAME. O son, do the saints pray thus?
Do you forget you were bought at a great price?
It is your friends who pay part of the price
in learning from you; this is their happy sacrifice,
and your profit on someone else's purchase.
ANTHONY. I wish only to give myself for their good—
THE FLAME. —and your goods to the poor and your body to
be burned, and if
the will of charity is not there still,
what good then will be the good you do?
Do you not know that not until you have sold
all that is in you for the poor, can you follow Christ?
All—including the knowledge that you give it to the
poor.
ANTHONY. Give me therefore grace—
THE FLAME. This is the grace—
this distraction that disturbs your prayer, lest the prayer
prove to you—poor child!—an unfair burden.
ANTHONY. —to be to them a tender father and wise;
grant that on the foundation they find in me
they may build a true church, low but well-roofed.

THE HOUSE OF THE OCTOPUS

Grant this, blessed Spirit, and bless
me to my task, whatever their present want.
THE FLAME. So let it be. But their want perhaps is more
than you could guess before, or can now.
ANTHONY. As for this trouble of a word, with me to show,
it may go well enough. The spirit matters
more than the letter. It were better to let slide
some jot or tittle, that has in its mere self
little significance than to split peace wide.
It is fit, if possible, not to antagonize souls
by the more-or-less, the give-and-take, of words:
better that quarrels should cease, and peace live.
THE FLAME. It is, we of heaven agree, a thing indifferent;
but any indifference may become sometimes a test.
Will God dispute over words? no; but man
must, if words mean anything, stand by words,
since stand he must; and on earth protest to death
against what at the same time is a jest in heaven.
Alas, you are not in heaven! the jests there
are tragedies on earth, since you lost your first poise
and crashed. Yet pray that his will be done on earth
as it is in heaven—tragedy or jest or both,
and so let it be. Do you know, Anthony, what I say?
ANTHONY. If they obey, I will strike the rock and cry:
'Water, flow!' So I have done, and so
will do now. Out of my poise of judgment
they shall leap certainly to their everlasting joys.
Amen. *[He remains silent*
THE FLAME. Amen. What do you say, Assantu?
ASSANTU. I will bring all my people back to me.
THE FLAME. That is honest, at least.
ASSANTU. We will feast by the fires
that shall flicker below the faces of the carved images
on the flesh of boars and bulls named and slain.

THE FLAME. Without shedding of blood is no remission of sins.
This, except in P'o-l'u, is understood everywhere;
P'o-l'u only has no sins to remit.
But be free, Assantu, be free; see what you can.
Come from the circumference, both of you, into the centre. *[He touches* ASSANTU's *head*
ASSANTU. O now the fire that walks in the jungle
astonishes my brain with promise. O Tantula,
Tantula, you shall be but one of a number; again
we will offer other sacrifice than boars and bulls.
THE FLAME. The blood of Tantula cries to me from the ground.
Look in it, Assantu!
ASSANTU. Sacrifice of men!
Others to be our offering, and their skulls made
more than boars or bulls our safe preservative.
We shall live and they die—
THE FLAME. So all!
Ask your hearts, my people, ask your hearts.

[to the audience

There are few of you here who do not prefer to walk
with the old man on the new way, and talk
with the ghouls and goblins of your own souls rather
than with us of heaven who were given to you for companions:
Count all—Anthony, Assantu, P'o-l'u, and you.
. . . Enough. *[He goes into the church*
ANTHONY. Go, Assantu; call my friends.
ASSANTU [*near the church*]. Siru! Siru!
SIRU [*coming out*]. That was a voice I knew.
It cannot be—
ASSANTU. Yes, Siru, it is I.

THE HOUSE OF THE OCTOPUS

SIRU. Why, Assantu! . . . What has happened?
ASSANTU.   As things do.
Our start too late, their disembarkation too soon,
the moon sunk and an ambush set in the hills
which we met.
SIRU.   You were taken prisoner?
ASSANTU.   And brought back
down the track we had followed three hours before.
SIRU. But our father?
ASSANTU.   O your father is here safely;
you need not fear for him.
ANTHONY.   Here, Siru!

                               [SIRU *runs to him*
SIRU.   Father!
                     [*He kneels for* ANTHONY's *blessing*
But tell me what happened. Are you come
to join us in death? is there to be no breath
in God's Church here but that of the Spirit himself
till a new mission be sent?
ANTHONY.   Do not despair.
A new way may perhaps be begun
where we least expect, and an all but spent fire
flare suddenly into heat. As for what happened—
it is easy to tell. Assantu led me safely
up through the first foothills towards the pass—
but I slow to go for age and heaviness.
When the moon sank we had come to the last strange
carved image, set on a platform of its own
where vegetation ceases and rocks begin.
There we rested; in the first thin light
pressing upward we went past that shape,
which, of all of them, looks most like a man,
an old petrified man staring at the sea,
and thinking our escape sure, stumbling on—

SIRU. But to delay there! Why, Assantu
  could go as far at night as any by day.
ASSANTU. No; not with a foreigner and an old man.
ANTHONY. Danger to go, danger to stay. We stayed—
  partly perhaps to let my breath come.
  O wisely, it now seems, I had hesitated here;
  I should have waited, as something in me bade.
  Suddenly they leapt on us out of the rocks;
  death in their rifles and in their faces, death
  in their hands on us, and their cries; well, there
  they bound us, and so, under God's will, we returned—
  to live or die, my sons in Christ, with you.
  You may guess if my heart burned in me by the way.
  It is well to be in time; perhaps, by that grace,
  our Lord will have us live and not die.
SIRU. This is strange and difficult! That they should lie there,
  not so difficult; they are subtle to do harm.
  But that Assantu should take no alarm—
  the very smell of their nearness in the morning air
  would have reached me, and I nothing to compare with him
  in swiftness of sense.
ASSANTU.   You must take it the Father made dense
  the skill of my flesh for the better fetching of his will
  for your designs.
ANTHONY.   Yes! and these things signs
  we shall sail perhaps on a course we did not think,
  to a new land, and not sink in the storm.
SIRU. I do not understand; what new land?
  One of us is already dead: what land?
ANTHONY. One of the Church?
SIRU.   Alayu, the daughter of Oloya;
  not an hour since, under P'o-l'u's rifles.

THE HOUSE OF THE OCTOPUS

ANTHONY. But—
SIRU. Come and pray beside her.
ANTHONY. I will,
immediately; the Lord receive her soul.
[*A moment's silence*
But—
why she? It was not for her faith? no;
he swore they did not persecute.
ASSANTU. I knew Alayu.
She had no faith; she wanted tender promises
till she was married. She was as soft as a plum
with as hard a heart.
ANTHONY. Where did she die?
SIRU. There:
where you are standing.
ANTHONY. But why and how—tell me.
Peace be with her.
SIRU. And on all of us the Peace.
One of their officers questioned us; catching at him,
she was struck down by his men.
ANTHONY. An accident then?
ASSANTU. I am sure in her fear she swore she did not believe.
ANTHONY. No; she would not, or—did she?
This was what I had much in mind!
I warned you, Siru.
ASSANTU. I know I am right; did she?
Answer us, Siru.
SIRU. She did; she denied all.
ANTHONY. Alas, poor child! The fear of this fretted me.
SIRU. So that now we do not know what 'to live' means
in your sense; we must have another 'to live'.
ASSANTU. No; I think you will not last long.
SIRU. Will you too wrong us? will you be apostate too?
ASSANTU. Wait a little, and we shall all see.

SIRU. And see everything, and see with clear eyes.
  You cannot surprise our Lord with the terror of death.
ASSANTU. No? There are others it seems possible to terrify.
ANTHONY. Hush, Assantu; this is wild talk.
  So young a child, and if I had been here,
  I might have set all right.
SIRU.   Our Lord, sir,
  will do that. It may be that her last scream
  was no more than a cry in child-birth, when he was born
  piercingly in her soul, and her very death
  her first motherly waking.
ANTHONY.   Hush, Siru.
  Apostasy is always apostasy.
SIRU.   I am sorry, father.
ANTHONY. Assantu and you are fallen to the two extremes
  of anger and apology. It seems it is time I took
  the shepherd's crook again. Go, call
  all the Church here: tell them I am here.
  I will pray presently by this unhappy girl
  who should—could she—have been a witness to Christ.
SIRU. She died, even if she lied; she is still a witness.
  Might not, sir, her first baptismal vow
  have swallowed her fault, instead of her fault her vow?
  If God is outside time, is it so certain
  that we know which moments of time count with him,
  and how?
ANTHONY. Enough; no more argument now.
  Call the Church. I will not speak by her body
  lest it raise quarrels—as here between you two.
                        [SIRU *goes into the church*
  You, Assantu, are a zealot; that is good,
  but we must not make your nature into a rule
  for all; you are blest in it; but for the rest—
  be tender, son. Siru is a good man.

THE HOUSE OF THE OCTOPUS

ASSANTU [*looking after* SIRU]. My zeal shall go further than Siru has gone,
and make his head into one of those. . . . You said?
ANTHONY. We must have quiet souls. Now I am back
they shall not lack counsel or command. O if—
if we might bring the Cross even to P'o-l'u!
No missionary has ever reached there—
ships cast away or turned from the port—
but O if now I, by a fair chance,
might . . . a little tact, a little care!
ASSANTU. Do you think to convert P'o-l'u?
ANTHONY. I hardly dare,
yet—It is true I have been for twenty-five years
a wanderer in these lands. O if now these hands
might pour the water of heaven on the sons of P'o-l'u,
that would be indeed a climax. Who knows?
ASSANTU. Weariness has made you mad.
ANTHONY. Blessed madness!
The Universal Church would well be eased
with this last miasma of mystical paganry
dispersed, and the last shire of the world held
by me for Christ! It cannot be, and yet he,
not we, chooses apostles and gives sons.
ASSANTU. It is clear, father, you take yourself to be someone.
ANTHONY. Who was it said the Fatherhood must have its way?
ASSANTU. To eat; but Siru or you will serve for me.
ANTHONY. Anything I can do to serve you, son, I will do.
ASSANTU. I think so; but which of us knows best how?
        [SIRU *returns with the* CHORUS
SIRU. I have told them what I know. Say your will.
ANTHONY. God's blessing on you, children.
THE CHORUS. And on you, father.
ANTHONY. I had rather a thousand times be restored thus

than safe across the mountains. Little children,
see how God rules all to good,
and that more than any of us understood.
Now we shall live or die together. Whether
death is as near as lately we were bound to fear
we shall see.
SIRU. We have seen. We saw Alayu die.
ANTHONY. Yes; well . ... that was tragic. Yet—
believe me, Siru, I do not think less
than how her death must grieve us all; the more,
in the manner it was. Yet—let us speak it out—
her death strips a weak branch from the Church.
It is the price of our wholeness. All is ruled
so that even our pain at such denial is our gain.
So it has been since Christ first built
the new man on his own plan of bones—
sacrifice after sacrifice. We must not make
a girl's sin or a soldier's folly or fury
the measure of the future; a future, I dare to say,
which has more to pay in joy than ever we supposed.
SIRU. Father Anthony, we saw Alayu die.
It were idle to think that these men will not kill
whenever they choose.
ANTHONY. Peace, Siru, peace.
I perhaps have been saved for this and sent
to be to you no abstract direction from afar
but a more visible father. I have come again
to be your father, you, my first-fruits of salvation.
I have a thought now that our new vocation
may spread over all the isles.
OROYO. On my own island
I have heard of what these creatures do to Christians.
Do not be deceived; they are devils all.
ANTHONY. Hush, son. Christ is their brother and ours.

TORNA. Indeed so; but we, you said, must be
   his witnesses—even if they kill us.
ANTHONY.   If they will.
   If they will not—
SIRU.   Father, you have come again
   to be our fellow and friend. So, good.
   But there is a knowledge in us we cannot share.
   We have seen blood; we have seen the end of this world.
ANTHONY. Do you think I, who am twice as old as you,
   have not seen death? I, when I was young,
   saw my mother die, and lacked her a thousand years.
   A child's tears are never wholly stayed
   through the man's life afterwards; his heart feels
   a full trench, and nothing heals the grief.
   Come; this is foolish talk; we must think
   the living need us.
OROYO.   That is true.
TORNA.   Say your meaning.
ANTHONY. This. If God show us a field to reap,
   I would have you ready, children, to yield to his will.
   I have talked with the leader of P'o-l'u; he wishes truce
   between themselves and us. I have thought of it
   and think we should do well to take his word
   rather than defy him and die.
SIRU.   We shall not defy.
   God, who only lives, cannot defy,
   and cannot die; nor cannot live with a life
   other than his own.
ANTHONY.   It is hardly fit, son,
   you alone should set yourself against me.
   I am older than you; I have studied the Faith more,
   and wear the priesthood.
SIRU.   What does this truce mean?
ANTHONY.   I am not to be questioned overmuch.

I will decide, and guide you. This leader of P'o-l'u
himself believes in some sort of omnipotent Father,
by whom in a short time we may show him ours.
You, Assantu, you heard him; is it not so?
ASSANTU. It is.
SIRU.   Sir, you have not to call witnesses.
P'o-l'u has its father, I concede; we saw
and heard something of him. Another captain
gave us details of where his servants lurk,
and the work they do. That is his truce; good.
We will give him no excuse to make another.
ANTHONY. That is flat insolence, Siru.
SIRU.   No.
Only Alayu's body lies between us
and the end of this world; and her true voice,
the voice of Alayu the Christian, takes my breath
perhaps from beyond death.
ASSANTU.   You are a fool.
No woman lives beyond ... but have your way.
The ocean, and certain things in it, will cool
this passion of yours.
ANTHONY.   Hush, Assantu! Children,
I have come back to you out of death—
SIRU. No, father, only from this side death.
We saw Alayu *die*.
OROYO.   And that is true.
Siru, I do not understand all you say,
but this day made a sudden breach in my heart,
and half of it is yours.
ANTHONY.   It is I who do not understand.
I came, if you must quibble, from this side death,
looking for the joy of your old obedience; thence
peace and the fruits of the Spirit.
THE FLAME [*coming out*].   Who named us?

THE HOUSE OF THE OCTOPUS

TORNA. Let the Spirit judge between us.
THE FLAME. So we will.
  Hither, spirits! come you all together. [*to the* CHORUS
  Take our will, the final skill to speak,
  the final compulsion upon you to speak truly,
  as if at very judgment. Now, Anthony,
  what do you wish?
ANTHONY [*slowly*]. I would . . . I would be again
  all that which I was to these once,
  their father, their centre, almost their creator.
THE FLAME [*to the* CHORUS]. Reply.
THE CHORUS. Wisely we did to send and you to go,
  and piety always we have for the past; but now
  we too are older; nothing can be as it was.
  A friend is come out of the Fatherhood; the Fatherhood
  lives only in the sweet duty to the friend.
ANTHONY. I wish you to spring from me and live from me.
THE CHORUS. The new life must be ours and not yours;
  God is our cause of being, and only God.
              [ANTHONY *tries to speak and fails*
THE FLAME. We lay our common will upon you; speak.
  Say the truth, and hear what you say.
ANTHONY [*as if under compulsion*]. I do not wish you to live from God alone;
  I wish always to be your means of God.
THE CHORUS. That, if it could be, we too
  would willingly enjoy. It is not we who long
  to mature, and endure the pure autonomy of souls,
  but only so shall we ever be true sons.
ANTHONY. Am I no more than you?
THE CHORUS. Nor we than you.
  Each of us all is a single conjunction with God
  to function so.

ANTHONY [*struggling*]. No . . . no . . . no;
I will not say . . . I do not mean . . . this.
THE FLAME. Say.
ANTHONY. It is not true.
THE FLAME. Say.
ANTHONY. No;
I could not mean . . . I could not . . .
THE FLAME. The art of heaven
knows your heart; heaven is always exact;
and shall give you an interpreter, whose mouth is more frank
to say wholly what you mean. Assantu, speak.
ASSANTU. I wish not to be eaten, but to eat others;
I wish to grow great and thrive on others;
and if others will not, I wish them to be compelled.
I will be a belly to them and they food to my belly.
THE FLAME. Our Father retracts himself in his own nature—
for his Son in himself and on earth for every creature;
this is the good of fatherhood—to be food,
and an equal friend in the end, and blessèd if so.
ANTHONY. No! but to lose the past—
THE FLAME. The past is now;
you will only enjoy either by being both—
else your sloth will be a creeping octopus.
Go on; say what you wish more.
ANTHONY. I wish them to be content to use the Name
for the centre of P'o-l'u; no blame in it
if we explain it away, and a chance that I
shall be called by and by the apostle of P'o-l'u.
THE CHORUS. Do you direct this as a priest of Christ?
ANTHONY. I claim at least the prestige of the priesthood.
THE CHORUS. There is no prestige in any blessed priesthood,
only the priesthood; no prestige in any

true thing, but God and the thing itself.
We saw Alayu die.
ANTHONY. Why say so now?
THE CHORUS. Death, friend, teaches us many things.
Ours is a world without opinions; here
everything is what it is, and nothing else.
And now, whatever may be at other times,
we will not use the same language as P'o-l'u,
who slew Alayu.
ANTHONY. After she betrayed the Faith,
and was by her own act excommunicate.
SIRU. You of other lands may separate so;
we cannot. We in these isles
live in our people—no man's life his own—
from birth and initiation. When our salvation
came to us, it showed us no new mode—
sir, dare you say so?—of living to ourselves.
The Church is not many but the life of many
in ways of relation. This new birth
was common to Alayu and to us; no sin,
no death through sin, no death in sin,
parts us. It is sin, you say, our Lord redeems
in his Church; how if he now redeem this?
ANTHONY. If indeed she had repented before she died—
SIRU. Sir, we lay there our hands on our mouths.
See, because of her death we live more strong
in his clear goodness—much less doubt,
less fear; this is God's way—
to cause his day to dawn in sheer blood.
It is she, let me say, as well as you, to whom
we owe now all that we know of grace.
ANTHONY. This is unbelievable and unbearable.
Do you say that this apostate woman and I
are equally profitable to you?

SIRU. Sir, why not?
  Thus it becomes us to be her friends and yours,
  her children even; she died without children,
  but her blood has mothered us in the Faith, as yours
     fathered.
ANTHONY. This is sheer and absolute lunacy and heresy—
THE FLAME. Assantu will say it better; speak, Assantu.
ASSANTU. You who have gone astray from the Father and me,
  you who will not be eaten of your betters, you
  who have wandered away from the images, and thrown by
  all that of old was true—there is a way
  waiting for you in the dead waters, and beyond
  is the land of rotting flesh and chirruping souls
  and the everlasting eating. A fire consumes me;
  I must have you for my own, wholly my own, none
  shall have you but I. I am the Father, and hungry—
ANTHONY. Jesu God Almighty have mercy upon me!
  I do not—I will not—know what I am saying.
THE FLAME. You were praying to my lord the Spirit for
     exactly that.
ANTHONY. I never wanted that—
THE FLAME. O but you did.
  Rid yourself, my son, of all deceit.
ANTHONY. But I may be right—
THE FLAME. Yes; you may be right,
  but to be right in the Devil is to be wrong in the Spirit,
  and yet, even in the Devil, right is right.
  Blessed and praised and glorious for ever be he
  who will have us right all ways, not only one.
  Glory, everlasting glory, for this grace—
THE CHORUS. —be to the Father and the Son and the Holy
     Spirit!
      [*The* MARSHAL *and the* PREFECT *come in abruptly.*
      The FLAME *hides himself*

THE HOUSE OF THE OCTOPUS

THE MARSHAL. All together? I hope, agreed? No doubt
some little hesitation? you will find it work out,
if you give it time. Can you say anything?   [*to* ANTHONY
ANTHONY.   I? . . .
What have I to say? What . . . I do not understand:
what decision do you need so fast?
THE MARSHAL.   Come,
you said you have reasons; so have I now.
The answer?
ANTHONY.   But what? to what? I am a poor
sinful man—
THE MARSHAL.   Never mind sin now.
Will you take my former offer or die? I see
you have no conclusion to report. Time is short,
but you shall have till morning. Before moonset I shall
   come.
I advise you to manage to agree to some compromise.
Your god is young and can afford to change his name;
ours is old.
SIRU.   That—
ANTHONY.   A moment, friend.
This, between brothers, is my office.
He has ended deception and mended what was amiss.
Our God, sir, has all time to his Name,
being the Ancient of Days and the Youngest Day.
There is no god but he.
THE MARSHAL.   We shall see that.
ANTHONY. I find that at last there is nothing else to see.
Come, brothers, let us before night
say the Rite together.
            [*He goes to the church. The* CHORUS *follow*
THE MARSHAL [*to* ASSANTU]. Wait, you.
            [*He beckons and a* SOLDIER *comes in with* RAIS
We found late this woman straggling. Your wife?

ASSANTU. She may say so; but a lord of the sacrifice has no wife.
THE MARSHAL [*to the* PREFECT]. Everywhere the same language! the Christians and he
babble one talk. One might think their speech
was flung, like falling fire, about the world
which all watch and catch, and syllable in frenzy,
each a match for the other. But we know
where all the mad significance of speech ends
in the emptiness of the hall of the infinite and sublime Nameless
among his cephalopods: space and nothing . . . I am dizzy . . .
Well, take her!   [*to* ASSANTU
          I bring her to help snare
the white priest mentally as you did physically.
Better lose no time.
ASSANTU.   Sir, now
  I think of other things.
THE MARSHAL.   The worse for you.
  Go!   [ASSANTU *and* RAIS *withdraw*
THE PREFECT. Excellency, why so much haste?
THE MARSHAL. Indeed, I had spaced it better; but to-night
  I hear messages and instructions through the air.
  The sea-borne Powers, the dying creatures of dream,
  have gathered a kind of fleet. It is thought well
  to swell our farther armies with ships and men.
  We must not cross the mountains. I leave here
  seven companies—and you, Prefect, at their head.
  I and the rest set out to-morrow for P'o-l'u.
THE PREFECT. But surely we destroyed them by sea and air.
THE MARSHAL.   Not enough.
  The Admiral muddled the affair; he is a fool.
  One of these new unfamilied men. Of course,

in the end . . . but I must not now spare the time
to prepare and school the Christians in their comic parts,
and watch their hearts sucked into P'o-l'u.
THE PREFECT. But I—
THE MARSHAL. Come. No; you are a strong man,
Prefect, but a little drastic for comedy. Farce,
perhaps. Come, you must write your report to-night.
You would not—would you?—forget your last opportunity?
I will do myself the pleasure of carrying it in person to
P'o-l'u. [*They go out*

ACT III

It is moonlight again. The CHORUS *are asleep about the stage, except* ASSANTU, *who is brooding near the trees with* RAIS *watching him, and* ANTHONY, *who is praying at the back near the church. The* FLAME *comes from the church.*

THE FLAME. This night is mine, and for mine. Dreams
are naught, except I put a thought in them.
Deeper and deeper let the pure night fall
in which, till the sun come, we are the light;
this is the night when souls become themselves,
and dreams become thoughts and thoughts acts.
Sleep; but awake, you spirits, in the world of spirit;
be aware of the great affair of conclusion. Earth
concludes, and feuds (except in P'o-l'u) end.
                           [*He moves among the sleepers*
Where there is yet sin left, where
you are not yet bereft of indirection,
see now that to which you cling.
Oroyo, you are apt to be impatient; do you feel
the angers? the moving rocks clapt together
and you barely safe? You were used to be shy,
Torna, among your friends, but I now
will have you rarely fine as a guide to others,
your brothers of to-morrow. And you, Siru, you have died
to sin, and soon I will set you free from sorrow.
And you, the messenger of our tongue, my son Anthony?
ANTHONY. Lord, let it plague me still to feel my folly.
THE FLAME. What in you was public is private in all;
it is a common dream; but whom we mean
to spare hereafter, we commonly endanger now.

THE HOUSE OF THE OCTOPUS

ANTHONY. I was a stranger and foreigner in the Faith I professed.

THE FLAME. No; only you were willing to rest in supposing
the Faith was for you and not you for the Faith.
Out of which dreams come, themes
of sad nightmare. Let us see now of what kind
such dreams, yours and all men's, are:
ask your hearts, my people, ask your hearts!
> [*He hides himself, and withdraws to the church*

This is the universal deceit; let us see
how it shows visibly. We—my companions and I—
withdraw; and do you, moon, fail from the skies!
Natural light dies with the supernatural.
Rise, fantasies! lies of the soul, rise!

ASSANTU [*muttering*]. Sacrifice: sacrifice: the sacrifice of a man!
That in the hour of death gives power
more than bulls to come past the All-Hungry
and be myself an eater in the empty isles.
O to consume and not to be consumed!
> [*The moonlight begins to alter to a glow of decay.*
> ANTHONY *rises stiffly and turns. The* CHORUS *raise themselves stiffly towards him. The voices become inhuman*

ANTHONY. Everyone adores me and I no one—
THE CHORUS. Everyone adores you and you no one—
ANTHONY. Except, of course, God.
THE CHORUS.   Except, of course . . .
> [*They get stiffly to their knees, stretching their arms out towards him*

ANTHONY. I am for each of you the only father—
THE CHORUS. You are for each of us the only father—
ANTHONY. Except, of course, God.

THE CHORUS. Except . . .
  [ANTHONY *moves slowly towards them; their hands touch him*
ANTHONY. Love me . . . love me . . . love me.
THE CHORUS. We love you . . . we love you . . . we love you.
ANTHONY. Except, of course, God.
THE CHORUS. Except . . .
  [*The* CHORUS *are silent. Their hands clasp him. The light has wholly changed*
THE CHORUS. Come down to us; come down to us.
ANTHONY. So I will; so I do; warm—
  it is warm here.
THE CHORUS [*dispersedly*]. It is warm; come down.
  Father, father, father, father, father!
ANTHONY. It is dark here: only your eyes are bright,—
  but they do not see me! there is no meaning in your eyes.
  Your hands are hard.
THE CHORUS. The better to hold you with,
  the better to draw you down.
ANTHONY. What do you say?
THE CHORUS. We say only what you told us to say:
  Father, father, father, father, father!
  here where we are meaningless, you are meaningless.
  [*The arms are wrapped round him*
  Press; squeeze.
ANTHONY. Not so tight.
THE CHORUS. Press; squeeze.
  Tighter; tighter.
ANTHONY. You are strangling me.
THE CHORUS. Dear father!
  we love you; we adore you; you wanted us to love you.

THE HOUSE OF THE OCTOPUS

How we love you! we only live in this love.
You loved love and love is what you shall have.
> [*The light goes out*

Father, father!
ANTHONY [*choking*]. Help!
THE CHORUS.   Thus we adore.
> [*The* FLAME *is seen in a fiery light*

THE FLAME. More perhaps, even in a dream, would madden you—
to see the spiritual octopus clutching a man's soul.
Anthony, can you hear me?
ANTHONY.   Yes . . . yes . . . O voice,
voice of something that was, draw me up.
THE FLAME. While you can hear me, you are not wholly damned,
even in a dream. Do you remember Alayu?
ANTHONY. Alayu?
THE FLAME.   She who died excommunicate.
ANTHONY.   Yes.
THE FLAME. Fall, fantasies! lies in the soul, fall!
Rise, again, moon! and, light, return.
Alayu!
> [*The ghost of* ALAYU *enters from the church. The moonlight returns.* ANTHONY *is standing in the centre, but the* CHORUS *are asleep as at the beginning*

THE FLAME. I stand between the living and the dead.
See each the other; see and speak.
RAIS. Why do you stare so?
ASSANTU.   I cannot see
the shapes I hear. I hear voices near
of the jungle and the ocean and the full moon: hush!
ANTHONY. Alayu!
ALAYU.   Sir, I am sorry I was afraid.

Will you forgive me and will the Church forgive?
I am sent to ask this.
ANTHONY. Sin is deeper—
and I caught in it—than ever I thought.
How can I have any right to forgive?
Ask our Lord; he is the only-adored;
he alone forgives.
ALAYU. So I do,
but a tongue of flame sent me to ask you.
ANTHONY. Can I, spent in sin, can I forgive?
I am worse than you.
THE FLAME. That is certainly true,
but how can you be forgiven if you yourself,
for whatever virtuous reason, do not forgive?
It is your function; be ashamed, but try.
ALAYU. Will you?
ANTHONY. Wholly; I solely am to blame,
and the shame is mine.
ALAYU. No. Just as I died,
I knew it was true, all the same.
ANTHONY. What?
ALAYU. What you said; what I believed; love.
ANTHONY [*shuddering*]. Love!
ALAYU. Love was so much better than you said,
I had been thinking of it and waiting for it,
expecting and selecting it, drinking the dream in
at the blessed feast, losing the feast in the dream,
confusing it with you and Siru: O stupid!
and then suddenly I was knocked into commonsense;
I knew, whatever it was, it was not so.
I may learn yet. What I owe to P'o-l'u!
Tell me, friend and father, what can I do
to show I am sorry I was such a sensual slut
while I thought I was only being Christian.

THE HOUSE OF THE OCTOPUS

ANTHONY.   But—
  I see and speak to you, yet I know you are spirit.
  You are one of the dead.
ALAYU.   Yes truly; but you said
  we were dead in Christ; there is nothing new in being
    dead.
  I know that now. But what shall I do?
ANTHONY. Blessed daughter, can I give orders to the dead?
THE FLAME. No, but I will; or at least propose parity.
  I stand between the charity of the living and the dead.
  Alayu, you who could not bear death
  through falseness of love, if this man were to die,
  could you bear his natural fear?
ALAYU.   Be afraid again?
  O!
THE FLAME. Or continue a slut in death.
ALAYU.   O! . . .
  I suppose so, by God's help, if I must.
  Must I?
THE FLAME. Or be a silly tippler in love.
ANTHONY. That was I—a drunkard in adoration.
  O salvation is rare, bare, and steep.
  What are you, spirit?
THE FLAME.   One of the masters of exchange.
  Let it rest at that. You talked much, Anthony,
  in a grand rhetorical Christianity, of what you owed
  your fellows and children in the Faith. Now will you owe,
  in no vanity of the general but in one particular,
  a debt to this—what did you call her?—apostate?
ANTHONY. I thought I spoke the truth.
THE FLAME.   I know you did.
  But then the Faith is much truer than you thought.
  If—as you may yet—you come to the octopus,
  will you be content that this girl shall bear

your fear? for (make no mistake) you will be afraid,
deadly afraid. You prayed for strength; here
is the answer God sends. Will you take the answer?
ANTHONY. I am to owe her my own salvation from apostasy?
THE FLAME. It may be. Will you?
ANTHONY. If she and God will.
THE FLAME. Blessèd is the intercession of all souls.
Alayu, you are dead; you have nothing yourself to fear
but something to do, and if that should be to fear,
it is still something to do. In a dream you desired
the Faith: will you redeem faith and desire
by saving another to be nothing but glad in death?
ALAYU. Yes. It will not—will it?—last long.
THE FLAME. As soon as you know it indeed, it will be past.
ALAYU. I keep on being a fool. I meant—yes.
THE FLAME. Blessèd they who confess the Christ so.
You shall find the blessing. This is the mind of the Church—
to discover always the way of the lover and the love.
The young shall save the old and the old the young,
the dead the living, and the other living the dead,
and my tongue shall tell in heaven the truth of all.
Return again, till I call you, to the cloud of ascension,
Alayu; and you, Anthony, to peace in prayer.

      [ANTHONY *kneels. The* FLAME *and* ALAYU *go to the
      door of the church*

ASSANTU. I begin to see the shapes: something moves.
There, over there, the fire's edge in the jungle!
RAIS. Where?
ASSANTU. There; it is burning through my brain.
cutting it in two. One side is dying;
the other is trying to know what to do.
My head! my head!
RAIS. Husband, turn to me!

THE HOUSE OF THE OCTOPUS

ASSANTU. I cannot run; I have not stopped running
  since last night they drew the snare tight.
  When they turned us there, my turnings ended,
  and ever since I have done nothing but run
  straighter and straighter; whatever I seemed to be doing
  I was running down the lonely track of the dead
  where is no way back, but P'o-l'u behind.
  Presently I shall run as fast as the fire.
RAIS.   No.
  Turn to me; I am your wife; here
  in my arms! I will hold you so that you cannot run.
                    [*She tries to embrace him*
ASSANTU. You? no; you are holding someone; whom
  are you holding? whose face looks—Tantula!
  it is Tantula; that is right; hold him fast.
  I told you to hold him: there is no room for me.
  Besides, you have no life but in your flesh.
  There is no canoe for you to the dolorous shore;
  you shall drift, as women do, along the waters.
  P'o-l'u and I do not want you.
RAIS.   P'o-l'u,
  now, has no use even for you.
  It will kill you soon.
ASSANTU.   Hold Tantula! O
  my brain is nearly cut through. But
  the old man was slow—so slow!
  it is he who keeps me back now, I know.
THE FLAME. Come quickly, come quickly, Assantu.
  In the jungle my companions and I do nothing but run,
  all the forces of nature loosed on a creature.
  Only in the church we run and are still at once;
  so it is willed where will and power are one.
  Outside, everything, without guide, runs.
  Run fast, Assantu, run fast.

ASSANTU. Yes, but I must rid myself of the old man.
  He is tied to my side. Since we were caught by P'o-l'u
  he has always hindered me. Rais cannot help;
  her embrace is round Tantula; her face on his.
  If now the old man were dead
  he could run quickly before me to the shore of grief.
  O! O!
RAIS. Husband!
ASSANTU.   Hush! . . . It is done.
  My brain is burned right through. Why,
  where is Tantula? have you let him go?
  he was not quite dead, was he? O
  but now everything is easy. Give me your knife.
  They took mine away, but left you yours.
RAIS. Not here; not now; wait!
ASSANTU. No waiting; P'o-l'u comes; and first
  I must make a sacrifice, a great magical device,
  to be the price of my freedom from the hungry Father.
  More; those who offer boars and bulls
  are safe; but those who offer men become
  then, as I will, eaters of flesh.
  I never knew this before; now
  I shall need no canoe; I shall walk safe to that shore
  over the waters on the path of the blood of a man.
THE FLAME. Without shedding of blood is no remission of
    sins.
  You too know the condition. It is known everywhere
  except in the quiet green hall of P'o-l'u.
ASSANTU. Wife, why do you keep me? quick! the knife!
                    [*He tears it from her clothing*
THE FLAME. Life for life: but we of the Holy Ghost
  know the laws of exchange better than you.
   Alayu, whom you mocked, knows them better, Assantu!
ALAYU. What is he doing?

THE HOUSE OF THE OCTOPUS

THE FLAME. Compelling a substitution
by his own effort—fool!
> [ASSANTU *begins to crawl between the sleeping* CHORUS *towards* ANTHONY

ALAYU. But what is he doing?
THE FLAME. He thinks—saving himself from being consumed.
You were blest; you were consumed before you knew.
Glory to the only God who made us and bade us
all be food and all eaters of food.
Is it a wonder Christ gave you your Eucharist?
ALAYU. He will kill Anthony!
THE FLAME. No. But since you give
yourself for Anthony, it is you shall let him live.
Go; whisper to Oroyo a thought in a dream,
say: 'There was no cry when the spy died.
Why?'
> [ANTHONY *has sunk into sleep.* ASSANTU *writhes near him. The spirit of* ALAYU *runs and stands over* OROYO

ALAYU. Oroyo, there was no cry when the spy died.
Why?
OROYO [*in sleep*]. No cry; that was strange.
ALAYU. Why?
RAIS. Husband, take care. The trees are thick with sound.
Come back. Look! my arms are empty: come.
Trees and sea and moon are thick with voices.
ALAYU. Oroyo, why was there no cry?
OROYO [*in sleep*]. Assantu,
where was Assantu then? why was Assantu
caught?
ALAYU. Why, Oroyo? wake, wake!
ASSANTU [*rising and making passes over* ANTHONY]. I give
you my name, white man! I make you me.

I prick your wrist and smear your mouth with blood
so that you speak in my blood. I whisper to you
the tale of the images; mine is the voice of the images
and mine their stone hand. I am living stone,
their stone, and you are I. Go,
away, before me, among the dead,
before me, to be consumed in my stead
by the nameless Father of terrors.
>   [*He whispers in* ANTHONY'*s ear*
ALAYU.   No cry, Oroyo!
Why? why?
OROYO.   Why?   [*He wakes*
>   Where was Assantu?
ASSANTU. In the fire in the jungle, in the running—
THE FLAME.   See me now!
me out of the jungle, the ocean and the moon,
me the uncovenanted flame of the Holy Ghost,
me the dreadful coast across dreadful seas,
me the consuming and consumed, me in power.
>   [*He runs in a circle round* ASSANTU *and* ANTHONY
>   *and comes to a stop opposite* ASSANTU, *exhibiting himself in his glory*

It was we whom the holy ones heard above Jerusalem
falling from the rushing flame-scattering wind
to teach the blessed the speech of heaven and us.
Can you see us? can you hear us? can you bear us?
>   [OROYO *catches* ASSANTU'*s wrist from behind. The*
>   FLAME *runs to the front of the stage*

                    Oho, my people,
can you bear us? can you hear us? can you see us? are
  your hearts pure
to endure everywhere the speech of heaven and us?
do you die daily and live daily in us?
are you consumed and consuming?—Or are you content

to get someone else to die instead of you?
Apostates!
> [*He hides himself and returns to the church. The*
> CHORUS *and* ANTHONY *start to their feet*

TORNA. Oroyo!
SIRU.   What is happening?
OROYO [*showing the knife*].   This. Here is the spy
Tantula met! here is P'o-l'u's man
who led our father into the snare! our Judas
doing murder in the night.
> [*The* CHORUS *exclaim dispersedly*
> Glory to God

I woke then.
TORNA.   Impossible. Why should any of us
be false. . . .
SIRU.   Tantula . . . P'o-l'u's men in ambush . . .
and this, . . . the knife . . . say something, Assantu.
> [ASSANTU *remains silent, staring at* ANTHONY *in
> a kind of ecstasy*

OROYO. And Rais! quick, get hold of her, you women.
Tantula did not die without his sister's leave.
SIRU. Did you know of this, Rais, and of what was meant?
RAIS. Do you think I shall answer you?
SIRU.   Treachery! always treachery!
Alayu's fall was little beside this.
Misery of falsehood!
OROYO.   Rais was none of us.
SIRU. Alayu and Assantu—
ANTHONY.   Say, that I too
was something less than you thought—but let me
   speak.
Those who have seen their sin know sin
and cannot be astonished. Why this man should hate
may be strange; that he should, cannot be.

Any temptation at any moment anywhere
may change the troth-plight: then the quality of faith
is to see, and not be abashed, and still smile.
When it knows what evil is, it is not surprised,
and till it does, it is only folly disguised.
Why did you betray the Church, brother? . . . why
did you want to kill me?

ASSANTU [*suddenly*]. I wanted a substitution.
I wanted salvation.

TORNA. But you had it; here it is.
What more?

ANTHONY. Yet tell us more. How could I help?

ASSANTU. Jungle-fire and jungle-blood about me!
I see the curling edge of the fire, the swirling
blood on the other shore. The image is I;
I am living stone. I stand at the edge of the land,
looking across the sea to the dead shore.
My stone mouth speaks; my stone hand
is stretched among the Christian folk and has fetched
something that something eats. I was hungry,
I shall be hungry again. My stone melts.
There, everywhere, a sea stained with blood
tossing up flesh, and birds wailing over me;
O the Father, the Father, I the Father,
I walking and eating: Oy! Oy!

TORNA. He is mad.

OROYO. Or cunning.

SIRU. Why does God try
his Church with all the worst evils at once?

RAIS. Give me my husband and let us go away.

OROYO. P'o-l'u's men will shoot; how will you go?
No; you must stay here where you chose to be.

ANTHONY. But take him to her: let them be together.
Watch them, Oroyo. Do you despair, Siru?

THE HOUSE OF THE OCTOPUS

Nonsense; it is not as easy as that for you,
who saw in Alayu's death a mode of redemption.
SIRU. The Church may stumble; can the Church betray?
ANTHONY. Do not say so; yet betrayal lay in the Twelve,
and Matthias took his brother's bishopric; then
among even those first men of the new creation
there was a bishopric for him to take. Beware
despair does not leave your own empty,
because, thinking you are someone, you become someone
to be caught by sin—and only someone so.
A nothing in God cannot despair. I heard
a voice cry when I saw the naughting of myself
that the Faith was truer than I thought. O truer!
A man is only himself to see himself
in his own naughting; what one, may not all?
See, we might have supposed the Church was good
in itself, or holy, or secure; but now never!
It shall be a nothing and blush to hear itself named
among men or angels; this is the burning joy
which if it has not to others it has not to God.
So to Assantu you; so I to Alayu;
so—O all to all and all to God!
Blesséd Spirit, enlarge and charge all
with—Well, but I see I am interrupted.
The eternal Peace be with you.
THE CHORUS. And with you the Peace!
    [*The* MARSHAL *and* PREFECT *enter with the* SOLDIERS
THE MARSHAL. Sermons? I hope to a true and useful close,
for now you must decide—you and your people.
ANTHONY.   Sir,
tell us clearly on what.
THE MARSHAL.   There are two courses.
One is to take the truce I now propose,
for the sake as much of your gospel as your lives. P'o-l'u

will undo the edicts against you; you shall freely teach
and practise your Rites. If you convert us all
I promise you the Sublimity will not take it ill.
But then on your side you shall be content
to use the same Name for your god and our lord,
the fatherhood in each titled by one word.
Dogmatic explanations you may make. We shall agree
that dogma is less important than fair living
and a free giving of exchange. I stipulate this
because some of your sect have proved obstinate.
You will pardon the discourtesy. Well?
ANTHONY [*smiling*]. And the alternative?
THE MARSHAL. O the alternative! I shall give you five minutes—
or less (the Prefect's men are very quick)
and then machine-guns will end everything. If
you prefer this, I will not, of course, interfere:
except so far as you yourself.
ANTHONY. I?
THE MARSHAL. Leave that; your answer—and pray be wise.
ANTHONY [*to the* CHORUS]. You have heard; we are agreed?
THE CHORUS. Yes . . . yes.
ANTHONY. Who will give the answer?
THE CHORUS. The Holy Ghost and you.
THE FLAME. In your voice, Anthony; mine in yours.
ANTHONY. Thus then, always under the Church.
Sir, this dying to trespasses is a long pain,
however it be all done; our hearts bleed
in a deed already finished—to explain this
were a riot of useless words here and to you,
who are so plausible to show us the inessential.
So. But where the potential of Christ is challenged
it becomes an act, one side death or the other.
The Church is congruous with the world and yet other,

because it has died. There is one here now
invisible, blazing-red with shame and glory;
she whom your men killed—Alayu, our friend.
Christ for us is only there. I see
that at other times the Universal Church
might agree with you in its own way; we,
if now we could take the invitation,
should agree only in yours; it must not be.
Salvation is never, any way, a bargain;
and if Christ must actualize himself in our death
it is we whom first he actualized in his own,
and still in his Eucharist; if we should now twist
the Fatherhood—

THE MARSHAL. These are fascinating metaphysics,
but my ships are waiting. You refuse then?
ANTHONY. Yes.
THE MARSHAL. Very well. You and I will talk further,
if you can speak without drink, on our way to P'o-l'u
and until the imperial cephalopods embrace you,
and you become food for the crabs, and the crabs
for the cephalopods. Fellow, take him in charge.
Conduct him to the ships, and put him on board my own.
Three men are to guard him day and night,
unless in my personal presence. Take him away.
ALAYU [*to the* FLAME]. I am terribly afraid.
THE FLAME. He is not; and he
will die purposefully, as you were meant to do;
he will die your death and you fear his fright.
This is the kingdom on earth as it is in heaven,
where this is joy—this—in him and you.
I shall meet you there.
        [*He dismisses her and she goes into the church*
ANTHONY. Christ in you!

THE HOUSE OF THE OCTOPUS

THE CHORUS. Christ in you! Christ!

[ANTHONY *is taken out*

RAIS. Lord, will you not save a man who served you?

THE MARSHAL. Who? this fellow? our dilatory spy?
Why, what has touched him? I have seen such eyes
fixed in a green ecstasy of religious trance.
Assantu! ... His glance does not change at all.
He has fancied himself into godhead, has he not?
The lot of such phantasts!

RAIS. Lord, save!

THE MARSHAL. He has swallowed himself. If I fetched him now
out of his own grave, he would come as a child,
speechless, staring, crying. Shall I show you?

RAIS. Must it be so? cannot the magic of P'o-l'u
do better?

THE MARSHAL [*talking slowly, his eyes fixed on* ASSANTU's].
Look, my dear Prefect!
Here you have the heightened religious mind
in its own kind, united in rapture with its god,
a paltry phenomenon, but unusual in such complete
consummation of unconsciousness else. Our own maxim
absorb was his; but the greater swallows the less,
so I him. There is one choice everywhere—
even between us, Prefect,—and that is to be
the swallowed *or* the swallower. I have heard say
that these Christians pretend an *and* enters—
swallow *and* be swallowed, consume *and* be consumed.
That is folly. See, how he shakes!
A god, are you? tell P'o-l'u you are a god;
Ho! the cephalopodic process could never make you
its prey! No; you cannot turn your eyes away.
You are falling out of your deity.

[ASSANTU *drops to the ground and dies*

THE HOUSE OF THE OCTOPUS
                                    If I had time,
I would make you a barking dog at my heels, or perhaps
a stone lying on the shore; little braggart!
If I had time . . .
RAIS.   Only you have not time.
There is something you cannot rule and dare not waste;
something, lord, that the great magic of P'o-l'u
cannot govern; there is need now for haste;
there is time and the end of time.
THE MARSHAL.   Wise woman!
but how do you know?—yet it is far away;
the day can hardly be thought that will bring it near.
RAIS. It will come.
THE MARSHAL.   When the world ends.
RAIS.   That will come.
THE MARSHAL. You loved your husband then? Well, you shall die
with him, here, among these Christians.
RAIS.   Be it so.
But you *must* go now; you *must*; you *must*.
THE PREFECT. Excellency, she speaks truth.
THE MARSHAL.   Yes. Thank you;
but whatever time may do at last to P'o-l'u
(always officially reserving the Secluded Emperor)
there is no exchange of eating between you and me.
Do not suppose it. Yes; I *must* go.
        [*He begins to go out; then pauses by the* SOLDIERS
                                                   Kill her.
           [*The* SOLDIERS *fire.* RAIS *falls across* ASSANTU
Take their bodies and throw them into the sea, over the
    edge yonder.   [ASSANTU *is carried out*
                       He can wander there
as bodies do, to knock against a rock,

THE HOUSE OF THE OCTOPUS

or be snapped in the belly of a shark.
>[*As* RAIS *is carried by, he strikes her face*

Hark, you,
will you tell us we *must*? will you say there shall be an end?
but I, you see, can send you before me to-day,
and still be at ease; the end is so far . . .
the end of P'o-l'u . . . infinities, infinities away . . .
we cannot think it. . . . But you, sink and be forgotten . . .
>[*He recovers himself and turns*

The rest, Prefect, I leave to you.
>[*He salutes and goes out*

THE PREFECT [*calling*].   Close in.
An end to you now, an end to your sin and salvation,
your so's and your not so's; there is only P'o-l'u.
And you are dead.

SIRU.   We have been dead a long while;
all you can do is to ensure that no guile
or violence of that old unhappy life
ever stirs in us again. Shall we not bless
you and your men and your master for such ease?
The faster the better. God's grace go with you,
and may his face hearten you at the end of time.
>[*The* PREFECT *goes out*

Now let us dead men sing.

THE CHORUS. Fire of the Spirit, life of the lives of creatures,
spiral of sanctity, bond of all natures,
glow of charity, light of clarity, taste
of sweetness to sinners, be with us and hear us.

THE FLAME. So I am; so I do; so I will; and so for all.
Come!
>[*A noise of machine-gun fire. The Christians fall*

I left you all to say your say:
that sometimes is the only way; but now

THE HOUSE OF THE OCTOPUS

I will have mine.
                  [*He discloses himself and comes down*
Rise, holy ones; rise, confessors and martyrs!
saints, arise! all is done; I am here; begun
is the gay day of our Lord; the air of felicity
is here now, and felicitous tongues to speak.
Now no longer is the deed hidden in the promise,
but the promise laughing in the deed. Now no need
is but of delight, and all the past
is but delight to satisfy present need.
O we do so well you cannot think;
Well, well, and again well! Rise.
          [*The* CHORUS, *except* TORNA, *begin to stand up*
Happy they whose first sight in heaven
is the flight or the stillness of the flames of the Holy
   Ghost;
as in Jerusalem, Rome, and all the Patriarchates,
so here; so in all the hearts who play
well their parts; rise, blessèd ones, rise!
The skies and the earth open, and there are we:
your past and future open, and there are we.
                           [*The* CHORUS *move round him*
Well, well, and again well at last!
fast is our sphere fixed, and fast it moves,
all loves circling in exchange of loves.
Come!
      [*He draws them into the church; then he returns
      towards* TORNA
    But you, Torna, I will have you
new-called to an old life: wounds
have you, and lie near the grave,
bleeding, lonely, and not even a priest
but the least of our house? Yet I will settle in you
a word, as private as you must, as public as you can,

of the Holy Ghost, heard above Jerusalem;
in you fidelity, in you magnanimity and mercy,
in you justice, in you beatitude. Rise—
up . . . up . . . up . . .   [*He waves* TORNA *to his feet*
                    your wounds shall heal.
You shall feel no hope; you shall be a hope
and a witness to us between sea and sea,
to the Maker of all and the only Taker of flesh.
What, can you stand? you see you can. On;
forward into the jungle: faint there,
if you must, from your loss of blood. Someone soon
will come across you, and hide and feed and give
as your need may be, and you, as may be, to theirs.
These affairs are easily settled in heaven,
given on earth a single conformable mind;
it were unkind else. Live till we come.
Our Lord will not leave himself without a witness,
and that (in the full fitness of compassion) you.
Now all begins again; go.
You are all and you are enough; go.
Go, and the blessing of adorable glory with you,
whom confessing the Church—hark! everywhere
sounds—and in you;   [*He swings on the audience*
                    and, if you dare, in you.
THE CHORUS [*as* TORNA *stumbles out*]. Composer of all things,
    light of all the risen,
key of salvation, release from the dark prison,
hope of all unions, scope of chastities, joy
in the glory, strong honour, be with us and hear us.

TERROR OF LIGHT

The text printed here is the final version. After the first performance the author amended the text; he died shortly afterwards and the revisions only exist in pencilled notes in the manuscript. The original text is given in the footnotes.

CHARACTERS

MARY
MARY MAGDALEN
JOHN
THOMAS
PETER
SAUL OF TARSUS
SIMON THE MAGUS
LUNA
THE APPARITION

TERROR OF LIGHT

The scene is laid in the orchard of John's house in Jerusalem

PETER. It seems a very long time.
THOMAS. It is only ten days.
JOHN. Ten! Is it as much as that?
THOMAS. You are as careless of time, John, as Peter is careful of it. To-day is the feast of Pentecost and of the first-fruits. It is exactly ten days since Jesus . . . disappeared.
PETER. We must wait. I am not impatient.
THOMAS. My dear Peter!
PETER [*with a definite impatience*]. Well, I will not be. We cannot hurry on whatever it is that is to happen. But I do not see his meaning in all this . . . waiting and watching.
THOMAS. I do not see his meaning in anything at all, and the longer we wait the less I see his meaning. I am quite sure that our lord was incredibly important, and I haven't the least idea what we ought to do about it. But that at present seems incredibly unimportant.
PETER. We ought to be at work somehow.
THOMAS. Ought we?
JOHN. The waiting and the watching are enough. Everything is changing every moment. I feel as if I had just died or were just about to die—
MARY MAGDALEN. Do not die, John, unless you must.
JOHN [*putting out his hand to her*]. This orchard now—it used to be a place with trees in. Now . . .
PETER [*staring at him*]. Well, what is it now? [*He looks round.*] It is still a place with trees in.
JOHN. Yes, but one looks . . . up through every tree, as well as at it, if you understand me.
PETER. I do not understand you in the least.

THOMAS [*rolling over to look at* JOHN]. John, are you becoming what the literary people call a Nature-mystic?
JOHN. Certainly not. I am not in the least the same thing as a tree, but. . . . Well, there used to be an inside and an outside, and one was either inside or outside, and now one is both at once, if you . . .   [*He stops*
THOMAS. . . . understand me. No, John. That sort of thing is your job; it isn't mine. Do you understand, Mary?
MARY MAGDALEN. Very well. Not so much about trees.
PETER [*turning back*]. Well, we must wait still. I will not be impatient. Please God, whatever is to happen will be soon.
THOMAS. There was that business of the election. Would this be a good time to go on with it? All the rest of the Companions are in the house, or about somewhere.
PETER. I should like to have asked our lady first. But why not?

> [*He turns and looks at* MARY. *As he does so, she speaks*

MARY. Peter, there is something I have meant to ask you. What has happened to Judas? Do you think [*They all look at her and away.*] I have not remarked his absence? I have not said anything because you have all been too much on edge till now . . . and no wonder. But now that you have had time to pause, and my lord has soothed you, tell me. Has he been arrested or has he run away? Or is he dead?
JOHN. He is dead, madonna.
MARY. I was afraid of that.
PETER. He could not be anything else. It is a mere chance that I am not dead too—no; it was not chance, it was because he did not speak to me. If he had spoken a word I should have destroyed myself. It split my heart in the garden—only to hear him, there with all the moonlight

on the swords, and Judas panting as if he were breathless, and Jesus asking him as one might ask anyone who seemed to want something. But afterwards he only looked at me, so I am not dead yet.

MARY. You are all of you very much alive.

MARY MAGDALEN. Yes, but, mother, you do not know what it was like to have him look at us.

THOMAS. It was perfectly appalling—it was like being put completely into one's own identity at that moment; perpetually settled in exactly *that* intention, *that* valuation. Pure heaven or pure hell. Fortunately he generally hooded his eyes.

JOHN. Thomas, which was it when you saw him—after you had refused to believe us about the resurrection?

THOMAS. That was almost pure laughter. [*He rises.*] You know—and he knew—that I have done many silly things but that was not one of them. In the state you all were then, I wouldn't have taken your word for anything. As it turned out, you were quite right to be in that state, but I was quite right not to believe you. And you know I was.

JOHN. Yes.

MARY MAGDALEN. He was terrible, mother, terrible. He never looked at you like that.

MARY. No?

MARY MAGDALEN } Mother!
JOHN } Madonna!

MARY. Wait, children, till you are older in this—state of things, faith or whatever you call it. I felt all this when he was a baby; it is afterwards, it is afterwards.... O you have only begun. Tell me of Judas.

PETER. He is dead and lying under a heap of stones—that is all. Outcast.

JOHN. Say, of some other fold. [MARY *crosses herself*

PETER. But there was something I was about to ask you, lady. Since it is so, since he is lost, and since your son chose twelve, it seemed to us that perhaps there should be twelve. We cannot be the bodyguards of his person; we were useless when it came to the point, and now his person is gone; well, and one of the twelve is gone. But do you think it would be wise to make a substitute for Judas of one of our friends, to complete the twelve points?

MARY. It is not for me to order the Church; that is for you and the rest. We are not like you, we have a quite different function. Mothers and victims are not priests and orators. Decide as you choose; whatever my lord proposes to you is best.

PETER. We are agreed, are we not? John?

JOHN. Yes. It is terrible to exclude Judas, but we can only agree to his choice. He is pent in God; he has gone down the wholly negative way, where there is nothing but God. Let us make the substitution.

PETER. Thomas?

THOMAS. I don't think it matters very much, but yes if you like, and the others of the company.

PETER. We will cast the lots now then. Thomas, will you find the others and tell them? Let us go inside.

[*The* APOSTLES *go in*

MARY MAGDALEN. What are you sewing, mother?

MARY. A scarf for you.

MARY MAGDALEN. Me?

MARY. Yes. You have taken to wearing very dull colours, and I cannot think why. You must know, as well as I do, that they do not suit you. I am sure John knows it, but I dare say he has a great regard for your independence of thought or your soul or something noble. That is very proper of him, but in me it would not be so proper and quite unnecessary.

MARY MAGDALEN. But, mother—
MARY. Well, darling?
MARY MAGDALEN. I mean . . . you see I *did* wear bright colours once, and I *did* look rather well in them. . . .
MARY. I am sure you looked quite beautiful.
MARY MAGDALEN. Yes, but then . . . O you know what happened!
MARY. It was all most unfortunate—natural, but unfortunate. That does not seem to me any reason for making yourself so depressing a sight to the Apostolic College or to any single member of it. If you love yourself because my lord loves you, you should know better. But it is never any use arguing with you girls.
MARY MAGDALEN. Yes, but, mother—I do not understand it at all—but my lord was killed, somehow, because of my fault. It would not be quite decent to wear bright colours after his death. [*She moves agitatedly*.] As it is, I am afraid . . .
MARY. Why?
MARY MAGDALEN. Well . . .
MARY. It is John?
MARY MAGDALEN. Yes.
MARY. Do you want to marry him?
MARY MAGDALEN. I do *not* want to marry him. I do not want to touch him. I don't know what is happening.[1]
MARY. No. I told you that you were very young in this new life. I have had thirty-three years of it [*breaking out*]—blessed for ever and ever and ever be He who made it. I am held here. I am held . . . He has an errand for me still, and He will show it to me.[2] [*She recovers*.] But you

[1] MARY MAGDALEN. No. I do not know what I do want. I do not know what is happening.
[2] MARY. No. I told you that you were very young in this new life. I have had thirty-three years of it. [*breaking out*]—blessed for ever and ever and ever be He who made it.

are dead and hidden in God; you may as well wear respectable clothes there, especially if I ask you to.

MARY MAGDALEN. O if you—

MARY. It is dear of you to wear those things because of what you did, and it will be dear of you to wear others because of what he and I have done. So either way all is well. There! [*She holds up the scarf*

MARY MAGDALEN. It is lovely. How good you are to me!

SAUL *enters*

SAUL. Good morning.

MARY. Good morning.

SAUL. You will forgive this intrusion, madame. I came to find if the Lord John Bar Zebedee was still in Jerusalem.

MARY. Why, yes. He is in the house at present, sir, but our people shall find him for you. Shall we have the honour to name you to him?

SAUL. I am called Saul and I am from Tarsus.

[MARY MAGDALEN *gives a little scream and her hands fly to her cheeks. He glances at her and away*

It will be kind of you, madame.

[*He looks back at* MARY MAGDALEN, *half-recognizing her*

Have I had the privilege . . . ?

MARY MAGDALEN. No! . . . yes . . . yes.

SAUL. I am abashed. . . . I know I have met you, but my memory for names—

MARY. Women's names especially, I think. Child, you had better tell this gentleman the occasion.

MARY MAGDALEN [*half-aside*]. Must I?

MARY. It would perhaps be better. The Nature of God is to have everything clear.

MARY MAGDALEN. O! . . . Well, it was in Jerusalem, a year ago.

SAUL. I was certainly here a year ago.

MARY MAGDALEN. You had just come out from an official dinner with the High Priest. It was rather late, and there was a Roman officer . . .

SAUL. You were the girl with him! [*He steps back.*] You!

MARY MAGDALEN. Yes. Will you forgive me? I am afraid I behaved rather badly.

SAUL. You were detestable. You made fun of me, and you . . . [*He cannot find words*

MARY MAGDALEN. I practically offered myself to you—yes. It seemed very amusing then. Publius thought it funny. Now I do not think it seems so amusing. Will you forgive me?

SAUL. But you were that sort of woman; you were that man's mistress; you—you are horrible.

MARY MAGDALEN. I know. I was.

SAUL. You—a Jewess and the mistress of a Gentile; a filthy little piece of fornication.

MARY MAGDALEN. I know.

SAUL. But what are you doing here? You are not . . . John hasn't . . . you . . . you . . . tell me!

MARY. Sir, you are talking about a great many irrelevant things. There is only one question—this young woman behaved most improperly towards you; do you forgive her? That is all. If (you will excuse me)—if we go into everyone's life history, we shall lose the main point.

SAUL. But . . .

JOHN *returns*

JOHN. Saul! My dear man, how unexpected!

SAUL. John!

JOHN. How do you come here?

SAUL. I was delayed at Antioch by my old trouble, and I very nearly turned back when I found I had missed the feast. But I was anxious to see you . . .

JOHN. That was delightful of you. You will stay here, of course . . .

SAUL. That is kind of *you*. But you have guests already—no, that is not the reason, though it is part of it.—John, are you still in with these—what shall I call them? Nazarenes?

JOHN. Yes.

SAUL. *Now?* Now, when he has been hanged?

JOHN. Yes, but such a lot more. You have no idea how much *has* happened.[1]

SAUL. I hear that the Council took action at last. John—you have not been outlawed, have you?

JOHN. No: the Council has not outlawed us, not yet. And on our side we have been told that he was the fulfilling of the Law.

SAUL. John, I beg you, I beg you! O this is dreadful! How can you talk so blasphemously of the things of God? Does the Law mean nothing to you now—the Law that you and I have tried to keep all our lives, the Law God gave us as a holy trust? Here is this world, with unbelief and vulgarity swelling up all round us; doesn't it mean anything to you—John, you must forgive me; I have no right to talk to you like this—but doesn't it mean anything to you that we are Jews, and Pharisees, and have some sort of honour? You who taught me more about it than I could ever have found out for myself! No; that is nonsense; what does that matter? John, he has called us to be his chosen—

JOHN. Yes.

SAUL. What?

---

[1] JOHN. O but such a lot more. You are behind-hand, Saul; it comes of living in provincial centres like Tarsus and Antioch. Now here in Jerusalem things *happen*. [*Thoughtfully*.] You have no idea how much *has* happened.

JOHN. Yes. That is the difficulty. You see he *is* the Law.
SAUL. What do you mean?
JOHN. I do not know quite. But if you can imagine that you were dead, day by day, night by night, living just the same, breathing, eating, but *dead*.
SAUL. And I suppose this woman is dead too!
JOHN [*staring*]. What woman?
SAUL. This—harlot. [*Pointing to her*]
JOHN. Mary? Yes, certainly. At least, she is alive now; more alive than I am—you can see that—but . . .[1]
SAUL. I cannot see it. Is she living in your house?
JOHN. Yes, of course. Let me present you.
SAUL. Present *me*—to her.
JOHN. Yes, you will like her. She is quite adorable. So is everyone, I know, but one sees it clearer sometimes than at others. Come. [*He takes* SAUL *by the arm.*] Mary?
MARY [The Virgin]. I think, John, I should not trouble—Mary and I are just going in. Come, child. Help me up; my bones are burning: something is going to happen. Sir—[*she makes a small curtsey to* SAUL. *He bows*]. If I may say so, I should take care of yourself.
SAUL. Myself! It is John I am thinking of, Madame. If you have any influence with him . . .
MARY. O, I? I should be no good. My son and he knew each other too well.
SAUL [*struck by a suspicion*]. Your son?
MARY. My son. I should recommend you to be careful of my son; though if, as I think, he is implacably determined to have you, all that will not help. John will tell you what it is like—knowing him. Come, Mary. Sir.

[*She bends her head.* SAUL *bows mechanically. The women go in*

[1] JOHN. O, Mary! O yes, certainly. At least, she is alive now; more alive than I am—you can see that—but . . .

SAUL. Who is that woman?

JOHN. The mother of Jesus.

SAUL. A harlot, and the heretic's mother. And you asked me to stop here. John—I would not have insulted you in that way.

JOHN. Do not worry. I should have told you before we sent for your luggage—at least I should have told you about our lady. Mary's business is, I think, her own. And I beg you not to go on saying 'harlot'. It is inaccurate.

SAUL. She has repented, has she?

JOHN. She has—but that is not quite what I meant. Well—you will not stop here?

SAUL. If she has repented I am sorry. I would not have spoken so. Though even then I do not see why she should be living in your house. But if she has not, I prefer to call things by their right names.

JOHN. You might as well call yourself a prig and me a blustering nincompoop. Neither of them is much better than a harlot; an intellectual sin is as bad as a physical. But even if you were right, there would be no sense in monotonously reiterating a name. You need a new vocabulary.

SAUL. I need nothing of the sort. The old names are good enough for me—the Law, sin, repentance, pardon.

JOHN. I know, I know. But you hear them and you feel them, and yet they don't kill you! You don't die into them. Nowadays I don't know if I am dead or alive.

SAUL. Emotional nonsense! You can obey the Law.

JOHN. I can *not* obey the Law. Can you?

SAUL. I can try.

JOHN. And if you saw the Law moving and walking and talking in front of you . . .

SAUL. John, this is very near blasphemy. You will be saying next that the High and Holy One himself may have been . . .

JOHN. Well, and at that—
 [*They are both shocked into silence*
SAUL. You don't mean that?
JOHN [*recovering*]. No; I don't. Only all these words one has used, they *were* walking about in front of me. You talk of sin and the Law—Saul, have you ever felt an absolute, complete, and utter fool?
SAUL. No.
JOHN. M'm. You will. And I don't envy you, or at least perhaps I do. You will be doing exactly what you ought to be doing: you will be full of the most proper emotions, and acting in the most proper way—keeping the Law or repenting of *not* keeping the Law or . . .
SAUL. John—
JOHN. . . . making other people keep the Law, which is quite likely if I know you!—And click! There you will suddenly be, staring at yourself—a blind stupendous imbecile. And will you know it! O I should have been so angry once. Sit on his left hand in the Kingdom, indeed! Idiot! Double-sized idiot! 'Burn the place down with heavenly fire!' Saul, I writhe even while I laugh. I said that. I walked about this incredible world saying things like that. But to resent it now would be to be as offensive in heaven as I was on earth. No resentment, even of myself!
SAUL. I know that all our righteousnesses in God's sight are like filthy rags.
JOHN. We all know that. They *are*, that is the whole point, they *are*. Saul, when you said that—forgive me, but when you said that, *did* you detect the slightest note of propriety in your voice? You do think you ought to feel like that, don't you?
SAUL. Of course I do.
JOHN. There you are! O not to know what one ought to do, not to feel one has done it—or hasn't done it, not to be

anything but a line of light in which things can be seen! But Peter feels more like you, so I suppose it is all right. There must be something in it. But I don't get it myself.

SAUL. John, this is quite useless. We are distressing each other and doing no good. It may be your Greek philosophers that have changed you; and you may think me pompous or a prig. I am sorry; I do not mean to be a prig . . .

JOHN. Only as much a prig as I was a blustering nincompoop!

SAUL. I do not think you *that* or I should not be appealing to you now. I say again—you and I should have some honour and a little loyalty: Jesus may or may not have been a good man in himself. I was not here during the trial and I won't pretend to decide. But even if you think the Council acted hastily—or I will go further, I will say even if you think they let themselves be influenced by a kind of mob hysteria and acted as they should not— still, I beg you to consider that the High Priest himself is not Judah and the grand tradition of the Law. The covenant of Abraham is our pledge—nothing less. Jesus may have been the best of men; he may not have meant to set himself against the God of our fathers; but at best he must have been rash, at worst—leave it. We are called by our God to stand by him—we the true Israel, the faithful remnant, the sons of those who came out of Egypt. John, you are a master, you can be so great an energy; do forget all this irrelevance. Did Jesus ever say anything that is not said better in the prophets? Did he teach anything that is not in Isaiah and Ezekiel and Micah? Forget him; forget all this riff-raff: help me, help us, help our God![1]

[1] SAUL. I do not think you *that* or I should not be appealing to you now. I say again—you and I should have some honour and a little loyalty.

JOHN. If I could we would talk. I cannot. I am dead and
alive at once. Have you ever been in love?
SAUL. No.
JOHN. If you had, you would understand better. You
might as well ask a man in love to forget that the girl
lived as me to—
SAUL. It is that woman who has done it. You are in love
with her, and you call that Jesus.
JOHN. Nonsense [*staring suddenly*]. At least—
[MARY MAGDALEN *comes out of the house*
MARY MAGDALEN. John!
JOHN. Mary?
MARY MAGDALEN. I was sent to tell you that there is another
visitor for you. He will not tell his name except to you.
JOHN. What is he like?
MARY MAGDALEN. A tall man, very beautifully dressed. He
has a thrilling voice and fine eyes—and a stately way of
walking. I think he must be one of the teachers one hears

You are a Jew as well as I am, even if you know more of the Greek
philosophers. And if *they* attract you, they are in danger too. It is
not only the Religion that is being attacked; it is Reason too—by all
these filthy new notions coming in out of Syria. We ought to recollect
ourselves and not go mad over our private emotions. Civilization is in
very great danger. Religion itself is being attacked. Jesus may or may
not have been a good man in himself. I was not here during the trial
and I won't pretend to decide. But even if you think the Council acted
hastily—or I will go further, I will say even if you think they let themselves be influenced by a kind of mob hysteria and acted as they should
not—still, I beg you to consider that the High Priest himself is not
Judah and the grand tradition of the Law. The covenant of Abraham is
our pledge—nothing less. Jesus may have been the best of men; he may
not have meant to set himself against the God of our fathers; but at best
he must have been rash, at worst—leave it. We are called by our God
to stand by him—we the true Israel, the faithful remnant, the sons of
those who came out of Egypt. John, you are a master, you can be so
great an energy; do forget all this irrelevance. Did Jesus ever say anything that is not said better in the prophets? Did he teach anything
that is not in Isaiah and Ezekiel and Micah? Forget him; forget all this
riff-raff: help me, help us, help our God!

of sometimes. There is a woman with him. I cannot see her face under the veil but I think she is beautiful too. He is very anxious to speak to you.

JOHN. He had better come out here. I suppose the house is rather full of the brethren?

MARY MAGDALEN. It is rather. Most of them are on the roof, but even so—

JOHN. Let someone tell him to come here. And thank you.[1]

[*They look at each other gravely. She goes in*

SAUL. The 'new religion' must find your house useful.

JOHN. I hope they do a little. There is nowhere else in Jerusalem they can very well meet.

SIMON MAGUS *enters with* LUNA

SIMON. The Lord John Bar Zebedee?

JOHN. Yes.

SIMON. I am Simon, called the Magus. You have heard of me perhaps?

JOHN. No. But I am glad to see you.

SAUL. Simon the Magus? The disciple of Dositheus?

SIMON. No such thing. Dositheus was a trifler, a bungler, an ignoramus. He only occupied his place till it was time for me to take it—a precursor, nothing more. Do not let us talk of him. I have come here to ask you about this new gnosis of yours.

JOHN. What gnosis?

SIMON. This secret wisdom. I hear you have, or rather your Master had, great magical powers. It has been going about the town that he revivified himself after death. He deigned to leave his body to be crucified, did he not?

JOHN. He deigned to be crucified. I do not think you can say 'left his body'.

---

[1] JOHN. Let someone tell him to come here. And thank you.
MARY MAGDALEN. Dear John! [*She goes in*

SIMON. You are not yourself of the High Grades, of the Perfected, that is clear; or you would not talk so.

JOHN. I am certainly not one of the Perfected, if only that I neglect my manners. May I—the Lord Simon the Magus; the Lord Saul of Tarsus.

[*He looks over at* LUNA

SIMON. This woman is the Moon of the divine science; her true name is not spoken except in the Rituals, but if you must speak to her, or speak of the Aeons and the Emanations which are conceived in her, you may very well call her Luna. She is nothing in herself but nothing can come into being without her, except the undisturbed Godhead and I who am that which is stable everywhere. That is why I am called the Standing One.

JOHN. I see. And you had some business with me, perhaps?

SIMON. I have only that business which goes on always and everywhere—the coming of men and women into the Perfection. If you are interested in that . . .

JOHN. Both Saul and I are interested in that.

SIMON. Then we may talk. Frankly I do not see what you can have to tell me, except perhaps in one particular. I do not wish to speak lightly of your master, but I understand he never performed any specially striking miracles. I mean—nothing but healing the sick, and arousing and abating storms and raising the dead, and so on, but that after his own death he chose to reinvigorate his body—and I have heard he removed *in* his body to some one of the heavenly spheres. Now this is very remarkable—both *how* he did it and *why* he did it. If you had any information about that, I should be glad to exchange with you any poor instruction that I chance to possess.

SAUL [*only half-aside to* JOHN]. Do you observe? It is like the insect-worshippers in the prophet Ezekiel. He absolutely *smells* of blasphemy.

JOHN. He will hear you—

SIMON. I should hear him—if I chose—if he were in his own room and only whispered the word into a mirror. But he isn't of any interest to me. You are.

JOHN. Well, but, my lord Simon, I do not see what I can do. If you have heard so much, you may have heard that we are waiting for—for whatever our Lord promised should happen. We cannot tell you—not even Peter can tell you—*why* he did things. He was himself the law of himself; that is where he was different from us.

SIMON. Were you one of his intimates?

JOHN. He had none.

SIMON. No; that is right, for all such as we are. We can have none. Yet he was betrayed, they tell me, by one of his company, a certain Judas Iscariot. It is what surprises me. Did he not know? I should know, and I should blast the traitor.[1]

SAUL. Obviously, John, your master was a quite inferior sorcerer. I do not think you will be able to tell the Lord Simon the Magus very much. Nor do I think I will wait to hear the argument. If this is the sort of associate you like I congratulate you on finding him. I had not supposed that John Bar Zebedee could sink to the foulness and folly of a rhetorical necromancer from the East.

THOMAS [*coming out*]. John! John!

JOHN. Hallo!

THOMAS. Our mother sent me to fetch you—so did Peter. The twelve are together except for you; Matthias is with them—and the wind is blowing back into itself at the last corner . . .

---

[1] SIMON. No; that is right, for all such as we are. We can have none. Yet he was betrayed, they tell me, by one of his company. It is what surprises me. Did he not know? I should know, and I should blast the traitor.

JOHN. What wind?

THOMAS. A wind is blowing out of the air—it is gentle but it is increasing; it loses itself suddenly; the house cannot be separated into it. It is the Holy Ghost that is coming.
[*He goes*[1]

SAUL. I shall not wait. I will see you again before I leave Jerusalem.

SIMON. I shall wait.

JOHN [*to* SAUL]. Yes, do. [*To* SIMON.] I will be back when I can.
[*He runs into the house.* SAUL *goes*

SIMON. They are working their Rites very uneremonially. [*He goes towards the house.*] No; I will not go in; I might spoil their magic, and I want to understand more of it first. The Holy Ghost? Luna![2]

LUNA. Lord.

SIMON. I will entrance you here.

LUNA. Lord, must you?

SIMON. Why, are you afraid?

LUNA. I would so much rather we were at home: couldn't we go home first?

SIMON. No, we have no time. I must know what is happening. I can bring the gods down to earth, but I cannot carry earth into the heavens. I cannot yet go up and down the ladder of all things in this body. If this Holy Ghost can help me to do that . . . Come; we will not waste time. You are quite safe here; you are the vessel of the knowledge and the instrument of compulsion, the

---

[1] THOMAS. A wind is blowing out of the air—it is gentle but it is increasing; it loses itself suddenly; the house cannot be separated into it. Come.
[*He goes*

JOHN. You will excuse me, gentlemen?

[2] SIMON. They are working their Rites very uneremonially. [*He goes towards the house.*] No; I will not go in; I might spoil their magic, and I want to understand more of it first. Luna!

TERROR OF LIGHT

rod of magic over the spiritual world. Come; remember yourself.[1]

LUNA. Lord, I am afraid.

SIMON. There is nothing anywhere for you to fear except the uncreated and me. And the uncreated does not know of you, and I am your lord and your lover. Come.

  [*She stands in the centre. He begins to hypnotize her*

LUNA [*suddenly*]. Simon. Simon!

SIMON. Hush! I am not Simon; there is no Simon here. There is only the Standing Pillar, the union of the worlds. I am the magical Adam; you are Eve in magic, the rod of the magic, the shape of the rod and of the woman, the union of the line and the life; you are the union of the seal of King Solomon; you are the vessel of the clear light. Look into the vessel; see what is happening in the light.[2]

LUNA [*her voice dying away*]. Simon! Simon!

SIMON. Priestess of the terrible art, reflect and see.

LUNA [*her voice changing*]. They are in a crowd in the house; they are hurrying to the roof; they are on the roof, they are on the stairs—within and without; the air they breathe is about them and the flashes within the air.

SIMON. Who are *they*? Where are you seeing them?

LUNA. In the house. They are the companions of the Spirit, voices of the light, dead and living in the light, all the Nazarenes. They are standing up—Simon the Magus, you are not the Standing Pillar.[3]

---

[1] SIMON. . . . earth into the heavens. I cannot yet go up and down the ladder of all things in this body. If it is true that the Nazarene has done so— Come; we will not waste time. You are quite safe here; you are the vessel of the knowledge and the instrument of compulsion, the rod of magic over the spiritual world. Come; remember yourself.

[2] SIMON. . . . Look into the vessel and into the light; see what is happening in the light.

[3] LUNA. In the house. They are the companions of anguish, voices of the light, . . .

SIMON. What! What do you mean?

LUNA. You are not the Pillar of the world. Each of them is a pillar, and the wind blows round and round them. There are millions of pillars, in the air within the air. You are not any pillar of them all.

SIMON. I am the lord of your trances; that is enough. I am the god to you. Examine their magic; tell me all.

LUNA. Every pillar is opening into fire: there are flames playing in the wind, and tongues singing. The pillars are crowned with flame, and there is a light beyond and below them.

SIMON. Be still; reflect and see.

LUNA. The light is within the air and breaking out of the air. The edge of the light, where it mingles with the air, is a company of twisting flames. The flames sit upon their heads. The edge of the light is in the air, and the edge of the air is in the earth; the edge of the earth is in the air, and the edge of the air is in the light. Their bodies are compacted of what is beyond the light: their voices are flame in the mingling of the light and the air. They are speaking.

SIMON. How is the body one with the light?

LUNA. I have gone into the edge of the light. I am going down into it, among the shapes and images. It passes me upwards; the invisible waves of it shake me. I am going down.

SIMON. Speak to the shapes. My magic is stronger than theirs; command them to speak to me in you.

LUNA. I am at the bottom. There is no light visible here. I am walking on the floor of the ocean; there are bodies and heaps of bodies. I can see something moving not far off. It is the shape of a man lying down; now he is standing up. He is coming.

SIMON. Who is it you can see?

LUNA. Those who cannot live in this world, the drowned by the new death. They are creeping and crawling here. Simon, Simon, I am dying too.

SIMON. Do not die. Return.

LUNA. I cannot rise; someone else is rising. Simon, save yourself. He is coming up instead of me. Simon, save me! Do not leave me here at the bottom of the terror beyond light. Simon, do not leave me alone! Save me, save me!

SIMON. I am the master of the heights and of the depths. Return.[1]

LUNA. He has gone past me; he is ascending. I cannot stand upright here. I shall be one of the dead creeping things.[2]

The ghost of JUDAS ISCARIOT *enters*

SIMON. Who is this? [*A silence.*] Answer me: what is this?

LUNA. That is what came from the bottom of the universe.[3]

SIMON. I know that. What is it? Answer me.

LUNA. Ask him.

SIMON. I ask you. [*He swings his staff.*] Answer me.

LUNA. Ask *him*. [*She falls*

SIMON. So! Very well then, you; if you will not speak to us by any voice but your own, answer in that. Who are you?

JUDAS. I am Iscariot.

SIMON. Why have you come here, Iscariot?

JUDAS. Because you called me.

---

[1] SIMON. Return.

[2] LUNA. He has gone past me; he is ascending. I cannot stand upright here. I shall be one of the dead creeping things. Simon, remember me. Be careful: he is coming for you.

The ghost of JUDAS ISCARIOT *enters*

SIMON. Who is this? [*A silence.*] Answer me: what is this?

[3] LUNA. That is what came from the bottom of the light.

SIMON. We did not call you. What god has presumed to send you?

JUDAS. I was alone at the bottom of the light when your will came down feeling and fishing for me, and I came up it because I was the only thing down there that could. All I know is that I am an Apostle.[1] An Apostle of Jesus.

SIMON. You are one of the fallen creatures, one of those that crawl about the bottom of the universe; you are the stuff of matter and of chaos kept to itself. We never called you. Go; let Jesus come and speak to us.

JUDAS. I am an Apostle, I tell you. I may be in hell, but even in hell I am an Apostle. I am dead twice over, but I am an Apostle in the second death. He sends me on his errands there. They have filled my chair above, and made another one for a lord of instruction in my place, but they cannot take away my office in the schemes of death. I am Judas Iscariot, an Apostle of the Lord.

[*He begins to shuffle nearer*

SIMON. Keep where you are. We know all you dead creatures; obey us. [JUDAS *stops.*] Why have you come here when we did not call you?

JUDAS. I was the nearest thing to what you did call.[2] You know very little, Simon. You are a great magical worker, but when you put yourself in the way of the light of the

---

[1] JUDAS. I was alone at the bottom of the light when your will came down feeling and fishing for me, and I came up it because I was the only thing down there that could. If the lights had chosen to go up it I could have stopped there among the stones, where I crawl about, in and out among the stones since they threw them down on me. I cannot find anything among the stones, and I am hurt in the middle where I fell. Sometimes I can almost stand but the pain pulls me down or a stone falls on me suddenly and strikes me down. All I know is that I am an Apostle.
SIMON. Whose Apostle?

[2] SIMON. We did not call anyone. We laid our will upon the Mother of Knowledge to tell us what things we wished to know. Why do you come without calling?

heavens you will suffer for it as we do. I call it light; it is not light; it is beyond light. It is what lay on the waters before light was. Do you know how the worlds were made, Simon?

SIMON. Go back; go to your dead; go to your stones in the bottom of the light. [*He swings his staff*

JUDAS. No, Simon.

SIMON. Go back.

JUDAS. No, Simon. [*He begins to shuffle nearer*[1]

SIMON. Go back. I am the Standing Pillar between all the worlds. [*He swings his staff*

JUDAS. You can command all the dead except me. I am an Apostle. God has shut me out of heaven and I have shut myself out of earth, but Jesus has not taken away my apostolate in the place of the judgment of the dead. I know my own who live at the bottom of the light among

---

[1]
  [*He begins to shuffle nearer*
  SIMON. By the names written on this staff, by the pronunciation of the titles of the Emanations, by the Mother of all the Aeons, by the shape of the woman who is the vessel of the Mother, go back.
  JUDAS. You can command all the dead except me. I am an Apostle. God has shut me out of heaven and I have shut myself out of earth, but Jesus has not taken away my apostolate in the place of the judgment of the dead. When the light began to move all mankind died, as when the light first moved all mankind lived. Now there are the dead who can live in the light and the dead who cannot live in the light. Every man and woman on earth is one or the other. No one knows which. Jesus knows his own who live in the light, and I know my own who live at the bottom of the light among the stones. That is where you belong and I have come to take you there, Simon. An apostle of Jesus has authority among the stones. The Devil himself cannot speak the name that I can speak because of that authority. He can torment me but he cannot silence me.
  SIMON. Get back. I am the Standing Pillar between all the worlds.
  [*He swings his staff*
  JUDAS [*breathing on the staff*]. When the light began to move it put an end to this. [SIMON *drops his staff*.] We both wanted to use the light, Simon. Now we shall have it.

PETER *and* MARY MAGDALEN *come out*

the stones. An apostle of Jesus has authority among the stones. The Devil himself cannot speak the name that I can speak because of that authority. He can torment me but he cannot silence me.

SIMON. By the names written on this staff, by the pronunciation of the titles of the Emanations, by the Mother of all the Aeons, go back.

JUDAS [*breathing on the staff*]. When the light began to move it put an end to this. [SIMON *drops his staff.*] We both wanted to use the light, Simon. Now we shall have it.

PETER *and* MARY MAGDALEN *come out*

MARY MAGDALEN [*breathlessly*]. What has happened?

PETER. It is what he said; the Spirit has come. The fires were the tongues that flickered at the edge of the light; we could not have borne the light itself. It came out of the air; the air gave up the light; the brightness of the cloud of light that received him. I saw everything—for one second, and then the fires were merciful and came between. Jerusalem is drunk with it. Did they call us drunk? He has given them a glory to be drunk on. But we cannot be drunk; the lines of his order are too severe, the death too certain. What did I say to them? I myself do not know.

MARY MAGDALEN. You told them—you told us—what Jesus was.

PETER. What did I say he was?

MARY MAGDALEN [*shuddering*]. I do not know; I cannot remember.

PETER. Nor I, now. I had said, long ago, it was not necessary and should not happen, and in that light I saw that it was necessary and must happen and was happening. I was afraid that he would die and that we should die with him, and in that light I saw us dead there and living there. I said he was lord and Christ—what does that mean? I must say so. I must say so.

MARY MAGDALEN. You spoke in a hundred languages: all the Companions spoke. There was a dance of terrible syllables; only it was not about Mary, and there was no fire on her.

PETER. Do not let us be afraid of the Gospel.

[*He comes down*

MARY MAGDALEN. When the flames rode out of the air and the speaking began, I saw millions of creatures in the air, listening.

PETER. Heaven and hell were listening to his promulgation of himself, and yet he has charged us with it. We will speak it everywhere, on earth and in heaven and in hell. . . . Here are two more. Have you come to be baptized? If so, go in and you shall be instructed in the way.

MARY MAGDALEN. Iscariot!

PETER. What!

MARY MAGDALEN. It is—body or soul it is.

PETER. Iscariot! . . . What are you doing here, Iscariot?

JUDAS. The Lord sent me, Peter. Do you know me still?

PETER. I know you, traitor. Are you dead or alive?

JUDAS. I am dead, apostate. Are you alive or dead?

PETER. I am alive, by the Compassion.

JUDAS. And I am dead by the Justice. What is the difference?

PETER. That. Yes, that only. [*He strikes his breast.*] No; more! For I repented in agony.

JUDAS. Was the agony that left you alive greater than the agony that drove me to death? Was that why you were quick to choose another in my place? Someone who had never been offered a bribe.

PETER. Traitor, none of us would have taken it.

JUDAS. Apostate, you were not offered it.

MARY MAGDALEN. O go, go! I cannot bear it; even with the

heavenly air fresh in my lungs, I cannot bear it. Peter, call him to go. It is horrible; he stands there between death and life, caught in that moment of dying when he became himself. Look! his face is the very passage into death. Send him away to the bottom of the light where he came from.

PETER. Why are you here at all?

JUDAS. I was called.

SIMON. No.

JUDAS. Yes. The acts of necromancy are oblique. Those who raise the body do not always raise the body they mean, and those who love do not always love what they think they love. Those who pierce the light in the universe find a voice moving everywhere in the light, and among the stones too like a worm stinging, singing and stinging. It says 'Friend, why are you here? Friend, why? Why? Why?'

MARY MAGDALEN. Voice in the light of the morning, singing and springing! Yes, it was that. 'Woman, why are you weeping? why? why? Answer for me, answer for me, my lord! glory of Love, answer!'

PETER. He has told us to-day; but the answers cannot live together. Judas Iscariot, I do not denounce you but you have no place here. The function that belonged to you had to be filled, and we have filled it. You would be separate from us and you shall be separate; you went out of communion, and out of communion you shall remain. In the name of Christ, we remit you to the judgment of God; in the name of the Church we assent to your own volition; we lay upon you the compulsion of your own act. Go.[1] [JUDAS *begins to go*

---

[1] PETER. ... the compulsion of your own act. Go.
JUDAS. Not without this man.
SIMON. Without me or any. Are you hoping to control us, creature of the

MARY MAGDALEN. Judas!

JUDAS [*with his back to her*]. Mary!

MARY MAGDALEN. Judas, I have been angry with you till now. But if there is a Union, I see now that the only way to it is to obey the Union. If you are doing that, will you do it more, and forgive me for being angry?

JUDAS. I am returning to death; if there is any life anywhere and I find it, I will live it. [*He goes out*

SIMON. I see that you can control the rebels of your own mystery. You have proved your illumination, I must understand it. What is this Holy Ghost?

PETER [*to* SIMON]. What do you know of the Holy Ghost? Did you do this? I thought you came to be baptized.

SIMON. If that is your initiation I am willing, but I hope that I may take the Grades quickly. I am not disposed to wait among the common crowd, and climb slowly up the mystical ladder of your method. I may speak to you as one of the Perfect adepts. You have some power that I have not, just as I have some power that you have not. Can you command the spirits down from heaven, whether the guardians of heaven choose to let them go or not?[1]

---

depths? Your own companions cast you off. Go, and since you came to us without calling be very sure that in future, when we call you, you shall come.

JUDAS. We shall see that in the future. I will not struggle against the Companions now, but you do not know the Companions and you shall find your own end. [*He begins to go*

MARY MAGDALEN. Judas!

JUDAS [*with his back to her*]. Mary!

MARY MAGDALEN. Judas, I have been angry with you till now. But if there is a Union, I see now that the only way to it is to obey the Union. If you are doing that, will you do it more, and forgive me for being angry?

JUDAS. I am returning to death; if there is any life anywhere and I find it, I will live it. [*He goes out*

PETER [*to* SIMON]. Did you do this? I thought you came to be baptized.

[1] SIMON. If that is your initiation I am willing, but I hope that I may take the Grades quickly. I am not disposed to wait among the common crowd, and climb slowly up the mystical ladder of your method. I may

PETER. I do not any longer desire to control heaven. When I desired heaven to remain secluded on the mountain top and when I wished to prevent heaven hurrying on into Jerusalem, heaven refused me both times. I am wiser since heaven has opened about us to-day. I shall try to control it no longer.[1]

SIMON. I can show you how to do so if you choose. I will exchange all my knowledge with you if you will let me know how the body is raised into the heavens. Without my body I am quite free, but it seems your Master has taught you how to be free with your bodies. Will you exchange magic with me?[2]

PETER. No, I have no magic to exchange. I can tell you a formula, Simon the Magus, but it will not help you.

> speak to you as one of the Perfect adepts. You have some power that I have not, just as I have some power that you have not. You can drive the dead back to their holes. I thought I could do so, but it seems that there are some I cannot easily reach. Can you command the spirits down from heaven, whether the guardians of heaven choose to let them go or not?

[1] PETER. I do not any longer desire to control heaven. When I desired heaven to remain secluded on the mountain top and when I wished to prevent heaven hurrying on into Jerusalem, heaven refused me both times. I am wiser since heaven has opened about us today. I shall try to control it no longer.

[2] SIMON. I can show you how to do that if you choose. Can you make a body out of air and earth and fire and water, and make a boy of it? No? Can you kill that boy in the Ritual of the Offering of the Blood, and send its spirit back to the place of futurity? No? Can you summon it again from heaven, and make it speak to you of what it has seen there? No? I can do all that.

PETER. What is it to me what you can do?

SIMON. I will exchange all this knowledge with you if you will let me know how the body is raised into the heavens. Without my body I am quite free, but it seems your Master has taught you how to be free with your bodies. Will you exchange magic with me?

PETER. No, I have no magic to exchange. I can tell you a formula, Simon the Magus, but it will not help you.

SIMON. Tell me then.

PETER. Others he saved; himself he could not save.

SIMON. Tell me then.

PETER. Others he saved; himself he could not save.

SIMON. That is not magic; that is pulpit-stuff, bourgeois-stuff. If the magician cannot save himself he is lost. He must learn the stress on the self by all the labours. No one can save others if he cannot save himself.[1]

PETER. Could you have saved yourself from Iscariot? from the body of the damned?

SIMON. Yes. Do you think you have saved me? Sooner or later, in an hour or in a thousand years, I should have controlled him. You must not think about time or pain or death, or anything but power, in the game which we play with the gods. Come, if you are so foolish as not to want more knowledge, if you are content to be a disciple and no master, if you are afraid of your Jesus, I will not offer you such things. Tell me the magic, and I will give you all the money you want.

PETER. Money!

SIMON. Even to the greatest magician a little money is useful. Come; name your sum and tell me the secret.

PETER. Perish your money and you! Do you think I will sell the mysteries for trash? I have told you the formula of the Kingdom, without payment. You will not be able to use it. That is your affair. You are like the creature that was here just now. I see indeed that it was right that he should come when you desired to inquire into

---

[1] SIMON. That is not magic; that is pulpit-stuff, bourgeois-stuff. If the magician cannot save himself he is lost. He must learn the stress on the self by all the labours, by the sharpening of the knife, by the cutting and polishing of the rod, by the making of the sheepskin, the purifying oil for the lamps, the learning of the Rites. Then the making the circle, the inscription of names, the dedication of the Ritual and the concentration of the purpose along the rod towards the spirit of the proper sphere: in all this he must be himself, utterly and wholly himself. No one can save others if he cannot save himself.

what you call our magic—and it is nothing but the knowledge of Jesus. He sold our Lord for money; you would make money a means to buy the strength and domination of yourself. But money will no more be used so than the soul itself. Money is a medium of exchange, and exchange is a kind of little love and a medium of greater love. It is a way of losing the self. (The lover who buys perfumes for his mistress in the markets of Jerusalem because she likes them is wiser than the greatest magician who secures them because he wills to control the spirits of heaven. Your money shall perish with you and you with it. But those who make it a way—mites of love, talents of love—shall find that the ways are paved with pure gold, their gold refined into stuff for their souls to walk on.) It may be said of any man others he saved; himself he cannot save, but others shall save him, and another shall save him. This is the mystery, Simon the Magus, and you cannot know it: this is the forgiveness of our sins which is the communion of the saints and the resurrection of all bodies and the life of the nature of the everlasting: the word of God and of Christ and of us the Church. Go to your ceremonies; seek your power; pronounce formulas; exercise necromancy. Others you cannot save; yourself you cannot save. Go.[1]

SIMON. I have given you an opportunity; if you will not take it you must do as you like. Keep your slavery; I will not trouble you again. [*He goes up to* LUNA.] Awake, Luna.

LUNA [*in the voice of* JUDAS]. Those who come down to us at the bottom of the light cannot easily return. The Holy

---

[1] PETER. Perish your money and you! Do you think I will sell the mysteries for trash? I have told you the formula of the Kingdom, without payment. You will not be able to use it. That is your affair. You say that you have killed others for your profit; we know now that he decreed his own death for our profit. You are like . . .

TERROR OF LIGHT

Ghost does not surrender what has been sent to him. She is not in pain, leave her.[1]

SIMON. By the name that is yours where the science of the Return is reflected in that which does not go forth, awake![2]

LUNA [*in the voice of* JUDAS]. She sleeps in the darkness at peace. Unless the peace commands her, she remains in the peace.[3]

SIMON. By the one most secret name—

[*He leans forward and whispers in her ear*

LUNA [*after a violent convulsion, speaking in her own voice*]. It is no use, Simon; you cannot use the name against itself. I can hear you, and see you, and speak to you, but I cannot come to you.[4]

MARY MAGDALEN. Peter, will you not set her free?

PETER. Am I the judge of the living and the dead? If this man cannot raise her, let her lie.

MARY MAGDALEN. But she will lie there for ever.

PETER. Let her lie there for ever.

MARY MAGDALEN. Must we?

PETER. The Spirit of Christ can free her if it chooses. We

---

[1] LUNA [*in the voice of* JUDAS]. Those who come down to us at the bottom of the light can not easily return. The Holy Ghost does not surrender what has been sent to him. She is not in pain; she is asleep among the stones at the bottom of the sea. Leave her.

[2] SIMON. By the seal of Solomon, awake! By the secret names of knowledge, return! By the name that is yours where the science of the Return is reflected in that which does not go forth, awake!

[3] LUNA [*in the voice of* JUDAS]. You sent her into the light when she could not bear the light, and the light was kind and hid itself and remained apart, and she sleeps in the darkness at peace. Unless the peace commands her she remains in the peace.

SIMON. By the one most secret name—

[*He leans forward and whispers in her ear*

[4] LUNA [*after a violent convulsion, and speaking in her own voice*]. It is no use, Simon; you cannot use the name against itself. I can hear you and see you and speak to you, but I cannot come to you. You were a kind master. Find a place for me on earth and let me lie there as my soul must lie here.

must not lay our power upon her for the benefit of unbelievers.

MARY MAGDALEN. Not even to heal the blind or the lame?

PETER. What?

MARY MAGDALEN. Not even to offer her the peace? The Mother of Love told me that we were dead and our lives hidden; Peter, would not our hidden lives live through her? We are not our own any longer.

PETER. Will you die for her?

MARY MAGDALEN. Yes—if that is the way. [*She goes up to* LUNA.] May I, Peter?

PETER. If you choose.

MARY MAGDALEN. Simon, mightiest of magicians, will you let me speak to the Holy Ghost for her?

SIMON. Do as you choose. If you can reach her whom the Invincible name cannot reach, I will say that there is no magician like you in the world. [*He crouches back*

MARY MAGDALEN. There is no magic, Simon; there is only exchange. [*She leans over* LUNA.] Luna, this is the veil that the Mother of Love sewed for me because her Son wished it, and because I was dead. Graveclothes for graveclothes. Luna, if our Lord wishes you to lie still, then lie on, but if not, then live. [*She throws the veil over* LUNA.] And declare the works of the Lord. And I will die for you or live for you in the Lord.

[*She covers her face*

LUNA. Mary!

MARY MAGDALEN [*dropping her hands*]. Rabboni!

LUNA [*springing up*]. Simon! [*He rises to catch her*

UNION. Are you free?

LUNA. There was a woman lying by me, and then both of us lived, both of us. [*She sees* MARY.] It is she. Sister!

MARY MAGDALEN. Sister! [*They catch each other's hands; then* MARY *breaks away and runs to* PETER.] Peter, it was he as he was in the garden and everything was alive. I was never alive before.

PETER. What do you say, Simon?

SIMON. I will not say anything now. There are semblances and apparitions and I will wait till I am sure this is true. But if it is, as I think it is, I will come back and find you out, and you shall teach me whatever you will. Come Luna.

LUNA. Sister. [MARY *and she embrace.*] May I keep this?

MARY MAGDALEN. My veil! O!

LUNA. I will give you a score of others for it!

MARY MAGDALEN. O but that ... No; I mean, yes, of course you may keep it. [*She looks longingly at it*

SIMON. Come. Farewell; if there is cause for gratitude, I shall pay in full.

PETER. You can never do that. No one can.

SIMON. No? Then I will be content to be a debtor.

[*They go out*

MARY MAGDALEN. O Peter, my veil! She has taken my beautiful veil! [*She bursts into tears*

PETER. But you offered her your life. Why are you crying when she has only taken your veil?[1] I do not understand you in the least!

MARY MAGDALEN. No. Our Mother will understand. I do not mind—no, really, Peter, I do not mind. It was only just at first. Please forgive me.[2]

PETER. You threw it over her, didn't you?

MARY MAGDALEN. Yes. It is all right indeed. [*She dries her eyes and begins to laugh.*] I wasn't quite ready.

---

[1] MARY MAGDALEN [*stamping her foot*]. O my *life*! What nonsense you talk, Peter, prince of the apostles though you are! And John has hardly seen me in it.

[2] MARY MAGDALEN. No. Our Mother will understand. I think our Lord is very severe. I do not mind—no, really, Peter, I do not mind. It was only just at first. Please forgive me.

TERROR OF LIGHT

PETER. I shall go in.
> [*He goes in to the house. A moment afterwards* SAUL *rushes in through the orchard*

SAUL. Where is John? Tell me, where is John?

MARY MAGDALEN. I do not know. Why do you want him?

SAUL. To get him away from the mischief that is going on here. I will have no more of it. I cannot get through the streets, they are so thick with people, all crushing here, all talking and shouting and the voices from the house—whose voice is it? Tell me, who is talking?

MARY MAGDALEN. Any of them or all of them. The twelve are always one; indeed I think all of us are one, but it is they chiefly who speak, and of them Peter.

SAUL. I do not know Peter. It shall not go on. I will rouse the Council against them. God of our fathers, why are our people tried thus? There is a single voice or many voices like one voice—it beats down on the street like a very wind; it is breaking the crowd into madness, and some of them are always near it, wild dwellers in the desert, lunatics from inmost Asia; and even the quietest men are aroused and staggering; and all the time the voice goes on. Were we brought out of the idolatries of Egypt and saved from the Greek Antiochus for this? It is always the same scream—God manifest, God manifest! Hawk-headed gods, beasts carved on walls; or the King Epiphanes, Ptolemy the Saviour, or whatever mad hero chooses to be a little deified; and now these, new tellers of an old tale, but this time flames and crowns of flame and winds and a shrieking tongue—he who died on a cross was a god! a god—that a Jew should say it![1]

---

[1] SAUL. I do not know Peter. It shall not go on. I will rouse the Council against them, but I will tell John first. God of our fathers, why are our people tried thus? There is a single voice or many voices like one voice—it beats down on the street like a fuming wind; . . .

MARY MAGDALEN. He did not—no! no! even Peter dared not say *that*.

SAUL [*taking no notice of her, but standing up as if in prayer*]. God, Almighty, Everlasting, Unchanging; God of Israel, save thy people! We have sinned and done evil, but hear thou in heaven thy dwelling-place and when thou hearest forgive. Thou art the only Exalted One; man cannot come near thee; thou art beyond flesh and blood and name and thought; thou art thyself only and there is none like thee. Thou turnest man to destruction; again thou sayest: *Come again, ye children of men.* Save thy people, save thine inheritance. Draw them from blasphemy and evil imagining, from the persuasions and inventions of sinful souls, from the idolatries of the Gentiles, and from the deceptions of false prophets. Blessed art thou, O God, and there is none like thee or second to thee in all the heavens and the earth. [*He turns to* MARY.] Go and fetch John.

MARY MAGDALEN. John is busy.

SAUL. Speaking or baptizing? Fetch him.

MARY MAGDALEN. I shall not. He will come when he wishes.

SAUL. Listen, you . . . vagrant. This sort of thing is not going on. I shall go myself to the Council and they will act. Then presently—tomorrow perhaps—I shall come with a guard and take everyone in this house. Because I have known John, I wish to tell him so; if he chooses to escape first he shall have that chance. Call him.

MARY MAGDALEN. I will not.

SAUL. Do you know what will happen?—What does happen to heretics? It will happen to John and to you. They will take you into a field—perhaps the field where your friend Judas died—and they will tie your feet and make you kneel down: perhaps, if you are very much afraid, you will fall quite flat. Then they will throw great stones on you. Stones. I have heard they did that to Judas too, but he was dead; you—and John—will be alive. The stones will fall on you, and break you, and crush you, and you will lie under them—probably not quite dead—until you do die. You will be in a great deal of pain—until you die. Your arms have been round many men: do you want to have them bruised and cracked and broken and crushed under the stones? Why do you let John bring you into such danger? Why do you bring him? Do you want to know that he is—

MARY MAGDALEN. Stop! Stop!

SAUL. We are Abraham's children: we must be honest. Almighty God has given us the Law to guard, and though I do not want to hurt anyone, yet as the Lord liveth I will do what I must. Go to John; save him; get him away.

MARY MAGDALEN. O do not be silly! Do you suppose John would come away for me?

SAUL. He is in love with you, I suppose.

MARY MAGDALEN. He is nothing of the sort! Do you know what has happened? Our Lord has happened; the Holy Spirit has happened. Do you suppose that John would betray them to save me?[1]

SAUL. He will do it if he loves you. But that is your business. Mine is to stamp this madness out. I shall do it, and I swear that if John is to die I will see that you die first. My God shall not be mocked while I am there to prevent it.

---

[1] MARY MAGDALEN. He is nothing of the sort! Do you know what has happened? Our Lord has happened; the Holy Spirit has happened. Do you suppose that John would betray them to save me? Saul, you may be a Rabbi and a learned man, but you do not know what a woman means to a man, and you never will. It is our worst grief and our very great joy. We should be completely happy if they were different, except that if they were different there would be nothing for us to love. John come away for me indeed!

MARY MAGDALEN [*laughing a little hysterically*]. It will be a bad day for your God when you are not.

[SAUL *leaps at her, as* THOMAS *enters*

THOMAS [*coming between them*]. What on earth is going on here?

MARY MAGDALEN [*recovering herself*]. It is all right, Thomas. This is a friend of John's—and of mine. He is trying to save us.

THOMAS [*a little coldly*]. I have heard of that kind of saviour before. They are quite common. Caiaphus is a little like it, and even Peter, my dear Mary, has a touch of it.

SAUL. Do not insult the High Priest.

THOMAS. I am not insulting him. I do not myself care for this crucifying and stoning and mutilating people to make them see the light. I think the true light—the light that is He—has a tendency to follow its own habits and not ours. But many great and good men disagree with me.

SAUL. It is proper that I should find an atheist here too!

THOMAS. I am not an atheist. I am, if anything, a limitation. I shall now permit myself to be a limitation. Has this gentleman any immediate business here?

MARY MAGDALEN. He is a friend of John's.

THOMAS. Really? He was about to strangle you on John's behalf?

MARY MAGDALEN. He would not have hurt me.

THOMAS. I shall see that he does not.

SAUL. Of course I should not have hurt her. This is not a private quarrel. The Council will crush you.

THOMAS. Well, if the Council is to crush us, we need not give you the trouble, need we?

SAUL. It is easy to sneer at what you do not believe!

THOMAS. Sneer is a harsh word. It is not so easy to be hot and cold at once, to be devoted and intelligent, to trust

God and keep your mind dry. But we do what we can. Please God the Holy Ghost will always let people like me hover between the dogmatists and their victims. Faith is a great danger and a great temptation; one can be more wholly oneself in the name of faith than in the name of anything else.

SAUL. Atheist! Prostitutes and atheists and drunkards—there are the disciples of Jesus.

THOMAS. I keep on repeating that I am *not* an atheist. Say lovers and logicians and the common people, and it sounds quite different. The truth lies between the two; I saw it to-day on the house-top, and why you called our lord a glutton and a wine-bibber. It is only a dead faith that is abusive.

SAUL. If I had a sword, I think I would kill you here and now.

THOMAS. O no, no. I have kept up my practice and I am probably better at the sword than you are. [*He unbelts his own.*] But I should not kill you, or even hurt you, unless you insisted on it; not before a lady, and not with any idea of being useful to the Holy Ghost. I could find it in my heart to love a little sword-play now, but I suppose it would not do. Sa ha, sa ha, for the scepticism of the Holy Ghost! Sa ha, sa ha, for the glorious intelligence of Love!

> [*He makes play with his sheathed sword, driving* SAUL *back*

SAUL. Put it down, you fool!

THOMAS. Protector of God, champion of faith, must the Holy Ghost be grateful to you for your defence of him?

SAUL. You will suffer for this!

THOMAS. I suspect your depth of passion; you may be one of us yet. Ambivalency and so on. When you are a disciple of Jesus—

SAUL. I a disciple!

THOMAS. —come to me, and say 'You were right, Thomas', as I know now that you are right. Then we will praise each other in the exchanges of heaven, and feed on each other in the substitutions of heaven. But I cannot do all the work alone. Scepticism is the need of faith, and faith of scepticism. Blessed and praised and hallowed be the Holy Ghost who is the entire compensation for himself! Meanwhile, this path will bring us to a gate in the wall. Sa ha! [*He forces him out*

MARY MAGDALEN. O Thomas . . .! The poor Saul! He has turned his back and is walking off. [*She begins to laugh.*] How dignified the back of faith looks!

JOHN [*coming in*]. Mary![1]

---

[1] The original version, given in the following footnotes, begins with the entrance of JOHN and continues to the entrance of MARY (p. 364).

JOHN [*coming in*]. Mary!

MARY MAGDALEN [*turning*]. John!

JOHN. How lovely to see you again!

MARY MAGDALEN. Have you missed me?

JOHN. No. But that makes it all the lovelier. Everything has turned over. We are all changed.

MARY MAGDALEN. You and I?

JOHN. A little. I never knew before how much I lived from you.

MARY MAGDALEN. I knew how I lived from you—ever since he went away. I knew it when I saw you in the light, among the creatures that were in the air; I almost saw him behind you, but you and he were exchanging yourselves; you were his substitute. O I see the words happening, but I cannot use them; I am a fool at words. John . . . it is so astonishing that you should be John.

JOHN. Not so astonishing as that you should be Mary.

MARY MAGDALEN. No?

JOHN. Yes then. I suppose it must be. I am in you and out of you at once. In the light one can be that, because one is nothing but in the light. I think I do not love you at all.

MARY MAGDALEN. I do love you. I must.

JOHN. Yet I cannot find any other word for it. If this is not love then there is something that is more love than love.

MARY MAGDALEN. John, my sweet! Love me like that.

JOHN. It happened when the fires took us. It is the fire in me that loves

TERROR OF LIGHT

MARY MAGDALEN [*turning*]. John! [*They look at each other gravely.*] Have you been looking for me?

JOHN. No. But it is wonderful to see you.

MARY MAGDALEN. John . . . it is so astonishing that you should be John.

JOHN. Not so astonishing as that you should be Mary.

MARY MAGDALEN. No?

JOHN. Yes then. I suppose it must be. We have known each other all this time; we have been together all this time; and it is only today that I have seen you—only since the light was in you and you in the light.

MARY MAGDALEN. He has exchanged us with each other. I have begun to live in him through you ever since that morning in the garden. After he had . . . gone you were the first thing I saw.

> you, and I because it drives me. It is unbelievable but it is so. Thomas would understand. Must I love everyone like that? and find eternity?
>
> MARY MAGDALEN. Perhaps. But I shall have been the first—yes? It will be lovely to have been the first.
>
> JOHN. Adorable glory, when it comes to eternity, I do not see how you can be even that. There will be no first or second there.
>
> MARY MAGDALEN. I shall know it happened so once—even in eternity. And I shall still be a little different. I shall be loved as myself, shall I not? You will love other people for themselves, the selves that the light loves. But you will have to love me for myself—even then.
>
> JOHN. Philosophically it is difficult to define selves in eternity. And, most adorable wonder, there is certainly no 'then' in eternity.
>
> MARY MAGDALEN. No? I shall never understand your . . . metaphysics, do you call them? There is a 'then' in everything I do understand. But I too saw something in the light, and I knew that all the thens were happy.
>
> JOHN. Are you sure of that?
>
> MARY MAGDALEN. Of course. Nothing can alter it—not even if they are unhappy. Is it he that is this?
>
> JOHN. It is this that is he. He must have come to so many like this. Did they know it? The Holy Ghost has taught us. Mary, Mary, make me love.
>
> MA·Y MAGDALEN. Love whom?
>
> *Note continued overleaf.*

JOHN. I had been very quick to run there, but you were there already. You were the first thing I saw after I had come out of the grave. Everything began to grow again, and everything was new. But you were the first.

MARY MAGDALEN. Do not say that. I am afraid of it. In the old days I always wanted to be the first. I am frightened of wanting it again.

JOHN. That is what we all wanted—to be the first. James and I asked for it and the Companions argued about it: and yet even then I think we knew it was foolish. In there—to-day—was there any first? I love you, but yet I do not love you at all.

MARY MAGDALEN. I have loved you ever since he vanished in the garden, and then—how long was it?—I saw you.

Note continued from previous page.

JOHN. Love. Is this what Peter meant when he quoted Joel, about the young men seeing visions? You are the vision, the vision of the City of God. You are to be loved because he loves you—and everyone is to be loved because he loves them. But I cannot do that yet. Mary, do you know how difficult it will be? It is much easier to love you because I love you.

MARY MAGDALEN. It would be much more delightful, I think—for a long time anyhow, perhaps for all our lives. It is all very well for you, dearest John; you do at least understand what you mean, but I—if it were not that you are so like him now I do not think I could bear it. You will be happy because you are loving me for God's sake. But I—I do not altogether want to be loved for God's sake.

JOHN. No?

MARY MAGDALEN. No. But I think it is right for you: to do it that way, and to know it, and to teach it. And I will do what I can. And you must never alter for me.

JOHN. Mary, there are moments when I suspect that you are being what I am talking about. I can see that I must love only because God loves; but you love as God loves. You love the plain simple thing that is there. O Augustitudeo, pray for me.

MARY MAGDALEN. Dearest, pray for me. Look, the Mother of Love is coming.

MARY *comes in*

JOHN. I cannot find any other word. If we do not call this love, we must call it something that is more love than love. But is very unlike all we mean by love.

MARY MAGDALEN. Love me like *that*! Oh, today I saw you when It came—among all the living creatures that were in the air. I all but saw him, but I did not; only I think I saw you instead. He will have it so.

JOHN. We are the witness to each other of the passage into life. Your face is the vision of the passage into life. It is unbelievable, but it is so. Thomas would understand.

MARY MAGDALEN. Thomas understands a great deal.

JOHN. Must I love everyone like this? And find eternity?

MARY MAGDALEN. Perhaps. We will try. But we shall have been the first to each other—yes? It will be lovely to have been the first.

JOHN. Adorable glory, when it comes to eternity, I do not see how you can be even that. There will be no first or second there.

MARY MAGDALEN. We shall know it happened so once— even in eternity, and we shall be a little different. I shall be loved as myself, shall I not? You will love other people for themselves, the selves that the light loves. But you will have to love me for myself—even then.

JOHN. Philosophically it is difficult to define selves in eternity. And, most adorable wonder, there is certainly no 'then' in eternity.

MARY MAGDALEN. No? I shall never understand your . . . metaphysics? There is a 'then' in everything I do understand. But I too saw something in the light and I know that all the 'thens' are happy.

JOHN. Are you sure of that?

MARY MAGDALEN. Of course. Nothing can alter it—not even if they are unhappy. Is it He that is this?

JOHN. It is this that is He. He lights everyone that comes

into the world. Did they know it? The Holy Ghost has taught us. Mary, Mary, make me love.

MARY MAGDALEN. Love whom?

JOHN. Love. Is this what Peter meant when he quoted Joel, about the young men seeing visions? You are the vision, the vision of the city of God. You are to be loved because He loves you—and everyone is to be loved because He loves them. But I cannot do that yet. Mary, do you know how difficult it will be?

MARY MAGDALEN. Oh, John, even now, even in Him, even with you, I am frightened of it. It is all very well for you, dearest John; you do at least understand what you mean, but I—if it were not that His Glory is in you now, I do not think I could bear it. You will be happy because you are loving me for God's sake. But I—Oh, I—still do not want to be loved for God's sake.

JOHN. No?

MARY MAGDALEN. No. But it is right; you must do it, and know it, and teach it. And I will do what I can. And you must never alter for me: you must keep me to it always. It is the only way of love.

JOHN. Mary, there are moments when I suspect that you are being what I am talking about. I can understand that I must love only because God loves, but you love as God loves. You love the plain simple thing that is there. Oh Augustitude pray for me.

MARY MAGDALEN. Dearest Apostle, pray for me. Look . . .

MARY *comes in*

JOHN. Madonna! [*They recede from her*

MARY. Perseverant, perseverant, is the Nature of God. The heavens are doubled and reflect each other; blessed are they who know it, blessed who see the mark of the other, who love the other, who rejoice in the other. Blessed is each in another. I have seen Iscariot.

JOHN. Iscariot, Madonna!

MARY MAGDALEN. Hush: I will tell you presently.

MARY. I saw him among the trees, an apparition of the dead among growths of the living. I came down from the roof and he was moving among the trees of the orchard. He came to my lord along the path of a garden among the fires of the torches in the moon, and I came to him at the will of my lord among the fires of my lord in the light of the Spirit. At the moment when he obeyed the voice of the Companions and of the Church which is more than the Companions—at that moment my lord exposed us to each other—

JOHN. He obeyed?

MARY MAGDALEN. He did obey!

MARY. He repented and threw away the silver; he chose as he could among the impossibles. You, children, can you love?[1]

MARY MAGDALEN. Yes, mother.
JOHN. Yes, madonna.

MARY. Be happy. Judas shall be like you; I saw him too in the way of the Spirit. My lord's mercy is more almost than we can bear, but Judas shall bear it. He shall love another; he shall love Matthias.

JOHN [*as it breaks on him*]. Heavenly richness!

MARY. Judas has betrayed my Son and his own place; very well—his place shall be given to Matthias. Matthias shall be a substitute for Judas; very well,—but Judas shall be glad of substitution and love it, and in degree as he

---

[1] MARY. He repented and threw away the silver; he chose as he could among the impossibles; and my Son tore him from the tree he was to hang on, and he chose again as he fell, and he obeyed Peter. He had yearned to choose another way; my lord brought him into the way of another. You, children, can you love?

loves it where can he be but in the substitution? Miracle of healing! His exclusion shall become his inclusion. Blessed and blessed and blessed for ever be the mystery of the life of my lord. I have spoken to Iscariot; now I have nothing more to do.[1]

JOHN. Nothing more?

MARY MAGDALEN. Nothing? O mother!

[*They recede further*

MARY. Nothing. Our lord the Spirit secluded himself till to-day in this flesh, but now he has given himself in a thousand places, and there is, I think, no need of me here. The glory has issued out of Themselves—

JOHN. Themselves?

MARY. Themselves who are He; and you shall go out with it—where you choose, or where you are commanded. But I shall go inward, to be secluded in the kingdom. Spirit outward through flesh and flesh inward through spirit . . . Call Peter.[2]

[MARY MAGDALEN *runs into the house*

JOHN. Must I lose my charge, madonna?

MARY. If I were to be of much use to you, John, I would

---

[1] MARY. They shall run a double course in each other for ever. They shall burn opposite Peter like a double star. Judas has betrayed my Son and his own place; very well—his place shall be given to Matthias. Matthias shall be a substitute for Judas; very well—but Judas shall be glad of substitution and love it, and in degree as he loves it where can he be but in the substitution? Miracle of healing! His exclusion shall become his inclusion; he shall be carried back again by the wind that drove him away. Neither shall be secure without the other; the rest of the Companions shall see the glowing mystery of the Spirit. Blessed and blessed and blessed for ever be the mystery of the life of my lord. I have spoken to Iscariot; now I have nothing more to do.

[2] MARY. Themselves who are He; and you shall go out with it—where you choose, or where you are commanded. But I shall go inward, to be secluded in the kingdom. Spirit outward through flesh and flesh inward through spirit—double courses of heaven, blessed in all the universes. . . . Call Peter.

stay—if my Son permitted. But I should not be—not now.

JOHN. I guessed it to-day—when I saw all the tongues of fire and not one on you. I knew then that the light had always been intertwined with your body, but we had not seen it; and that the wind of the Spirit had been in your voice, but we had never heard it. Nor could we. And now when we can, when we can see and hear, you will go!

MARY [*smiling at him*]. Suffer it be so now, for thus—

JOHN [*smiling back*]. —it becomes us to fulfil all righteousness. It does.

MARY. Besides, you see it elsewhere, do you not? You may have to teach other people to see it—or to reassure them that they do see it.[1]

PETER *comes in*

PETER. Lady, you sent for me?

MARY. Yes, Peter. I am dying.

PETER. Dying! But, lady, you must not . . .

MARY. Yes, Peter. Were you going to tell me that I must not die?

PETER [*conquering his intention*]. No. But—what will the Companions of your Son do? and the whole Church?

MARY. The Companions will direct the Church and each other. Do not forget that they are all directed in and through each other. And if there is anything that they cannot direct, let them be humble about it—and especially, dear Peter, you yourself.

PETER. Yes. I am a common man, mother. I am not a saint like John nor an intellectual like Thomas . . .

---

[1] MARY. Besides you see it elsewhere, do you not? You may have to teach other people to see it—or to reassure them that they do see it; you have much to do—you and Mary.

MARY. No. I do not see that that is anything to be proud of, or particularly pleased about—except in God.

PETER. Proud! pleased!

MARY. Dear Peter, you must try and endure the saints and the intellectuals. It would never do for the Church to be left to them, and my Son has directed them to their proper place.[1] But do not you forget their place. You and all the common men will, no doubt, praise them; but see that you do not pervert them. You are the better image of all the relationships, but I would not have you know it too much.

THOMAS returns; JOHN checks him

PETER. I will not.

MARY. Your children will despise Thomas and admire John and be as far from either as from you. The City can only be built on all the foundations. Thomas!

THOMAS. Lady! [*He goes to her*

MARY. You and I have been twins in the Spirit, Thomas. I asked a question of the archangel, and you would not believe for the mere noise of many voices. It is true you should have understood my Son better, but the Companions are not in a position to blame you for that. Without you there can be no peace in the Church, nor any proper scope of goodwill. I leave you my question: How shall these things be? That is your vocation: be blessed.

THOMAS. I am the least of your servants, lordliness.

MARY. I do not know where you will go, when the Companions begin their journeys. India, perhaps—you will have enough work there, my brother in scepticism. But

---

[1] MARY. Dear Peter, you must try and endure the saints and the intellectuals. It would never do for the Church to be left to them, and my Son has put them in their place. But do not forget their place. You and all the common men. . . .

the school of your followers will have even harder work within the Church. You and John. Love each other; love each other: when Thomas and John are divided, the Church wanders.

JOHN. Never, Thomas; wherever we go.

THOMAS. Never, John, though we are separated.

MARY. You and you. [*To* JOHN *and* MARY MAGDALEN.] You and Mary. [*To* THOMAS.] You and Peter. Peter and I. All of us[1] and He.

PETER. Tell us more of that which came to us on the roof.

MARY. It was that which lay first on the waters and moved, and there was light; and lay entwined in my body and moved, and there was my son; and lay about you, the Companions, and moved and there was the Church. Joyful and sorrowful and glorious are the children of His love. Light on the waters, light in the body, light in the Church. O my Son is waiting; he is waiting. I am keeping him too long. I must go in.

MARY MAGDALEN. Mother!

MARY. Dearest! Where is your veil?

MARY MAGDALEN. You know. You know how it had to be given to the woman who was the companion of Simon the Magus; and she has it.

MARY. Yes. My lord never leaves anything with us for very long,—and yet for ever. Well . . . John must buy you another before you go.

PETER. But where shall we go?

MARY. Rome, I think, for you, Peter. There is something about both Rome and you that would suit each other. But for the rest—do I know? Only let each keep his own witness; no one can witness for another till the great

---

[1] MARY. You and you. [*To* JOHN *and* MARY MAGDALEN.] You and Mary. [*To* THOMAS.] You and Peter. Peter and I. All of us. O he is waiting; he is waiting. I am keeping him too long. I must go in.

substitutions are known. It was said that the light is the calling, and the calling is the light; there is one light and many callings. Go, go!

PETER. We will go.

MARY. Babylon and Bactria and the islands of Thule; to the little men in the jungles and to the myths beyond the sources of the Nile; to all the pulses of all the peoples. I must go: he is waiting. Come with me as far as my Lord allows.

JOHN. Mother of our Lord, leave a blessing to the world.

MARY. Son of my body, have mercy upon the body of the world.

ALL THE COMPANIONS. Alleluia!

MARY. Let us go. [MARY *and* JOHN *support her.*] Blessed be God . . .

ALL THE COMPANIONS [*murmuring*]. Blessed be God.

MARY. . . . to whom be ascribed, as is most justly due—
    [*Her voice stops suddenly.* JOHN *looks at her and looks up at* PETER

PETER AND ALL. All might, majesty, dominion, and power, now and for evermore.

THE THREE TEMPTATIONS

A Play for Broadcasting

CHARACTERS

PILATE
CAIAPHAS
HEROD
JOHN THE BAPTIST
THE VOICE OF CHRIST
THE EVIL ONE
JUDAS
CLAUDIA
Chorus

THE THREE TEMPTATIONS

The voices of three men and a woman talking

FIRST MAN. But what then is to-morrow?

SECOND MAN. To-day is the Feast of All Saints; to-morrow is the Commemoration of All Souls. Some take it to mean all Christian souls, but I think rather all those who have ever lived or will ever live.

THIRD MAN. Or died or ever will die. It's the same thing.

THE WOMAN. One gets older so quickly, and what has one done with all the time there was? There seems so little left.

THIRD MAN. Hardly time enough to be comfortable. When the war is over I am determined to be comfortable.

FIRST MAN. Can one?

SECOND MAN. Perhaps. But you must take care not to believe anything. Belief and comfort do not go together.

THE WOMAN. Tell me, do love and comfort go together?

THIRD MAN. Rarely, and not for very long. Love—proper *love*—is too harsh for comfort.

SECOND MAN. Yes; it is like peace.

FIRST MAN. Is peace so uncomfortable?

SECOND MAN. Even the peace of man is terrible. When we talk about peace we forget how terribly we shall have to work for it. As for the peace of God—

THE WOMAN. That may be as hard, but then if we worked for that we might find both.

FIRST MAN. I thought you Christians believed that Jesus came to give you peace.

THIRD MAN. And a sword.

THE WOMAN. That was what his mother knew—the peace in her heart which pierced like a sword.

SECOND MAN. That is his peace; there is another kind. He himself was tempted three times to take it. Each temptation, when he refused it, became his enemy.

THIRD MAN. He and they could not live together. The three lords who slew him—Caiaphas, Pilate, and Herod—all refused his peace. They were very sensible; it is a great thing to know which side one is on.

THE WOMAN. But there was a woman, Pilate's wife, she who dreamed, perhaps she knew it. Mary Magdalen knew it; his mother knew it. O Mother of God, pray for us!

FIRST MAN. Perhaps Judas Iscariot knew it, and was afraid of it.

SECOND MAN. Perhaps, if we had been in Jerusalem, we should have known it. . . .

THIRD MAN. If we had been in Jerusalem, we should have hated it. . . .

THE WOMAN. If we had been—if we had been in Jerusalem. . . .

[*The voices die away. In a moment there is a great noise, out of which they rise again*

FIRST MAN. The Roman soldiers have barred the street; look!

THE WOMAN. What are those other spears?

SECOND MAN. King Herod's guard.

THIRD MAN. Look, there in his litter is the king himself.

THE WOMAN. They are chanting somewhere.

SECOND MAN. The Jewish Sanhedrin is coming—some at least; and there is the high priest Caiaphas.

FIRST MAN. He and the king have gone into Pilate's palace, and the soldiers have made a screen before the gate. What does it mean?

THIRD MAN. Wait, and perhaps you'll know and perhaps you won't.

THE THREE TEMPTATIONS

SECOND MAN. Pilate has called them to council.
FIRST MAN. But why?
SECOND MAN. What cry has gone through the land
but the news of John, the new prophet by Jordan?
THE WOMAN. My father was once in Cairo and saw a prophet.
He sat on a stone alone and talked magic.
Presently he grew feathers all over him, and changed
into a vulture, and away he flew to Sahara.
THIRD MAN. Your father! This is not that kind of prophet.
I cannot find he has been anything like as amusing.
FIRST MAN. Yet I have a mind to go out and hear him.
SECOND MAN. If you can get near! But if you will go, so will I.
THIRD MAN. Pooh! it is only a cash profit that matters.
THE WOMAN. I should like to go—
THIRD MAN. Do not be a fool!
SECOND MAN. Come, let us go together—
THIRD MAN. No! it will be tedious.
FIRST MAN. But worth saying we have been—
    [*A hubbub of voices; it stops. After a pause*
PILATE. I have invited you here, my lord Herod,
and you, my lord Caiaphas, that we three
may talk over this affair. This country of yours
endures, more than any other I have known,
shocks of restlessness. The crowd flocks to hear
any peddler of promises for the future. Now, when the
wars—thanks to the divine Caesar—are done,
I had looked for a time of quiet. Do I find it? no;
I feel a long tide of trouble stirring under us.
CAIAPHAS. It is true, there are tiresome rumours and strange humours

everywhere; men talking in corners; sometimes
a shout, or stones flung. What it is about
no one seems to know, but the peril is there.
PILATE. Do you hear of the new teacher out by Jordan,
a mad preacher from the desert? It is said he declares
that a king or a kingdom is coming soon.
HEROD.   Whose?
PILATE. It is officially reported to me that he spoke
of the kingdom of heaven—
HEROD.   O only that!
He is probably one of the eccentric friends of Caiaphas.
CAIAPHAS. What, Herod, do you mean by my friends?
HEROD. Well . . . heaven, and so on. It is—is it not?—
rather in your line? I had always supposed
that the clergy kept the design in their priestly pocket.
CAIAPHAS. The God of Abraham—
PILATE.   If you will permit me, gentlemen.
This enthusiast is becoming popular; crowds
are pouring out fast from all the towns.
Ought we to take action? I do not wish
to interfere unwisely and provoke revolt,
but I cannot afford to let a new cult
grow up in the city. Duty—
HEROD.   Duty!
We are private; let us be truthful; we are afraid.
Any crisis is, for us, a mistake.
You, Pilate, know how you dread Caesar—
the public petition or the private letter (in the street
a few too many dead, or in the hills
a rebellion spread)—and where is your office and power?
Gone—so!
PILATE. Well—and so? have you
no fear for your houses, your pleasant gardens,
your clothes and dishes and carved chairs?

HEROD.   Yes,
  of course. I said so. I am afraid for my wealth,
  and you are as much afraid for your reputation.
CAIAPHAS. I only then am without fear.
  Your enjoyment of security may disappear,
  but my calm habit of belief lasts—
  blessed be God—and save me from grief everywhere.
  He has settled my way, and day by day I take it.
HEROD. Pooh, you are as much afraid as we;
  only you were so made as to take refuge
  in religion, as we do in money or fame.
CAIAPHAS. I afraid? what do you mean?
HEROD.   What I say.
  Your soul has fallen in a coma which you call peace;
  poor stuff for religion to thrive on. You alive?
  You faithful? If God showed you a new
  sanctity, called you to a new gain in spirit,
  would you welcome those throes, that pain? Smile,
    brother.
  You think you have come to terms with God; now
  if he withdrew that comfort, if some new
  abandonment, trifling in itself, terrible to you,
  were offered—
CAIAPHAS. Are you talking of the strange prophet?
  Could *he* frighten *me*?
HEROD.   He does frighten you.
  Your soul shakes like a bird in a trap.
PILATE.   Enough.
  Do not press the priest outside his pulpit.
  Let us agree, both my lords and brothers,
  we are all three afraid. What shall we do?
HEROD. That is it; that is the very word.
PILATE. What is? What delights you so?
CAIAPHAS. He thinks he sights a solution.

HEROD.   I do; I do.
  We agree we want to know if this maniac of Jordan
  is dangerous, if his kingdom is a fable or a truth.
  Send we all three messengers, to ask:
  'What do we do? Friend, what do we do?'
  If his answer is vain vapour, leave him;
  if he utters any kind of definite command,
  he is dangerous; destroy.
PILATE. And supposing he only says
  what Caiaphas, if we asked *him*, would say—
CAIAPHAS. Pilate!
PILATE. —or would think he ought to say—believe,
  pray, obey God?
HEROD.   If our messengers
  delay with him, or come back converted
  or even scared—though I do not think mine will be scared—
  I shall say again *kill, destroy*.
                                          A voice
  prophetically singing, bringing a call to rejoice
  in the high hard way to a common good
  should be choked in the prophet's own blood. Kill—
  unless indeed you want the kingdom of God.
  I do not; I confess I prefer my comfort.
  Is it agreed?
PILATE.   It is; let us choose messengers.
  A soldier or two for me.
HEROD.   For me a few
  of those crafty old tax-collectors.
CAIAPHAS.   And for me
  two or three of my priestly brethren will go.
HEROD. So. And then we shall see. No kingdom
  —whatever it may be—ever comes unless men act.
  That we must stop. Brothers, for the present, good-bye.

THE THREE TEMPTATIONS

If this trouble should last or another should rise—
worse, perhaps; who knows?—we will again meet.
Vain is the kingdom of God against our power;
most men prefer our life to strife for the kingdom.
Good-bye.
CAIAPHAS. Herod!
HEROD. What is it?
CAIAPHAS. Only suppose
this prophet bade you send back your brother's wife!
HEROD. That undoubtedly would interfere with my comfort:
with any luck I should stop it, and I think somehow
I should certainly have the luck. Good-bye.
      [*A pause: the voices of the crowd swell again; then
      the voice of St. John the Baptist*
ST. JOHN. Repent; the kingdom is at hand.
    Repent; the kingdom is at hand.
      Repent; the kingdom is at hand.
FIRST MAN. Tell us more.
SECOND MAN. What *is* the kingdom?
THIRD MAN. Who are *you*?
ST. JOHN. I am a voice in the wilderness;
Prepare the way, make straight the path, for the Lord.
THE VOICES. What way?
    what path?
      what Lord?
ST. JOHN. Love and wrath; he that comes quickly.
Repent, repent! where is charity, where
is meekness? they fled to the desert air;
they sit alone with locusts on a stone,
and the wild honey holds them. There comes one
who springs as a locust, who speaks as honey;
he descends on palace, praetorium, and temple.
Repent! the kingdom of heaven is at hand.

THE THREE TEMPTATIONS

The axe is ready at the roots of each tree
whose fruits are wanting, justice and charity wanting;
but the crooked shall be made straight and the rough smooth,
and all flesh shall see the salvation of God.
Repent, believe; the kingdom of God comes.   [*Voices*

A PRIEST. You, get out of my way. I am a priest
sent to speak with the Prophet.

A TAX-GATHERER.   By your leave,
good people. I am a collector of taxes
come to speak with the Prophet.

A SOLDIER.   Shift there!
in the name of Caesar. I am Caesar's centurion.
Hey there, you, prophet, mountebank!
If I wanted this kingdom of yours, what should I do?

ST. JOHN. Do violence to none; be content with your pay.
Make straight the way of justice, the path of the Lord.
Love and wrath are at hand; repent, repent!

THE TAX-GATHERER. But pray, sir, I, a poor collector
of taxes, if I desired the kingdom,
what should I do?

ST. JOHN.   Be content; cheat none;
speak truthfully; praise and follow charity.
from all to all; let him with two coats
give to him that hath none; all live by all;
therefore let all give what they may to all.
Make straight the way for the love and the wrath to come!

A PRIEST. What shall I do then, I a priest?

ST. JOHN. O generation of vipers, who, who
hath warned you of the wrath? Away, repent!
The kingdom of God is at hand; repent, repent.

THE PRIEST. Blasphemy, blasphemy! Israel-in-the-Temple,
and the comfort of Israel, is the only kingdom: away!

THE TAX-GATHERER. A comfortable house is better than any
 kingdom: away!
THE SOLDIER. Caesar is the only giver of kingdoms.
 Away!
THE CROWD. Tell us more, Prophet!
                              tell us how
 the kingdom will come.
                    Will Pilate's palace fall
 in an earthquake?
                  Or will our own King Solomon call
 on the spirits of the air and shut Herod in a pot?
 Will those who have repented squat on new cushions?
 Will the Gentiles be made the slaves of those who believe?
 Will those who receive the new king be viceroys?
 Will the Glory of God shine suddenly out of heaven
 and affright all our enemies with a bright light?
 Or will nothing at all ever happen anywhere?
FIRST MAN. Who is that man?
SECOND MAN.   Who? where?
FIRST MAN. He there, with hair of hazel-colour;
 He who is going to the Prophet.
THIRD MAN.   Beyond the crowd
 he is come on the Prophet's level; there,
 look at them both!
FIRST MAN.   Look, the Prophet stops
 in his cry; he drops his arm and bends his head.
 I am afraid.
SECOND MAN.   I am afraid.
THIRD MAN.   I am afraid.
ST. JOHN. Behold the Lamb of God!
THE VOICE OF CHRIST.   My lord, bless me
 and baptize me.
ST. JOHN. I—bless? baptize?
 I am not worthy to loose the shoe's latchet

of any just man—you are no just man.
What you are is terrible both to the just and unjust.
I—baptize *you*?

CHRIST.   Let it be so now.
The gospel of justice is yours, and you mine,
and you and all just men may dine in my kingdom,
and the greater must always be blessed and baptized by
   the lesser.
This is the ceremony of the necessary kingdom; thus
It becomes Us to fulfil all righteousness.
Bless me, my son.

ST. JOHN.   I bless you then for being;
I bless you for being with the benediction of praise,
necessary being with necessary benediction.
Have mercy upon me, my Lord, and come to the river.
                [*Confused voices and the sound of thunder*

THE VOICES. What are they doing?

                                It is his familiar spirit.
No; it is the king in his kingdom.

                                  It is his lieutenant.
He is putting spells on him!

                          In running water?
No spell can stand against running water.
Hush, the Prophet spoke.

                          It was not his voice:
it was above us;
            it was out of the air;
                        it was heaven.
Whatever it was, what did it say?
                          It said
This is my Son.
        Look, look, there!
The light is too bright.
                   Something is moving in the light.

THE THREE TEMPTATIONS

Flying.
        Flying down on the new Prophet.
An angel!
      No; a fiery dove.
                    Get back;
it may do us some harm; get back.
                          Get out of my way.
I cannot see.
        There is nothing at all to see;
only a man walking away to the wilderness.
How fast he is going but how quietly!
                            It is all over.
ST. JOHN. Repent and prepare! the kingdom is at hand.
                                  [*A pause*
CHRIST. Father, glorify thy Son.
My glory was in thee before the worlds were,
and now I am come here to manifest thy glory;
I am come to begin the work thou gavest me to do,
and to bring to thee thine own.
                         Glorify thy Son
as thy Son glorifies thee; as we are one
let all thou hast given me be one in our love.
Father, glorify thy Son.
I have seen Satan as lightning fall from heaven;
he and the world do not know thee, but I—
I know thee, Father, and those who are mine
know; thine are mine and mine are thine,
and my work is begun; the glory thou gavest me
I have given to them, that they may be as we.
Father, glorify thy Son.
The work must be; that they may be as we
The Son of Man must go to the desert and the cross
and the loss of thee. Father, I must unknow
thee and myself, that the others may know thee.

THE THREE TEMPTATIONS

    Now is the hour when the sin's power begins
    to undo me, but I declare thy Name
    and shall declare it. Father, glorify thy Son.
THE EVIL ONE. Sir, it is a cold night. I may make bold
    to ask you—have you no shelter or food?
    not even the prophet's locusts and wild honey?
    Money is a poor thing the saints despise
    and rise above, but, Sir, it is good
    to use our proper power for our proper comfort
    and some small comfort is needful for every heart.
    We masters of a magical art can be
    fed by ourselves; turn these stones to bread.
    It is certain you could do so with very little trouble,
    or I for you, if you would but ask.
CHRIST. It is written that man does not live by bread alone,
    but by every word that proceeds from God.
THE EVIL ONE.   Sir,
    that is wisely said, and yet our needs must be
    provided for as wisely; now some comfort
    may make you the stronger to-morrow to preach longer.
    It may not be the comfort King Herod has,
    but I hope you have as much right as he
    to your own; think now a little of yourself.
    What you need, you and I could bring to pass
    easily, do but lose a few moments' prayer.
    Indeed, if you choose, I can offer you greater things.
CHRIST. This is your hour; whatever you think is yours
    propose and proffer, if *you* choose, while it endures.
    Afterwards I will deal with the offer as I choose.
THE EVIL ONE. Sir, since you talk with so easy a grace,
    bear that I show you, from a high place of spirit,
    such as becomes me and all my folk,
    with what I could well requite kind worship,
    which is my right everywhere in this world.

THE THREE TEMPTATIONS

Feel now, Sir, how I fill your mind
with the thrust and thunder and wonder of great thrones.
Look, in Britain and Gaul and all Asia
are those that are piled under Caesar; and now feel
what it were to be Caesar and have kings kneel.
And beyond Caesar (even Caesar is not all)
lie the imperial majesties of Persia and China,
strange outrageous marvels. To have these
all in one, and alone, is the glory I give.
None can take it from my hand; stand and see—
Sir, it were all yours, did you worship me.
Conceive now, in what comfort of great fame—
much more than poor Pilate's miserable reputation—
might you not abide, and your name glorified for ever.
CHRIST. It is written: ye shall worship only the Lord your God,
and him only serve.
THE EVIL ONE.   Are you not wise!
Comfort of flesh and comfort of grand spirit—
gust of bread and bold glory—these
you refuse easily; and these pass, it is true,
when a man dies, or indeed before. Sir,
I see you were made one of the true masters:
Those who are stayed, beyond all disasters,
on the comfort of safe religion. You have compounded
with God to belong to you, and bid him rid
trouble away. He gives his angels charge
over all such, and they with a soft touch
upbear them and spare them pain or heart's danger.
Your faith comforts you much, does it not
Why, if from this his temple's pinnacle
this glory of faith, you flung yourself down,
he would save you from bruising your mere foot on a stone.

THE THREE TEMPTATIONS

He who holds the throne of the whole universe
will always help in the nick of time, will he not?
Take that trick of comfort now, in God's name.

CHRIST. It is written: Thou shalt not tempt the Lord thy
God.

THE EVIL ONE. Why, it is no more than Caiaphas promises
his people; you ask only safety and peace
after a spiritual kind; it was sworn so.

CHRIST. Caiaphas answers for his deeds, and I for mine.

THE EVIL ONE. But somehow, somewhere, there is some
comfort you want
to grant your disciples at least, if not you.

CHRIST. I will send my own Comforter one day to my
own.

THE EVIL ONE. Nay then you will be—will you?—exempt
from every stress of world's joy: have it or have it not,
it is all the same to you. Sir, you shall!
O indeed, Sir, so you shall!
A little new interval, a year or two,
and I will try you with exemption from comfort indeed.
Your drink vinegar, your bed cruel wood,
your fame a criminal's—an obscene lost thing;
and if then you mean to take comfort in God—
no, even there you shall grow lost and obscene,
seen by yourself as the sin worse than any
you shall seem to yourself to have done all I will
and had, more than all men together, skill in iniquity.
Disciples?—you! I will despoil your toil
of all disciples! they shall set you on a soft seat
high-riding and kingly, and cry *Hosanna*—
all three comforts just there!
and then you thrust down, and they
opening a new day with *Crucify*. Hark—
I will put an end to you!—hark, do you hear?

THE THREE TEMPTATIONS

THE VOICES. Hosanna!
>Hosanna!
>>Hosanna!

PILATE. Herod and Caiaphas, my brothers, come immediately.

>This is a worse noise; what is this?

CAIAPHAS. This is a worse prophet than John.

HEROD.   Much worse.
>John taught share and share alike,
>a just price and equality of sacrifice;
>made our thrones brittle, but he was little
>to this man, who will not spare us even with a share
>of our hearts' comfortable loves; this man talks
>of himself and complete surrender and total loss,
>of the cross for all men and all men on the cross.
>This is total ruin: what shall we do?

CAIAPHAS. I have acted already.

HEROD.   O excellent Caiaphas!
>Show me anywhere a man who is spiritually scared
>and I will show you one who has dared everything.
>He must act; he cannot wait. What have you done?

CAIAPHAS. I have fetched you a man here out of this crowd,
>Who stretched his ears after Jesus awhile,
>and stopped them presently.

PILATE. Why?

HEROD.   Fear—and greed.
>Like us. Am I right?

CAIAPHAS.   Near enough. Have him in.

PILATE. Ho, you! bring in the fellow in the waiting-room.

HEROD. Is that he on the stair? Poor wretch!
>Why, he looks there like any foreman or clerk
>in my storehouse or in your office, Pilate,
>or a smug Levite. Everyman! Everyman, I swear!

CAIAPHAS. He is not Everyman; his name is Judas Iscariot.

HEROD. Everyman, all the same; let him enter.
　He is the one centre we all work on—
　Everyman hoping that God will leave him alone
　with Caiaphas, and that either Pilate or I will lean
　down from a throne to give him some security.
　Everyman hurrying to betray the voice he heard.
CAIAPHAS. Do not talk nonsense, Herod. Judas Iscariot,
　you have been with Jesus of Nazareth, have you not?
JUDAS. My lord, for a little while.
CAIAPHAS. 　　　　　　　　　You grew afraid
　of his teaching?
JUDAS. 　　　　Yes, my lord.
CAIAPHAS. 　　　　　　　　　You made a proposal.
　We now prepare to accept the proposal
　if you, for your part, dare carry it out,
　to give up Jesus into our hands.
　　　　　　　　　　　　Your demands were also—
JUDAS. O no demands, my lord!
　I only hoped for a little show of goodwill
　and a quiet future.
CAIAPHAS. 　　　　　You can give yourself quiet
　if you stop walking with Jesus and talking of a kingdom.
　There is no necessity for people like you to be saints.
JUDAS. No, my lord; on the whole I thought not.
CAIAPHAS. Be content with a reasonable piety. As for reward—
　I will give you a comfortable place at the Temple services,
　and ten silver pieces. These gentlemen
　of their grace will each give you as much more.
HEROD. Economizing fellows you priests are! Listen
　Iscariot: I am King Herod; I will give you
　ten pieces, and a comfortable house in Galilee
　with a slave or two—girls, if you prefer.

THE THREE TEMPTATIONS

PILATE. Iscariot, I am Pilate. I will give you
ten pieces and a comfortable title—to be
a Roman citizen in the next degree of the kind.

JUDAS. O my lords, you are generous. It is not, indeed,
that I hate the man Jesus or am against reforms.
But we must wait God's kingdom in a peaceable style
and a moderate goodwill; is not that a better way?

CAIAPHAS. Much.

PILATE. Much.

HEROD. Much—and the goodwill
will after a time moderate still more.
My lord High Priest will tell you that in a while
when you have chosen warily once or twice
God ceases altogether to trouble you with new choices.
He speaks from experience.

CAIAPHAS. Herod!

HEROD. My dear Caiaphas,
we all depend on Everyman. Why shouldn't Everyman
have his place in damnation as well as we?
If you think it damnation. I do,
and prefer it. You do—and pretend it's faith.
Pilate does, and he pretends it's duty.
Judas Iscariot is of the same flesh as we,
and prefers the quiet temporary comfort of damnation
to the crucifixion of glory: don't you, Judas?

JUDAS. My lord, I . . . damnation, my lord? . . . I hope
I am only thinking of what's best for everyone.

HEROD. Pleasing phrase! There, I am teasing you. Good-bye,
but deliver the body of Jesus into our hands.

PILATE. Deliver the body of Jesus into our hands.

CAIAPHAS. A guard will be sent with you to receive his body.
It is he or you now, you understand.
Go. [*A door shuts*
Why, Herod, do you talk so?

HEROD. Because I wish us all to know the worst.
   The temptation, and the fall—and we curst for ever—
   is here for us, and for Judas surnamed Everyman.
   We yield, as does he, and all the world.
   Let the Kingdom perish, if we may cherish our comfort.
   Well—I am Herod. I will know what I do,
   rue it though I may—but you, you refuse to know,
   hypocrites of the State and the Church! fools both!
CAIAPHAS. Your eyes are burning!
PILATE.   You are out of your mind!
HEROD.   No.
   Too deep within. My mind sees too well
   the shape we cannot conquer and cannot escape,
   the dreadful inevitable kingdom. Judas Everyman
   is going, is hurrying, is running—how running!—
   with all his greed and fear running with him,
   armed images of himself scurrying along
   there, out there! Share and share alike
   was John Baptist's cry; he is dead; and I
   killed him, but this other horror of abandonment,
   this mortal shape that awaits Everyman
   beyond the gates of his neat comfortable heart—
CAIAPHAS. Enough, Herod: let us speak plausibly.
   The kingdom of God—
HEROD.   What will the kingdom say
   when Everyman gets to it? there the flurry of heart
   stopped, and the scurry of thought checked there?
   What has it said already? what bread
   of the wilderness—or none? what glory or faith
   in the wilderness—or none, will it offer?
PILATE.   None; none.
   The guard will have him; he will say nothing.
HEROD.   He will say
   one thing only: he will only wait and bring

THE THREE TEMPTATIONS

all his eyes to bear against Everyman,
and cry: *Friend, why are you here?—why?*
Why have you come? O when that kingdom speaks,
what will you say, Caiaphas?
CAIAPHAS.   Do not talk nonsense.
I shall not be cross-examined by a criminal.
HEROD. You will be yet; yes, high-priest, one day
you will see the work we are truly about. O
then the eyes burn and the mind spins,—
hark, what a shout! They have caught him.
PILATE. Already?
HEROD.   Already.
Steady now to your work, both of you. Kill;
in the name of Judas Everyman, kill the kingdom,
and save your piety and your fame and your modest
    comfort.   *[The noise of a crowd*
CAIAPHAS. Quiet there! My lord governor, we bring
this man before you as a traitor to imperial Caesar,
because he professes to be a king. By your law
he ought to die therefore; and by ours too
because he calls himself the Son of God.
He turns the whole world upside down.
Blasphemy, heresy, treason. Pronounce sentence.
HEROD.   Quick, Pilate.
PILATE. Yes— but some trial;
We must have some trial to save my face.
CAIAPHAS. Quick, Pilate.
HEROD.   Any trick of a trial.
Think of your reputation and your place in the world.
PILATE. Yes, but justice—
HEROD.   Justice! are you too a prophet?
A noise about justice asks only a noise about justice.
A SOLDIER. Sir, her excellency your wife the Lady Claudia
is coming.

PILATE.　　　　　Claudia! What—
CLAUDIA.　　　　　　　　　　Do not touch him!
　　He is sacrificial; loose him; do not touch him.
　　He is not yours, my lord; he is not Caesar's;
　　he is no one's but his own. I am frightened; let him go—
　　him—it—the thing there—the sacrifice!
PILATE. Lady, if I loose him we may lose everything beside.
HEROD. Do not mistake us; he looks young: he is old—
　　he is the ancient world-wide call to surrender all;
　　our comfort, our safety, our loves depend . . .
CLAUDIA.　　　　　　　　　　　　　　Misery!
　　Misery if you touch him. I was asleep—
　　peaceably, comfortably, pleasurably asleep—
　　when he came through the curtains . . .
PILATE.　　　　　　　　　　　　*He* came!
　　When?
CLAUDIA. When? just now—while he was here!
　　He comes and speaks at the same time to everyone.
　　He came to my bed and did not say a word,
　　but his face became the face of each of my friends,
　　each in turn, each pale, each in its agony,
　　each staring at me. I knew their pains,
　　the separate secret stubborn pains of each,
　　and yet it was no one all the time but he.
　　Their pains were in his body; and I too—
　　Husband, I too, I in him—
　　I felt my muscles cramp, my bones burn,
　　my head rack as if thorns stabbed.
　　Their pains in his, his in mine;
　　he stood, and his face changed and never changed—
　　he was each and all and none. I was his slave,
　　his thing, his nothing. O I have suffered terrors
　　this hour because of him. My dear lord,
　　do not speak to him, do not look at him, let him go.

THE THREE TEMPTATIONS

PILATE. I dare not, Excellency; look, you dreamed.
You are not called to abandon yourself; you dreamed.
This fellow shall not trouble your comfort.

CLAUDIA. Comfort!
I shall never know comfort unless he allows;
let him send it—O now, if ever, his!
I cannot bear my friends' pains; let him go!
Cannot I love my friends without hurt?
The sword of his peace pierces me; to love my friends
has been my hope; now—O Pilate,
are my friends he? is he my friends?
is he the love and the comfort of friends? he
love? is this pain his comfort?
I cannot bear it; I will not bear it; I must.
Pilate, save me! [*She falls*

PILATE. Lady! Bear her carefully.
I am sorry, gentlemen.

HEROD. A woman's sensibility! charming!
but a little alarming too, if I may say so.
This inconvenient uncomfortable union of friends
is not at all the lot that Everyman wants.
Nor we. Make an end. Give sentence.

CAIAPHAS. Make an end.

PILATE. I must take the general opinion, to be sure of myself.

HEROD. Do then; ask the crowd; ask Everyman.
ask a multitude of Everymans, all the Everymans
who are listening now; ask them, ask them, do!

PILATE. They shouted Hosanna.

HEROD. Yes indeed, my simpleton.
Then they were running no risk; now they are.
Now he means death of some kind; now they can think,
and what your wife said may sink in.

PILATE. All you who hear me, what shall I do with this man
who comes to bring his kingdom and destroy ours?
THE VOICES. Away with him!
> Put him to death!
> Kill him!
PILATE. Go, all of you; take him and put him to death.
> [*The voices of the crowd fade*

Are you content, gentlemen?
CAIAPHAS. Let all prophets
end as this one does—dust on a dunghill.
HEROD. And Judas Everyman with his thirty pieces.
I am only afraid, for a few days yet,
you may find the Lady Claudia somewhat restless.
But time and certain judicious pleasures will cure her.
Visions pass.
PILATE. How still the world seems!
Only a slow chant rising from the Temple.
HEROD. As if out of a tomb.
CAIAPHAS. And the feet of your soldiers
changing guard.
HEROD. As if about a tomb.
O damnation is a quiet pleasant thing
at present.
CAIAPHAS. How dark it grows!
PILATE. Indeed the sun
seems to have done its work and to be on the point
of giving up the ghost.
CAIAPHAS. A host of lamps
twinkle in the houses; torches are lit in the streets.
> [*A faint crash*

PILATE. What was that noise?
HEROD. I can hardly see, but I think
one of your men in the courtyard has fallen in a fit.
CAIAPHAS. Why is it all so dark?

THE THREE TEMPTATIONS

PILATE.   Lamps there! lamps!
HEROD. Are you fainting, Caiaphas?
CAIAPHAS.   I can hardly stand. Help!
PILATE. What is happening? where are those lamps?
A VOICE.   Sir, the wicks—
  the wicks will not catch light.
CAIAPHAS.   Life and light—
  O God of Abraham!—are going out together.
PILATE. The gods are leaving the world.
HEROD.   Wait; it may pass.
  We ran this risk when we began the work.
PILATE. What risk?
CAIAPHAS.   What work?
HEROD.   We knew it was always possible
  we were fighting against the complete and only kingdom,
  the kingdom John prophesied and Jesus brought—
  justice on earth and more than justice in heaven.
  If we were, we shall each be left lonely in the dark
  with the mere recollection of our sometime comfort. Hark!
  someone is running to join us in our darkness. Who is there?
JUDAS. I have sinned; I have betrayed the kingdom. Where
  is the Governor? Where is the High Priest?
    Where is King Herod?
HEROD. Is that my little friend Judas Everyman
  come to join the great lords in damnation?
  What do you want, Judas?
JUDAS.   To give back the price.
  I have betrayed the kingdom.
HEROD.   And now you are afraid.
  Well, and so, Everyman, are the soldier and the priest.
JUDAS. I have sinned; take the silver and the comfort back.

HEROD. No; now when the sun and moon are out,
   and the soldier almost dead, and the priest in a swoon,
   it is too late to talk of giving things back.
   The silver, and the girls in Galilee, and the Roman citizenship,
   and the pleasant comfortable place at the Temple rites,
   are yours; if you cannot use them, can we help that?
   What more do you want?
JUDAS.   Only to be
   free, as I was before, from innocent blood.
HEROD. You notice the smell, do you? the smell of blood
   creeping up now through the dark of the world,
   as if we were standing on Golgotha, among the bones
   of the dead who starved in our cities or were killed in our wars?
   the smell of the shed blood of the innocent everywhere.
   Someone else is coming.
CLAUDIA. Pilate!
PILATE.   Claudia!
CLAUDIA. Why did you do it, husband? it meant so little
   not to do it; done, it means so much.
   The sun is out; thick darkness is all about,
   in and beyond your souls.
CAIAPHAS
PILATE   What has happened?
JUDAS
CLAUDIA. Judgement. It is finished. Now all we,
   all we who are here, have what we chose.
   This for some of you was your last chance; now
   the path is straight; now the love and the wrath
   come on a straight path. Once there was a voice crying
   in the wilderness, now there is only dark in the wilderness
   and a dying everlastingly, a slow perishing
   and less and less cherishing of comfort; at last

THE THREE TEMPTATIONS

the stress of the glory is past; this is hell.
I am sent to say softly to anyone who hears—
you would have it; have it then; hell
is always there for the craving, and the having is easy.
For me, the peace of the sword in the heart drives me
out among other lives. Time was; time is past.
Farewell; no prophet shall ever disturb you again,
nor ever the pain of other hearts trouble you.
You wanted your own; have your own; farewell.

www.ingramcontent.com/pod-product-compliance
Lightning Source LLC
Chambersburg PA
CBHW032014230426
43671CB00005B/81